CONTENTS

PREFACE

There are many good, yet complex, books on strategy; however, in a connected, busy world, reducing complexity to simplicity arguably has a higher value. I have therefore tried to keep this book simple. Fast-moving markets have left many strategy concepts gasping for breath and leaders are forced to rely on agility and their wits to survive as old models and pre-conceptions collapse. This book aims to redress the balance by looking at the future more effectively, thus enabling leaders to bring strategy firmly back onto the map. The aim is for leaders to secure clarity, confidence and energy in their business method, outlook and approach.

To convey the underlying idea behind the book, I want you to imagine a team ball game. If we could anticipate just a little ahead of the other players on the pitch where the ball will be in the game, we would be able to position ourselves in the right way, place and time to take the advantage and thus beat our opponent. Not forgetting, of course, that the other players are all trying to do the same. The very best players in life – whether through nature or nurture (practice) – do this almost subconsciously. It has become second nature for them. However, when you and your organization are seeking to move up a level – which is probably why you have invested in this book – we must explore more consciously the patterns involved and our role in the business game.

Throughout the book, I have stuck to the law of focus and only included the main points. If you need further information, I have included source references that will allow you to explore the topics mentioned in greater depth. Focus is a really key point behind the title. Consider the following questions: Where can you and your organization *focus* to create an absolute first-in-class position? How can you get ahead of your competitors in a *focused* way, in order to create a niche, and offer a better service to your customers and end users? These could be perceived as marketing questions, but as leaders we must find the answers to these questions. The answers are at the heart of securing advantage in the business game.

In my explorations I have deliberately included some tried and tested case studies to demonstrate particular points, but I have peppered the ideas with metaphors, which I hope will create better context and recall. Overall, my aim with the book has been to demonstrate that despite fast-moving times, strategy and leadership still remain key to gaining advantage.

12 The advantage sum   223

07 Elementary decisions 121

08 Changing the game 143

Much of what we discuss is inherently known in business. I hope it is the sum and a fresh perspective that inspire you to take more time out and look at your strategy anew. Collectively, our goal in business leadership is to effect real changes that will make a difference to gain advantage and build more purposeful organizations. Crucial to this process are our sense and belief that we have the ability to create positive outcomes and build the future.

Finally, I must thank my family for their patience while I wrote this book. I would also like to thank the many teachers who have helped me be in a position to write – from clients to mentors, friends and editors.

Feedback is always useful so if you have any observations or questions, please let me know. It is from questions, not answers, that we actually learn the most.

Extra material

You can download more resources to go with this book at
www.koganpage.com/cca

Creating competitive advantage

Introduction

In our highly technical and global society, business markets and sectors are becoming increasingly complex and dynamic. The fast pace of change has brought new challenges for business leaders and strategists, increasing the need for faster reinvention, better ideas, anticipation and agility. How do we strategically lead and anticipate market direction ahead of others? How do we consistently secure the right ideas, strategies, products and services at the right time to gain competitive advantage?

What strategies, tools and outlooks are required to understand what our customers and end users are thinking about and what they might want, as opposed to what we want to sell to them? How do we match business design, products and services with future needs more effectively, in order to stride ahead with advantage? In a knowledge economy, what ideas are going to be most valued going forwards?

How do leaders get a clear view of the line of probability in market direction and customer trends ahead of the competition and what tools, data and techniques can you employ to assist the process? How can leaders and strategists secure the time and mindfulness within their roles to anticipate events more effectively? How can strategy stay ahead in fast-changing environments?

This book aims to answer these questions, setting out skills and techniques, supported by case studies and tools. Figure 1.1 encapsulates the steps needed to create competitive advantage. The rest of the chapter then introduces each step. Thereafter each step has its own dedicated chapter.

FIGURE 1.1   The process of creating competitive advantage

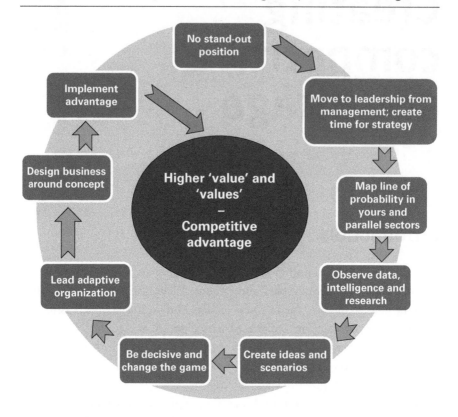

The 'ahead' advantage

When an organization develops valued traits – that is products, skills, services or a combination of these that are desired and different – it will have an advantage over its competitors and usually outperform them. The best foundation for this position is to develop a better and clearer understanding and identification of your customers and end users, and what they want now or are likely to want or value in the future. Today, your customers want faster and better products, support and services, and they want them delivered on their terms. Repeated studies show that in most cases, being first with new products, services and strategies provides market-share advantage and once this position is achieved it is typically sustainable. Numerous cases demonstrate this: from Ford's batch production first introduced in 1908 with the release of the Model T automobile, Dyson's launch of the first bagless vacuum cleaner in the United Kingdom in 1993, to Apple's launch of the Macintosh – the first mass-market PC with a graphical user interface and mouse – in 1984.

The advantages of being first mover and standing in front of the competition are, from experience, compelling. So how do some people and companies seemingly achieve this status successfully time and time again? Essentially some people are intuitively aware of what is coming, accessing and combining experience, research, trial and knowledge. They are aware of the need to be ahead and combine this insight with either a cost differentiation approach or products that others are unable to offer or are not yet offering. Alternatively, they innovate, beating others to the market with entirely new and sometimes disruptive products (typically in such sectors as technology). Others achieve 'first' status by simply securing processes and skills that make customers want to work with the business as a preferred choice. They possess the intuitive ability to be ahead, securing advantage and creating the future rather than following it.

This intuitive skill can be developed and rationalized. For example, while developing his vacuum cleaner, Sir James Dyson went through 5,126 failed prototypes and all his savings over 15 years. This was predominantly a research approach but what kept Dyson to his agenda? Insight and belief. The 5,127th prototype worked, and the Dyson brand both invented and leads the bagless vacuum sector. In 2014, Forbes estimated Dyson's wealth at £4.5 billion, and he leads the largest bagless vacuum manufacturer in the United States and the United Kingdom, with Japan close behind. Dyson has the intuition, ideas and vision to be ahead.

Leadership not management

To create competitive advantage, leaders and strategists need to anticipate customer needs more effectively. This involves listening, research, humility and taking the time to think creatively. Effective leadership requires good organizational skills. However, too often organizing becomes managing; that is, everyone reporting to the leader asking what they often already know or should know, or managing stakeholders, governance and politics. These practices leave minimal time for leading; that is, setting clearly the direction, vision, products and services ahead of the market and the competition. How many strategy meetings are held about who is doing what job or what the problems are? This is management, whereas leadership anticipates customers' changing needs and trends, and examines the emerging opportunities. Leadership, then, designs the business around clearly communicated strategies that make the most of the changing opportunities, to create advantage.

> To create competitive advantage, leaders and strategists need to anticipate customer needs more effectively.

The boundless and accelerated developments occurring in our global economy provide a significant opportunity for improved business, but only if leaders move with or ahead of the zeitgeist, the flow of the moment. With rapid market change, leaders need new techniques, skills and strategies in order to anticipate and communicate the right changes and strategy ahead of their competition – to lead as opposed to follow. For those of you who have played strategic games such as chess, you will actually be very familiar with this concept. In strategic games, by thinking four moves ahead and making the right moves accordingly, against a player who is only thinking one move ahead, you will nearly always beat that player, and it is the same in strategic leadership.

To achieve 'ahead' strategies, leaders need to create an environment, the awareness and the space for this thinking and analysis of possible moves with the right support beneath them. Therefore second-tier management must be aware that the leader must be able to think, research and plan for change. Leaders must ascertain in which direction things are moving, so that they can determine how their organizations can take advantage. This 'how' might involve new products, services, acquisitions and/or alliances. If the 'how' is not clear, the leader must determine both what research is required and how the time and resource will be found to conduct such research.

Leaders keep open minds; they listen and observe very carefully. While what you have seen before in your business's and sector's direction of travel may seem clear, appearances can be deceiving in many ways and some possibilities may yet be unexplained. Herein lies the greatest opportunity. With the world of work being completely transformed, only those who learn openly and continuously will experience better opportunities in the future.

The line of probability

To understand better where the market is likely to go we must understand where we have come from and where we are now, both on a macro whole-of-market basis and on a micro, sector/service basis. To demonstrate this concept, let's compare business to the human story, the ultimate macro picture.

Science records that life on earth began about 3.8 billion years ago, with single-celled prokaryotic bacteria cells. Mammals evolved 200 million years ago; Homo sapiens 200,000 years ago (0.004 per cent of the earth's history). The advanced social state of civilization is relatively new, driven by the invention of agriculture and religion some 10–13,000 years ago. Since civilization began, humans have become utterly prevalent on the planet, with the global population rising from some 2.5 billion to over 7 billion in the last 50 years alone.

Almost directly in line with the multiplication of our population, technology, business and social complexity have grown. Since the written word, and particularly following the invention of the printing press by Johannes Gutenberg in 1436, the speed of ideas, technology and social change, along with population growth, has accelerated exponentially. Computers and the transmission of ideas globally in the blink of an eye via the internet have accelerated this change to the point where magic is almost a reality. We can now clone a species, split an atom to power a city, transmit moving pictures instantly, swap a heart, or download a 3D printing template published in Brazil and on the same day print the object in Madagascar. I use the word 'magic' deliberately; of course individual experts understand how all this is done, but the complexity is beyond any one individual and therefore, to most of us, such developments are magic.

The pace of change has increased and thus anticipating the line of probability in business sectors more effectively has become more critical. In the past, the reasonable historical average human lifespan was about 50 years; however, with the level of communication and knowledge share that humans now enjoy, this has increased in the West to nearly 80 and it is growing by two years every decade. One in four children born in the West today will live to over 100 years old. With longer lives and more change, the world you were born in will be significantly different technologically and sociologically to the world you leave. Similarly the company you lead may need to be wholly different to its current form in just 10 or 20 years. It is important that we remain conscious of all new and growing developments – both those that concern our own individual industries and the broader trends – as it is easy to be caught by surprise and fall behind. When we are surprised we lose ground to competition. Consider 15 years ago when there was no smartphone, Skype or Google. Amazon and eBay launched in 1996, when there were 16 million internet users; there are now over 3 billion users – transformations that materialized in very short periods of time.

The full context of the past explains more fully where we are now and therefore increases the accuracy of our understanding of where we are likely to go. While we can't predict the future, the cumulative pace of change we are now experiencing means we face a period of fundamental disruption in social and economic positions. However, the overall context enables us to at least see how everything fits better. This is mapping out the 'line of probability' and by applying more technique to this we can make better business decisions. This is a qualitative, subjective method (art) against information, whereas trend analysis is a quantitative calculation (science) against data. With a truly open mind, think about where your sector and comparative sectors are today; where they are *really* going and what strategies you could employ now, ahead of the competition.

Trends and big data

Knowing what our customers are going to want in the future requires research, data and trend analysis. According to a study conducted by PwC and the Economist Intelligence Unit in 2014, 58 per cent of executives still use either their own intuition or those of a colleague to make big decisions that bring significant risk (PwC, 2014). There is an increasing opportunity to use analysis and research to build a better picture of the line of probability. By using the right systems, and by asking the right questions about those systems, we can target the strategy and decisions more effectively. 'Big data', as the current business jargon affords, is, as you would expect, big, but what makes it interesting is the ability to turn the intelligence into something manageable and translate it into better decisions. The ability to capture, manage and analyse large and complex data sets allows for improved decision-making and business practices, as well as tailored products and services in many different industries and fields. What are people's buying patterns? How does the pricing of goods affect sales in real time? What are customers searching for and how often do they want to buy?

The key with *big* data is to actually think *small*. There are very few important numbers needed to understand the possibilities. The IT sector can in its complexities lose sight of the reason why we want and need the data, disappearing into overload. The top role of the data is to have a better dashboard and thus visibility of what is occurring in our market and our organizations today. What is the demographic of our customers? How much do they have to spend? What is their average spend against what overall market size? How much can we spend to win a customer vis-à-vis our average sale, and at what time are they most likely to buy? The overall opportunity is in tracking this data over longer periods than a year to start seeing the trends, better defining the customer relationship and therefore the opportunity to better engage. In predictive analytics, the other main concept is to try to collaborate the data to create a profile of your customers. This proves to be particularly insightful during the process of trying to differentiate the good ones from the bad. Who do you need to focus on, and recommend more to, and who is wasting your time? Understanding this helps reduce inefficient operations and increases conversion rates, but it also provides the future opportunity of knowing who the real customers are today so that we can plan better products for them tomorrow.

Intelligence is dangerous if it is unreliable and unfocused. The key is the question 'What do we *really* need to know?' not 'What can we collect?' If you have read Douglas Adams's *The Hitchhiker's Guide to the Galaxy*, you will recall that a group of hyper-intelligent pan-dimensional beings demanded to learn the answer to the ultimate question of 'life, the universe, and everything'. They built a supercomputer, Deep Thought, to tackle the challenge. It took Deep Thought 7½ million years to return with the answer 42. Deep Thought pointed out that the answer seemed meaningless because the beings who instructed it never actually knew what the question was.

IT and data collection can create major advantage if prioritized correctly. Designing your systems so they create visibility simply and effectively is critical. The approach is one where you seek to both see and then join the dots; for example, marketing data is usually separate to financial data, but why? If we can understand how much a customer costs to win, for example, we can seek to both drive that cost down and use the number to run far stronger marketing budgets with clear return on investment. Because the internet and systems are so strong at collecting and holding data, large corporates are now employing data scientists to help manage the data mining and design the predictive algorithms and variance models.

Analysis can go far beyond what is occurring in your organization to detailed analysis of others. Research can be as simple as travelling to other countries and organizations to see how it is done elsewhere. How many great businesses start this way? Seeking out people in parallel sectors that seem to be ahead and asking what they have done. Look in more detail at your competitors. We all say we are leading but who is really leading and why? To examine this, leaders and strategists need to be clearer on how much time and resource they allocate to research and trends analysis.

Customer surveys and research can significantly contribute to the data sets but we must be mindful as customers don't always know what they want. A famous first was when Chester Carlson invented the photocopier in 1939. At the time, multiple copies were made using carbon paper and manual duplicating machines, so people did not see the need for an electronic machine. IBM and General Electric both rejected Carlson's technology. In 1947 a small New York-based manufacturer and seller of photographic paper took out a licence to develop and market the copying machine, thus founding Xerox. In some respects we must find ways to ask customers what they have *not* thought of and what they have *not* said. It is silence that we must seek to interrogate. The customers who are vocal will be either very unhappy or very happy, but what about the majority who say little: what are they thinking?

Strategic planning and scenarios

The aim of predictive models is to create simplicity from complexity in order to help leaders make the right decisions.

In our quest for competitive advantage there are two main models that are helpful. The first is essentially a dashboard of the current picture. Imagine a car with all the key performance data, metrics and feedback for the driver in one clearly designed and visible picture. As we are trying to ascertain where things are going, this model will combine the three pictures of the line of probability, research and intelligence. The second is a ranked scenarios' synopsis; as a result of the dashboard, what is, or are, the likely outputs, ranked and prioritized after brainstorming and analysis.

The overarching goal is to provide value and insight to the business to understand the probable direction and therefore the possible opportunities and scenarios. The foundation of the predictive modelling is the recognition that many factors may combine in complex ways to create sometimes surprising futures. We are seeking to both reduce the surprises and identify the opportunities and potential new insights about the future, deep shifts in values, unprecedented regulations or possible new inventions. Simplified models can also be used as exceptional communications tools so that all employees gain insight into future possibilities, enhancing adaption against discontinuity.

The world has been transformed from slow, loosely connected and reasonably predictable local economies to an unpredictable, global, fast and complex web of relationships and information where the effects of singular events can be felt almost instantaneously. On 11 September 2001, the Islamist extremist group al-Qaeda hijacked four airliners and carried out suicide attacks against targets in the United States. Two of the planes were flown into the towers of the World Trade Centre in New York City and over 3,000 people were killed.

FIGURE 1.2   How predictive modelling drives competitive advantage

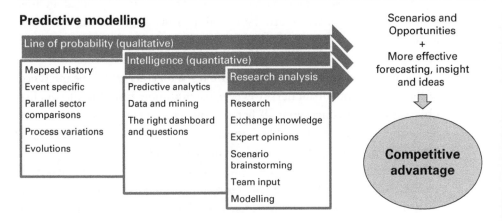

The effects of the attacks were felt around the globe and rapidly transformed our security, culture and financial markets. Unexpected events will occur and with the right dashboard and scenario models we can be better prepared for them.

As Figure 1.2 demonstrates, predictive modelling can help drive competitive advantage by integrating historical consciousness, business intelligence tools and forward-looking analysis.

Elementary decisions

Mapping out the line of probability and fusing this with better intelligence increase our awareness – ahead of the competition – of the opportunities in changing markets. Leaders then seek new ways, changes and ideas to do things differently and exploit these opportunities to gain competitive advantage. There may, however, be a myriad of possible strategies; thus we must select the best ones and focus on these. We have increased visibility and can better see the patterns and categories, but now we must assemble all the pieces to create focus. Focus is important as too often there are too many initiatives and ideas, which can cause as much inertia as too few. Focus is about selecting and backing up the few exceptional ideas with absolute determination. Strategic initiatives need to be clear, short and based around a few very elementary ideas only.

Leaders read the clues, select, decide and focus. They is done by following a process. First, they broaden the range of options in the business game by securing better awareness and anticipation of the opportunities. They then

– working with the team – decisively narrow this down to a few simple conclusions and strategies. There are lots of pressures involved in this process, not least of which are the vested interests of all the players in the game and the difficulty of concentrating on the quiet new options when the old problems are so loud.

The line of probability and intelligence fused together create the inference of the potential opportunities. However, we must now turn this into quality observation and conclusions. What are our customers really thinking or likely to be thinking and what opportunities and ideas do we have as a result? Then, how do we decide which ones to take?

The strategic decision-making process is rather like the old detective stories, most notably *Sherlock Holmes* by Sir Arthur Conan Doyle, in its use of deductive reasoning. We broaden the whole picture by asking lots of questions and being truly observational, objective and open to secure all the evidence and clues. We then add expertise and logic to calculate a narrow range of possibilities; yet, as Sherlock Holmes summarized, 'It was easier to know it than to explain why I know it.' In other words, deduction, analysis and calculation improve our ability to make the right decisions, but so does intuition. Most leaders have experienced making some very positive decisions based on a 'gut feeling', drawing from lengthy experience and proven habit.

However, as already mentioned, the fact that the majority of business leaders admit that most of their decisions are largely intuitive is a concern given the potential inexactitude of intuition. Assessing future trends is inherently difficult and therefore better decisions are likely to be made when we actively seek a balance and blend of an analytical approach with intuition. Diverse boards help create this blend: who is your analytical person? Who is the instinctive one? Who is the young maverick? Who is the wise sage? Some entrepreneurs do seem to balance this mix individually, but it is exceptional and a team approach is usually far better. All initial suppositions and theories should be tested by logic and analysis of facts with a balance of styles. The strategies ultimately decided upon after the process may not be right but it is better to have tried and failed than have failed by not trying at all. Finally there is a clear agenda that conclusions and set strategies must and shall be reached in reasonable timescales.

Changing the game

There are far too many businesses that are doing the same thing in the same way and not particularly well. Why is this? Overall there is comfort in staying with the crowd; it seems less risky so why push ahead and stand out? Why take risks when the status quo works? There is, after all, safety in numbers. Besides, if we do things differently and attempt to stand out, we will be noticed by others and what if they criticize us? Indeed, when they criticize us will we rush back to the crowd? 'Everyone else does it like this so it must be right' is a common but fallacious mindset as it assumes that there are rules and that everyone else will stick to these rules and play the same game, yet our inherent experience is actually different. We may always be surprised as to how, but someone always seems to work out new and better ways of doing things, which affords them game-changing advantage.

> There are far too many businesses that are doing the same thing in the same way and not particularly well. Why is this?

To be curious and to improve is part of being human. Why shouldn't it be your organization that strategically leads the change? Charismatic leadership is hard to learn, but the quiet, innovative and strategic approach, asking the right questions with greater clarity, is proven time and time again. Where is the market going and therefore where should we go? What are our customers likely to want? How can we gain advantage when combined with belief and toughness? Pixar were significantly ahead in computer animation and taking significant market share from Disney, who later bought Pixar for £7.4 billion. Both companies deserve credit for their successes: Pixar for its innovation and Disney for identifying Pixar's value. Dyson were first with the bagless vacuum cleaner, again taking enormous market share from the leader Hoover, whose name is practically synonymous with 'vacuum cleaner' even today. Dyson's restless innovation and focus, as well as a global approach, helped the company surpass the £1 billion turnover mark for the first time in 2011 (BBC, 2012).

Changing the game and being different take determination and a willingness to invest in research and development (R&D). This is not just the responsibility of the technical departments, it is also inherent in the role of leadership. If you combine R&D with active awareness of a market's probable direction, you reduce the inherent risks. R&D becomes an investment, rather than just an expense.

Established firms may struggle with moving ahead with innovation, simply because there is so much effort involved in managing just to stay still. This may play a part, but the lack of willingness or vision to disrupt themselves is usually also a big contributor. In the late 1970s IBM felt that hardware –

its core business – was the future. When IBM launched the first personal computers it left one Mr Bill Gates of Microsoft the licensing rights to the operating system it had developed, despite using it as its core platform. Microsoft overtook IBM rapidly as the world's computing giant. Fast forward 20 years and one internet revolution and you see Microsoft still entrenched with the PC and enterprise software, rapidly losing market share to Google with its strong lead in cloud computing and its strong position in mobile operating systems. In 2014 PC sales fell by 8 per cent to mobile devices. Were Microsoft complacent and unwilling to disrupt themselves? The consequence is that the firm is currently in the mobile space now condemned to 'me-too' entry products, for which survival (not thriving) can be the only reward.

Many leaders sit in the present and carry with them the history of how they arrived at it. This history can lead to preconceptions, and vested interests in the present can hold them back from taking difficult decisions. The skill lies in stripping away the layers to see the truth: where is the company really going, how can it move ahead and do what it needs to do take advantage?

Adaptive organizations

Leadership's increased strategic anticipation helps us secure new ideas and make the right decisions ahead of the market. However, sometimes the ideas are there, but organizational inertia and the vested interest of people in maintaining the status quo mean we fail to gain competitive advantage. To make changes we need supportive, adaptive management and good implementation. Leaders are perhaps rarely good managers; in recognition of this, Google hired one of the world's top CEOs, Eric Schmidt, despite the company only being three years old. The hiring of Schmidt was pushed forward by venture capitalists, who had just invested in the company and recognized the need for an experienced manager. Despite initial reluctance, the founders Larry Page and Sergey Brin came to recognize that wealth and success lay in leading continued innovation first, but not without exceptional processes and management to help support their company's development.

Competitive advantage is usually found in businesses where the attitude of 'we will do what is right', as opposed to 'what we like doing', is set at the heart of its team and decision-making. This is very difficult to achieve, particularly as many executives' careers are better aligned with maintaining the current position and their current roles. It requires leaders to constantly identify, reward and encourage entrepreneurs – the innovators within the businesses – and to promote managers who create adaptable teams.

Anticipation can also fail, and from time to time there will be dramatic shifts in any given sector. For example, in recent years retail has been transformed by the internet, and the scale of this transformation in such a short period has meant that very few anticipated it, thus most have been forced to become followers rather than leaders. From time to time there will be dramatic (usually technology-led) interventions in the line of probability or market flow that catch us by surprise. When surprised, by being more aware, and creating more agile and flexible organizations, we can be early strategic adopters and with any new arena there is nearly always the opportunity to be better. This enables us to quickly place ourselves first. Strength in business today comes from knowledge, agility, communication and responsiveness; not simply size. The ability to create wholly adaptive businesses connected to the knowledge economy puts businesses ahead. How is it, for example, that private equity can often multiply well-established, owner-managed businesses threefold in very short spaces of time? Private equity, of course, improves access to capital, but often it is their application of clarity of commercial direction with focus on who does what and why in the top team that creates results.

Business by design

Once the ideas and the strategy exist to create advantage without pre-conception, it is time to look again at the whole business. How does the design and business model fit? Do you have the right establishment, culture, people, distribution, systems, brand and structure? This is essentially an interdisciplinary approach with a holistic view. You have decided where the market is probably going and what you can do to take advantage in terms of products and services, now we need to examine and design the business infrastructure to best deliver.

Many good objective ideas and strategies have failed because changes to the business design have been neglected, partly because changing business design can require the most difficult decisions. New products distributed in the wrong way, layered on an old system simply because it's there or with the wrong people, will fail. Good business design will ensure the right people in the right roles with the right infrastructure, and capacity based on our aspirations and the advantage we seek, not on the history, models or infrastructure of previous strategies. In this design phase of creating advantage, it is important to recognize that it is often better or necessary to go backwards before you go forwards, and there are no rules.

The concept of business design is essentially for the leaders to audit every component of the business and ask whether it is right for where you or where the market is going. A great example of a company that consistently achieves the right design is 3M. If you review their history of innovation it is extraordinary, from paper mills to product manufacture and now IT, but what is even more interesting is that they make the change before they actually need to. The company's structure follows its strategy, rather than the reverse. 3M has shown a consistent willingness to not only divest less attractive businesses, but also to reinvent itself by investing in new industries and long-term R&D. By embracing rather than rejecting change, 3M has adapted and grown over 11 decades (since it was founded in 1902) into what is now a multinational conglomerate that boasts a turnover of over $30 billion.

Since 1952 there have been only two companies that were in the UK Stock Indices FTSE 100 that are still there, namely GKN and Tate & Lyle. The remainder have either been acquired or no longer trade: change or fail. In the United Kingdom, Unigate the dairy believed they were in the milk business, not the logistics business. At their peak Unigate had a nationwide distribution network with environmentally friendly electric vehicles capable of delivering anything. Where is Unigate now? The model was great; the product, however, should have been an online supermarket. Ocado foresaw the opportunity in an online supermarket product; founded in 2000, by early 2015 it had a market capitalization of over £2.4 billion. Meanwhile Greencore, who acquired Unigate in 2011, is currently valued at around half that at just £1.2 billion.

Competitive advantage is not just about being strategically objective in the quest for new positions and products; it also requires you to be honest about your business model, systems and people. Too often we see organizations where the leaders are managing the business because the management are not held accountable and as a result are failing to lead and get the strategy right. Business design may require divestment, closures, reorganization and looking hard at your people and their real abilities, but it is vital to support advantage ideas. Competitive advantage can be found without ground-breaking new disruptive products but in innovative and forward-thinking business models.

Decisive action

In seeking competitive advantage we engage better today in tomorrow's business. However, many people are caught in the present. This means change can be very difficult when you are pioneering new concepts. Creating competitive advantage requires a carefully nurtured culture and awareness of decision-making styles and objectivity towards your approach to risk and diversity. Are you and your organization pioneers, followers or current riders? Do you embrace risk to push boundaries, manage them or avoid them? Do you invest ahead for the long term or simply the next 12 months? Have you achieved alignment among the board members and management, and are communications between all decision-makers clear and transparent? Do new ideas need testing or is it time to be bold? How do you communicate and implement the plan without the usual inertia that sticks to change like glue?

Creating advantage also requires diversity in the team. In one recent meeting of a 250-employee partnership in the property sector, the board asked for help innovating, feeling that they had grown stale. As I stared at the 10 board members, all male bar one, and all aged 55 and over, I felt compelled to ask the diversity question, which was met with a wry smile only. Beyond lack of diversity, there are other common factors that can stifle organizations, such as risk aversity. Advantage requires the willingness to embrace some risk. Working with another client, a £4 billion revenue plc, I asked the same innovation question. In this case, new ideas were plenty, with a healthy mix of ages and both sexes in their key team. The problem was that despite running regular innovation workshops, failure was deemed entirely unacceptable, and therefore not one of their innovation workshop ideas had been instigated. The risks were all deemed too high.

In dynamic markets we need to be able to change more quickly. Advantage is achieved when we see more clearly where the market is going and develop the business in that direction quickly, but it requires the ability to decisively, simply and clearly communicate to align the organization to the changes required.

The advantage sum

No one can accurately predict the future with ease, or time events by their will, but some people appear to time and time again. They do this by a combination of research, planning, clarity and confidence. In this thesis we earn advantage by placing the drive to be ahead and stand out at the heart of the organization. Open-minded leaders with the free time and space to think, research and engage in making changes and – rather than managing the status quo – strengthen the ability to identify the right strategies. Mapping the probabilities and fusing this with intelligence enhances visibility and creates the ideas. Focus and decisiveness select and turn these ideas into strategies, the right business models and plans.

When we think or look more moves ahead, we might also need to consider the purpose of business, particularly as knowledge-driven consumers become more focused on ethics and transparency. Capitalism mostly has a free market economy. This means people buy and sell goods and services under their own freedom of choice according to what they most value. Consumerism is the assumption that the more goods or services exchanged the better off that society; however, increasingly overconsumption and greed are being negatively attributed to both capitalism and consumerism. Overall this means that in seeking advantage leaders will need to accelerate growth, profit and shareholder values in alignment in the future with a more purposeful contributing approach. Sustainable advantage will require strong ethics and values.

Competitive advantage in dynamic markets requires:

- vision and determination to create something better beyond the immediate;
- dissatisfaction with the status quo and ideas;
- being prepared to act in opposition to convention;
- open minds, careful observation and intense listening;
- clear roles and responsibilities with the permission to strategize;
- acceptance that failure is part of learning;
- research and creativity, analysis and intuition;
- leaders who manage yet embrace risk to achieve;
- willingness to disrupt and change even when things are working;
- a complete open mind about tomorrow; and
- teamwork, focus, responsibility and belief.

Organizations with a track record of disrupting and leading successfully ahead of the market make a difference, are more purposeful and sustainable, grow more quickly, and are more valuable. Building such an organization, however, requires a less conventional, even contrarian, approach. This book will support you with the tools and strategies necessary for positive change – to help you change before you have to – and help you to illuminate what must be done to create competitive advantage.

In the next chapter, we will explore how certain organizations are able to get ahead and achieve 'first' status through clarity, innovation, anticipation and dynamic leadership.

References

BBC (2012) Dyson sales and profits boosted by US and Japan. BBC News Business, 07/09. Available from: www.bbc.co.uk/news/business-19515485 [Last accessed 26 August 2015]

PwC (2014) 'Guts and Gigabytes: Capitalising on the Art & Science in Decision Making' [Online] www.pwc.com/es_MX/mx/servicios-tecnologias-de-la-informacion/archivo/2014-10-big-decisions.pdf [last accessed 26 August 2015]

References

Being ahead

02

Introduction

Business leaders all share the common need to find their way ahead of others in order to succeed in changing times. However, some leaders are better equipped and more attuned to the need to be ahead than others. Organizations and leaders who anticipate change early, move into action and adapt at the right time usually succeed more quickly and effectively. As the pace of human change has accelerated, we must be ready to make changes quickly and ahead of others – again and again – to secure advantage. How can we move ahead, and what are the advantages?

The benefits of being ahead

Customers now dictate and lead. They are better informed, more connected and less loyal than ever before. This means they are far more focused, value driven and demanding on what they do and don't want. The modern customer demands new products and better services on their terms; effective leaders and organizations anticipate what these demands are and will be. In this scenario, being a first mover (whether strategically or through new products) and thus standing in front of the competition is well documented as a successful method of securing growth, advantage and growing more effectively against the modern customer's higher expectations. Innovation and inspiration are the access keys to being a first mover to meet new demands. Today's successful leaders combine experience with research to gain better strategic insight, foster innovation and make better decisions.

Innovation at the right time, ahead of others, is undoubtedly an effective route to competitive advantage. If you are selling products before anyone else, you can, in theory, acquire market share before would-be competitors gain traction. You also have the time to build superior brand recognition and customer loyalty, and time to perfect the product. eBay is a textbook example: the company was started in 1995 by Pierre Omidyar from his living room.

It was the first internet marketplace for the sale of goods and services for individuals. eBay has both streamlined and globalized traditional person-to-person trading, which was traditionally conducted through local garage sales, collectibles shows and flea markets.

First movers, innovators or organizations that make the right strategic moves ahead of others and before they have to, typically benefit from:

- early profits;
- time to increase customer loyalty;
- the opportunity to improve products and services, using early profits to build even greater customer value;
- superior information on competitors;
- the ability in the new market to select the most attractive niches;
- scale and market share advantage; and
- increased strategic flexibility to create the future.

The future is unpredictable. It is essential and useful to think about the change and uncertainties around us both in our sectors (content), and parallel sectors (context), with a view to creating ideas and innovations first that put us ahead. By thinking about the possibilities and examining how to be ahead, we create better decisions today and we adopt a planning advantage, which helps to create the future rather than follow it. Whoever is first in the field will be fresh for the fight; whoever is second in the field has to hasten to battle and will arrive exhausted.

Ahead in the right way

Organizations and leaders can gain significant competitive advantage through innovation and strategic moves ahead of others, but this can be a daunting reality as we are not all pioneers. An 'innovate first or die' mindset, as many proponents preach, is too simplistic an approach. There are some great examples of focused and lean companies that sustainably succeed without being exceptionally product innovative, such as Coca-Cola and HSBC. They operate in seemingly mundane industries, selling carbonated soft drinks and providing financial services, respectively. While we might not think of these companies as being 'first' today, they are ahead with their business models, customer services and/or processes and hence creating more trust in the minds of their customers and employees. Coca-Cola boasts one of the most powerful worldwide distribution networks in the world, in addition to its superb marketing, advertising and customer loyalty. HSBC was one of the few banks that did not require a bailout in 2008. A lot of its success in terms of growth and stability can be attributed to its effective marketing and global diversification.

The term 'first-mover advantage' is a well-known, studied and proven strategic concept. There have been plenty of great success stories in the 21st century, including eBay, and even over 175 years ago in 1840, Sir Samuel Cunard sailed the first great transatlantic steamship, the *Britannia*, granting Cunard first-mover status. On the other hand, there are good examples of some exceptional innovations that failed, either because they were perhaps too far ahead of their time, or the business strategy behind the innovation was flawed. A classic British example of failure was successful computer pioneer Sir Clive Sinclair's 1985 C5, the first small, electric, people's city car. We all know today that in a carbon reduction economy, electric has a place. However, the C5 had too short a range as it was too heavy, lacked a roof to cope with British weather, had safety issues and worst of all was launched in winter. The fundamental idea was good but the technology was not quite there and the marketing just was not able to communicate the benefits enough to an (at that time) unprepared consumer. Today, virtually every major car manufacturer has a successful small, electric city car.

Organizations should seek to be ahead of others but in more precise, balanced and guaranteed ways than is typically understood or presented. 'Disrupt or die' is too simplistic and is better balanced with strategic methods such as research and modelling, to increase anticipation and awareness. We need tools and techniques to secure these methods. Figure 2.1 shows the key components that are important to driving positive change, and shows that there is more to disruption than simply being different. The innovator's dilemma is that both risk and uncertainty are hard to disentangle, and it is only with hindsight that we can truly know what was right. Successful strategic innovation will arise when combined with better awareness of profit opportunities, in conjunction with the use of the right business models and approach, to secure competitive advantage and to dictate future success. It requires the right ideas, implemented in the right way, at the right time.

> 'Disrupt or die' is too simplistic and is better balanced with strategic methods such as research and modelling, to increase anticipation and awareness.

FIGURE 2.1   Planning advantage: the key components of driving positive change

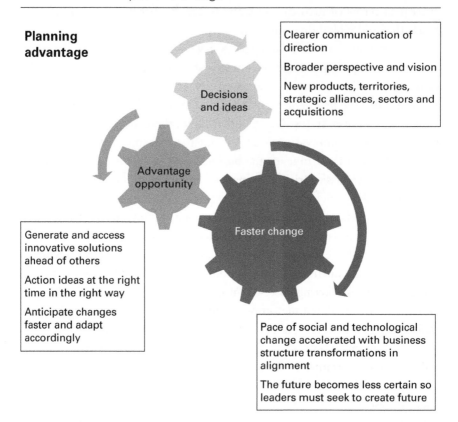

Planning advantage

Decisions and ideas

Advantage opportunity

Faster change

Clearer communication of direction

Broader perspective and vision

New products, territories, strategic alliances, sectors and acquisitions

Generate and access innovative solutions ahead of others

Action ideas at the right time in the right way

Anticipate changes faster and adapt accordingly

Pace of social and technological change accelerated with business structure transformations in alignment

The future becomes less certain so leaders must seek to create future

The zeitgeist

The zeitgeist is German for, literally, 'time spirit'. Internationally it's a word used to define the spirit, attitude, or general outlook or movement of a specific time or period, reflected in politics, society, literature and business. Every year has its moment and things change, but understanding the current of that change in the present is critical to effective business strategy. Before we can be ahead we have to have strategic understanding of what we are trying to move ahead of, and this requires a deeper understanding than we usually care to develop. I have used the word 'zeitgeist' rather than 'the present', as it better describes the need to look through a microscope at where we are now, as well as examine on a whole-of-market basis the currents in the economy. We are looking beyond the facts to the spirit beneath, so to speak.

> Essentially to be ahead we challenge what many believe as truth and seek the reasoning as to why.

Everything that has a beginning has an end, yet it is easy as leaders to see things as we see them and assume that that is that – yet things are not as we see them. I can recall saying in 1993 that the internet would not revolutionize things as modems were so slow. At the time it only communicated 1 per cent of telecommunications information; today it's 97 per cent. I was limited by my ignorance of the forthcoming technical advances in both modem speed and the grid that the net would sit on. What I saw was the truth through my own lens, which was not only skewed by my tendency towards impatience, but was more importantly limited by the narrow window of my perspective. The future might even be here already; sometimes you have to take a closer look. For example, I was surprised to find in December 2014 that the US Navy was set to install its Laser Weapon System (LaWS) on ships in the Persian Gulf to battle enemy drones and ships. What was once probably considered fantasy has now become reality. We must study the present in more detail and with more open minds, preferably with the same rigour and vigour shown by the military. This is needed in order to both widen and narrow our view on what is currently happening around us. Imagine literally switching a camera from wide angle to narrow angle in your mind. This increases our ability to be ahead.

Essentially, to be ahead we challenge what many believe as truth and seek the reasoning as to why. The truths can be harsh – reality often is – but to shy away from it is to neglect our role as leaders and the responsibility we have to our organizations and customers. Today's fundamental truths are simply not tomorrow's – history tells us that – so if we look at the present more effectively, we secure insight and opportunity to make better strategy. Figure 2.2 shows just some of the trends I believe today's organizations and businesses need to move ahead of.

Strategic future thinking

Strategic thinking entails coming up with alternative viable strategies, initiatives, business models or products that deliver customer value. It is deeper than planning as it implies thinking more effectively than the competition, to find alternative and better ways of competing to provide customer value,

FIGURE 2.2   The zeitgeist – current business and social trends

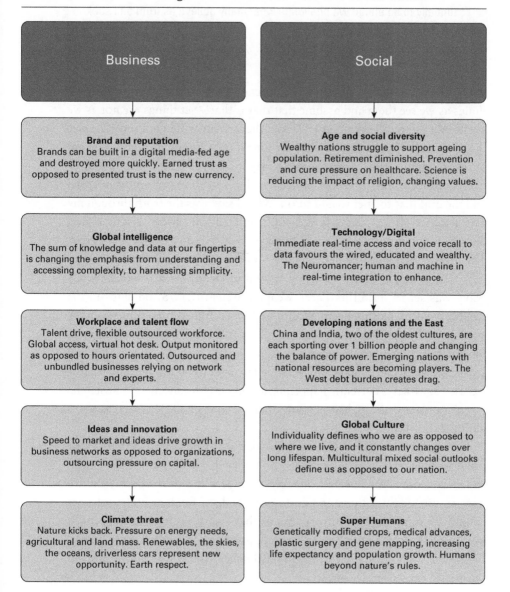

Business	Social
Brand and reputation Brands can be built in a digital media-fed age and destroyed more quickly. Earned trust as opposed to presented trust is the new currency.	**Age and social diversity** Wealthy nations struggle to support ageing population. Retirement diminished. Prevention and cure pressure on healthcare. Science is reducing the impact of religion, changing values.
Global intelligence The sum of knowledge and data at our fingertips is changing the emphasis from understanding and accessing complexity, to harnessing simplicity.	**Technology/Digital** Immediate real-time access and voice recall to data favours the wired, educated and wealthy. The Neuromancer; human and machine in real-time integration to enhance.
Workplace and talent flow Talent drive, flexible outsourced workforce. Global access, virtual hot desk. Output monitored as opposed to hours orientated. Outsourced and unbundled businesses relying on network and experts.	**Developing nations and the East** China and India, two of the oldest cultures, are each sporting over 1 billion people and changing the balance of power. Emerging nations with national resources are becoming players. The West debt burden creates drag.
Ideas and innovation Speed to market and ideas drive growth in business networks as opposed to organizations, outsourcing pressure on capital.	**Global Culture** Individuality defines who we are as opposed to where we live, and it constantly changes over long lifespan. Multicultural mixed social outlooks define us as opposed to our nation.
Climate threat Nature kicks back. Pressure on energy needs, agricultural and land mass. Renewables, the skies, the oceans, driverless cars represent new opportunity. Earth respect.	**Super Humans** Genetically modified crops, medical advances, plastic surgery and gene mapping, increasing life expectancy and population growth. Humans beyond nature's rules.

and thus to accelerate growth in a business. Futurology considers the possibilities of the future, seeking to identify the probable, to understand what is likely to continue and what could plausibly change. It is considered a social science focused around systematic and pattern-based understanding, requiring imagination, creativity and speculation. Many business leaders are highly practical and find such speculative activities leave them cold and that they belong in the realm of science fiction. Furthermore, their experience of planning, which rarely survives for long in a competitive environment, can also leave them with little tolerance or patience for a strategic planning process that requires them to consider long into the future.

Yet, conversely it is looking into the future and creating the future where ambitions and dreams are achieved. If you fail to plan to gain advantage you are planning to fail. However, strategic thinking and looking ahead take time. I address the issue of ensuring we have this time in the next chapter. Table 2.1 outlines the differences between effective strategic future thinking and planning; the final row relates to the game of chess.

In the game of chess, it is proven that the player who can stretch the game further ahead in their mind will always have an advantage, so long as they remember to spot the simple, one-step moves as well. If you think four moves ahead rather than one, you will increase your chances of making the right moves. If leaders visualize this in their thinking, they build a better chance of gaining competitive advantage, effectively out-thinking their competitors. It's impossible to make the right move every time, but engaging more effectively in strategy will help you succeed ahead in the face of the unpredictable. It can be helpful for executives to see the difference between strategy and planning by keeping meetings of each type separate. Studying the above list prior to and at the end of meetings can help executives do this. 'Is Bob any good at his job?' is a management and planning meeting. Conversely, strategy meetings are far broader and more thought-provoking: 'What new products, services, strategic alliances, acquisitions and territories – against what overall and overriding direction – do we want to take the firm to and why in the long term?' Too many meetings are all about what we are already doing. The chess analogy reminds us that there are always other players in the game; gaining competitive advantage requires you to study their moves much more closely.

Strategy has changed as the pace of human and competitive movement has accelerated. To compete successfully in the digital age, you have to know what to do when you're not sure what to do, and you have to decide quickly. This can be done if you increase your research foundations in both data and the environment, thus building a greater understanding of probabilities. We examine this research in much more depth in later chapters. In the end, however, successful companies 'give it a go'. There are some great companies that lost their momentum quite simply because they didn't move fast enough. Ford is still a strong company but it is no longer a first-class business, despite at launch being a first mover with mass production. Its executives – despite representing good, stable and experienced management teams – simply did

TABLE 2.1   Strategy versus planning – key differences

Strategy	Planning
A broad range of facts and critical analysis	Generally a specific challenge or initiative
Consideration further ahead than 18 months	A focus on what next, now
A focus on shareholder value growth as well as profits	A target towards shorter-term profit
Scenario planning, learning and thinking	Looking hard at the current challenge
Futures and environment methodology	Resolving current issues without looking beyond the resolution
Objectivity, listening and preconceptions removed	Objectivity, listening and preconceptions removed
Competitive analysis and advantage comparisons	Focus on organization
A willingness to disrupt, even your current business model	Often involves resolving the content issue (symptom) not context (cause)
Evolving the firm to adapt to and shape its environment to sustain advantage	Internal specific initiative
Setting the overall direction of travel, culture and values	Usually a singular move not a multidirectional move
Decisions despite uncertainties	More certainty of the outcome as singular
Four moves ahead; whole-of-market game	**One move ahead; own game**

not react fast enough in the 1970s and 1980s. The influx of better and cheaper Japanese products resulted in Ford's slow decline from the leading position.

The future belongs to those who see possibilities before they become obvious. We need to increase our ability to anticipate and detect the need to change earlier. Possibly the most important aspect of strategy is to be objective and willing to embrace significant changes of direction, however fundamental or painful those changes might be. To disrupt others and thus own the future, we may have to disrupt ourselves (this is covered in more depth in Chapter 8, Changing the game). In dynamic markets, competitive advantage leaders and organizations put aside the past and their egos. With completely open minds and eyes they seek to own the future, taking action quickly and decisively as a result.

Why being 'first' counts

In this book, being first is not about the brilliant new saviour product that only a genius could arrive at after years of expensive research and development. Instead, we seek better understanding of where the market is heading and thus what actions need to be taken to gain advantage. If you like, it is about leadership and the senior team spotting and engaging strategic opportunity first, before aligning the business to take advantage. We might be first in a new process, marketing initiative or distribution system without any product initiative at all and still gain competitive advantage from the sum of the move rather than the one saviour product. Companies often follow a typical cycle. First, an idea is born out of innovation and creativity. The idea is then developed and materializes as a new offering; this results in a new start-up, or an advantage for the more established organization. However, the managers executing the idea then get caught in the day-to-day operations, which reduces creativity, until one day someone comes along with a better idea that reduces the business to diminishing returns.

A parallel can be made between biological and economic evolution. It is not the strongest of species that survives but those most responsive to change. We examine this in more depth later in Chapter 9, Adaptive organizations. Business is a merciless competition; those that fail to earn high returns are destined to crumble, to make way for the new. In 1942, in his book *Capitalism, Socialism and Democracy*, Joseph Schumpeter coined the term 'creative destruction'. This is defined as the 'process of industrial mutation that incessantly revolutionizes the economic structure from within, incessantly destroying the old one, creating a new one.' This is really just an extension to the old adage that 'business is war'. You might not be competing against the US Navy's LaWS, but you should still perform on the assumption that your competition is executing with the same rigour and vigour that the US Navy brings to bear.

Much of the problem with the concept of first-mover advantage is that it may be hard to define. Should a first-mover advantage apply to firms entering an existing market with technological discontinuity, for example digital word processing software replacing physical typewriters, or should it apply solely to new products? The imprecision of the definition has certainly named undeserving firms as pioneers in certain industries, which has led to some debate over the real concept of first-mover advantage. Apple (until I suspect Google takes over) is the world's most valuable brand, as calculated by Forbes in November 2014 (Forbes, 2014). We tend to associate the Apple brand with being the first mover in consumer technology; however, none of its products were new; others had already launched computers and personal digital assistants (PDAs) before Apple. What Apple did was take new functioning products into supreme design simplicity and added value, through form as well as function. What they were new and first at was combining electronics with art; not ground-breaking transformational technology. Was this a new idea? No, think what Ferrari did to the motor car.

To get to the point: you don't have to be transformational and disrupt entirely new markets with ground-breaking technology to be first. You can, in the sum of your approach, be first, as long as you are focused and clear on how you are different and why this adds value to the consumer. Apple took the tablet, the PDA and the phone and designed them vastly better than its competitors who had already reached the market. They had the additional advantage of being able to see how others did it first. They observed, watched and learnt and then did it better. Market pioneering is neither necessary nor sufficient for long-term success. Understanding first what customers will gain better value from is. Another example is how Microsoft bundled its desktop applications into single packages. The applications themselves were not particularly innovative or first to market, but Microsoft was able to deliver the software in such a way that maximized customer value. In 1998, the United States Department of Justice (DOJ) ultimately took Microsoft to court. The company had gained so much market share through its various bundling strategies that it had effectively become a monopoly.

Timing can be as critical as the product itself, if not more important. This is particularly true when the revenue base can be protected by high switching barriers, or driven by network effects as is the case with numerous internet companies. Microsoft, Google, Facebook, eBay and Amazon are all prime examples of the network effect, whereby the value delivered by these products and services increases exponentially as the number of customers and/or users increases. If you are not first to market, being better (near the start) can also be a strategic advantage. Hubert Cecil Booth may have invented the vacuum cleaner, but this didn't stop William Henry Hoover from improving and simplifying the design. Hoover released his own vacuum cleaner, marketing the product far more effectively than his competitors. The product truly resonated with customers and it was not long before the Hoover brand became synonymous with the product itself. The vacuum cleaner maker Dyson was founded many decades later than Hoover. Nonetheless, the company was able to invent its own niche and with just 5,000 staff, in 2013 Dyson achieved a turnover of £6 billion and a profit of £360 million (Warman, 2014).

People want what is new. If you bought your phone just one or two years ago, it is probably considered outdated today. Notwithstanding the rapid technological advancements in the 21st century, this is not because of major changes in performance, capabilities or even design. Many of the new devices on the market today are really just incremental improvements of past models. It is the loyalty of the consumer to the company and their enthralment with the product and service that allow for these reiterations to succeed. Additionally, it is these regular, albeit minor, upgrades and improvements that cumulatively result in long-term innovations. Not all innovation is necessarily breakthrough or produced overnight. The Japanese coined the term 'Kaizen', translated literally as 'good change', which is often used in a business context to describe the process of continuous improvement. The idea is that if an organization's culture is committed to regularly questioning its work and making incremental improvements every day, these small efforts will yield large results over time. Kaizen is often described as a type of cultural philosophy and way of life, rather than a management tool or one-day workshop. If you cannot predict the future, you can instead strive to create it every day, simply by doing things better and communicating this to your customers. If you are not new, make it look as though you are new. This could be even more effective than actually being better.

Being first is a perception, not always a reality. I am sure some Volvos are technically better cars than Mercedes, but the Mercedes brand is synonymous with prestige in the eyes of consumers, so the technicalities become irrelevant. On the other hand, Volvo did very well with the first mainstream 4×4 7-seater, the XC90. The seats disappeared into the floor well, which was new

FIGURE 2.3   Getting ahead through differentiation, innovation and operations

Ahead

Where are you different?		
Differentiation	Innovation	Operational
• Existing product • New ways	• Better products ahead of others	• More efficient pricing/process/distribution
How do you communicate this?		

at the time. Therefore there is no sure-fire strategy for being first. Figure 2.3 shows how there are different ways to attack the objective of getting ahead. It is not just a matter of intellectual property, it can be equally about new functionalities or building an organization and culture that resonate with customers. Intangibles such as brand recognition, customer service and cultural values can be just as important as raw specifications and technical features. The fashion industry is a very pure example of identifying with customers by focusing on distinct target demographics and customizing marketing campaigns to these demographics. Many of Lacoste and Ralph Lauren's products are fundamentally homogeneous, yet they still manage to differentiate, for example through their heritage, branding, marketing, advertising, packaging, etc. Both have loyal customers.

If your organization achieves first status, it is then well positioned to invest heavily in continuing this tradition, to further its advantage over its competitors. The Coca-Cola Company is an example of a company that has been able to reinvent itself numerous times in the beverage space. The company has an almost unparalleled global distribution network and is home to over 500 brands across 200 countries. By continually reinvesting in marketing, advertising and acquisitions, Coca-Cola has built an economic moat around its business and become a formidable opponent to its competitors. Success therefore is not built on fads; it is built against long-term trends. We demand form and function and as we get more complex we will insist upon it. Where can you be first? Where can you be different and add value to customers in a way that builds loyalty, so that you are seen repeatedly until you become trusted? Even when you are first, you must watch the

FIGURE 2.4   The ahead advantage

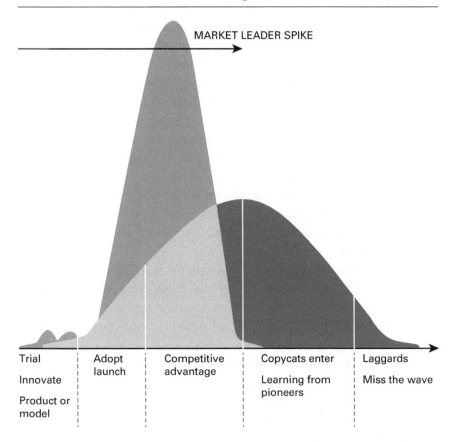

MARKET LEADER SPIKE

Trial	Adopt	Competitive	Copycats enter	Laggards
Innovate	launch	advantage	Learning from	Miss the wave
Product or			pioneers	
model				

competition continuously. Do not underestimate them, as their moves may dictate your moves. Figure 2.4 shows the typical cycle of when either a new product or process creates significant advantage or a spike. Typically the position creates new customers or a new niche and thus a surge before copycats catch on regains some market share, with even laggards or late adopters securing some part of the market.

Customers' expectations

Competitive advantage leaders recognize that the digital age and more dynamic markets have changed the way customers think. Old traditional loyalties have gone. With more information, customers are more fickle. The biggest expectation from customers is that they no longer want to be *told* what they want and how to think. Instead they want to engage in a dialogue and *decide*. Therefore, organizations need to create new models that allow for two-way, not one-way, dialogues. How do you get information to clients and in a way that they want (text, e-mail, social media, etc), while influencing and not persuading? Customers are now empowered, particularly with social media, on an open basis to communicate, not just to one person but to thousands of people, in just one comment. This has immense capability for companies, with some growing exponentially off, for example, simple celebrity endorsements, but there is also a need to respond to negative commentary as well. This has even given rise to specialist reputation management services, provided by many internet marketing and communications firms today, allowing brands to respond quickly to customer complaints and to garner online feedback for use in product development.

Two-way communication lies at the heart of the digital age. Its effectiveness, though, relies on such communication translating into behaviour change. Customers can order virtually anything to arrive the next day. They can receive call back and use live chatting software to ask questions all from the comfort of their living rooms; organizations have to respond and move with this trend. In many respects this is the greatest challenge organizations face in being ahead. It is a business paradigm shift, if you like. It has not always been the case that the customer is right, nor indeed are they; some do have unreasonable or flawed expectations and beliefs, but regardless they can undoubtedly express their views beyond the traditional face-to-face method of engagement. They can now create communities around their views – reasonable or not – and this creates both an opportunity and a threat to being ahead.

CASE STUDY   Gillette

The Gillette Company has a long history of being the first to market in its own areas of operation. The company's achievements include producing the first successful:

- safety razor (1901);
- twin-bladed razor (1972);

- twin-bladed disposable razor (1976);

- pivoting head razor (1979);

- pivoting head disposable razor (1980);

- razor designed specifically for women – the Sensor (1992);

- triple-blade razor; the Mach 3 (1998); and

- battery powered razor; the M3 Power (2004).

The timeline above also demonstrates how innovation has accelerated with shorter gaps between the product designs and launches (Procter and Gamble, 2015). As well as being first to market, Gillette has also continuously produced products that feature improvements to existing technologies. These generate new customer demand and interest, which means stores take the lead in bigger displays, increasing the advantage. Razors benefit from switching costs because each manufacturer restricts the blade heads to the design of their razor. This builds and locks in loyalty – consumers will keep buying the same razors so as to avoid these switching costs – and a brand is thus created. It is critical to note that Gillette has a real, long-term commitment from leaders and management teams to high standards and effective research and development to create revenue-generative concepts and ideas. As many of you will know, it is very easy to lose money designing products, systems and processes that don't work, so real time and care need to be taken to ensure the right direction and investment.

CASE STUDY   Apple Inc

While we have mentioned them before as the world's largest value company at the time of writing, we have to include Apple in our case studies. Apple is an example of a company that has been committed to innovation from the very beginning. The company was founded in 1976, just one year after Microsoft. In February 2015, Microsoft had a market capitalization of around $350 billion, while Apple was valued at roughly double that, at around $700 billion. Both companies have been innovators, yet Apple has performed far better than its counterpart over the long haul. There may be many reasons for this huge differential; however, it is clear that Apple was always different. By combining electronics with art, Apple prioritized design, aesthetics and the overall user experience over raw performance or technicalities. The company's Macintosh, which was first released in 1984, was the first mass-market PC to have a graphical user interface (GUI) and mouse. Apple was never first in terms of engineering or raw computer power, but it never needed to be. Most technical features become commodities quickly. Competitors such as Samsung produce hardware and devices that are just as powerful as Apple's products. The reason Apple is able to charge higher prices and stimulate greater demand is because it has built the most powerful, almost evangelical, brand around its unique product designs and experiences that it is very hard to commoditize.

CASE STUDY   Eastman Kodak Company

A real-life example of creative destruction is the history of Kodak, which was founded in the late 19th century. The first Kodak camera model appeared in 1888. By 1975, Kodak dominated the photography film space. That same year, Steven Sassoon – then an electrical engineer at Kodak – invented the first digital camera, marking an inflection point for the industry. However, despite being largely responsible for the advent of digital photography, Kodak was slow in making the necessary transition.

Kodak saw digital photography as a substitute rather than an outright replacement of the older technology that was film photography. The company's demise was largely due to its reluctance to challenge its (false) assumptions. The Kodak brand became increasingly associated with the older technologies, while competitors such as Sony entered the market and stripped market share away from Kodak. The company's foray into digital photography was half-hearted, and mainly consisted of products such as Photo CD that merely tried to create synergies between the newer and the older technologies. Additionally, Kodak was reluctant to adapt to the industry's changing consumer demographic, which was changing from a largely female to an increasingly unisex and male market. Overall, the company was not bold enough; Kodak avoided uncertainty and failed to evolve, which ultimately ensured its demise. The company finally entered Chapter 11 bankruptcy proceedings in January 2012, and is still currently working on a turnaround effort.

CASE STUDY   Velcro

While hunting in the Swiss Alps in 1941, the electrical engineer George De Mestral noticed several spiny seeds had stuck to his clothes. Noticing the odd adhesive properties of the seed, he took them home and examined them under a microscope, where he noticed hundreds of hooks that caught onto anything with a loop, such as fabric, fur or hair. Mestral saw the possibility of binding two sheets of similar material reversibly – with tiny hooks and loops – as a replacement for buttons, strings, zippers and other fasteners. His colleagues ridiculed his idea, but he took it to Lyon, France, the centre of weaving and textiles and created two prototype cotton strips which worked correctly; however, the proper match of hooks and loops was nearly impossible to manufacture. Mestral finally, as a last-ditch idea, created two identical strips of loops, cut the loop tops off the second strip with scissors, and created perfectly matching loops and hooks. The process took nearly a decade, and Velcro was finally patented in 1955. First-mover innovation can be singular and require determination beyond the belief of others.

CASE STUDY   Hawksmoor Restaurants – London

Being ahead is not always about great product innovation, it can be the sum of the approach, and Hawksmoor is just one of many small but fast-tracking businesses that demonstrate this. Founded in London in 2006 by childhood friends Will Beckett and Huw Gott, the motto is simple: 'Work hard and be nice to people.' It's a philosophy that seems to have been effective – Hawksmoor's business has grown by 51 per cent in the past year.

As well as four restaurants in London's Guildhall, Seven Dials, Spitalfields and Air Street, the company opened Foxlow in Clerkenwell in November 2013, and added 135 employees to its payroll, giving a total headcount of 398. Informal daily briefings and meetings at a grass-roots level, along with a bi-monthly newsletter and a blog are designed to help the whole company feel involved in the business. Pizza Fridays, where all head office staff make themselves available to chat and share a takeaway pizza, are popular. People are treated as individuals – bosses aren't looking for identikit waiters in black ties and employees aren't given reams of rules. Rather, they are expected to display 'Hawksmooriness', with senior leaders sent on a course devised to help them to understand the values. All general managers, restaurant managers and head chefs are internally appointed. Interestingly, Hawksmoor has at its heart purposefulness, and it is the sum of this that gives it competitive advantage. They want a business they can be proud of – whether that's making sure the food they serve is as good as possible, that the animals the food comes from lived a decent life, or that everyone who works for them enjoys what they do.

Purposefulness is a combination of ethics, corporate responsibility, workplace approach and the right business model to build sustainability. It is a very powerful ingredient to create advantage. Hawksmoor are not alone in using purposefulness or doing the right thing to secure competitive advantage. Dun & Bradstreet and Accenture are both substantial corporates that have used a combination of ethical policies and clever workplace management to make them stand-out companies.

Chapter summary and questions

Competitive advantage is won by those who find the time to look more effectively and decisively at strategy. It requires leaders who are willing to take and enjoy taking difficult decisions in the face of uncertainty and accelerating markets. These leaders recognize that building a stronger foundation of increased awareness of the environment is the only way to manage change with reduced risk. You must seek first-mover advantage either in process, initiative or product, and invest in both this effort and any other differentiators that will move your business ahead of the crowd. To achieve advantage, leaders need to contemplate more the past, present (the zeitgeist) and the future in order to create the right access signals to understand what to do in the right way. Furthermore, once the ideas are secured, they rapidly engage these ideas into action for change. They are willing to disrupt others and even their own organizations to add value profitably, to meet the ever more demanding and informed customer, anticipating both their current and their likely future needs.

Competitive advantage leaders and organizations:

- anticipate change ahead of others, while maintaining an awareness of timing;
- enjoy change but with balance;
- invest in seeking new directions constantly;

- research to secure greater commercial awareness;
- disrupt in combination with the right support actions;
- manage the risks of change while still adapting quickly;
- recognize the importance of innovation and move beyond fear, to openness;
- use the past to see better the future;
- create strategies that excite customers and employees;
- challenge old beliefs, preconceptions and conventional wisdom;
- notice small changes early, helping them recognize how to adapt to the bigger changes that are to come; and
- keep moving quickly and decisively, again and again.

Being first in a market at the right time is generally better than having a better product than the competition, with eBay as a great case in point; however, while Hubert Cecil Booth invented the vacuum cleaner, William Henry Hoover improved and simplified the product with far better marketing to the point where the Hoover brand name became synonymous with the product. This shows it is possible to catch up and overtake by strategically positioning yourself to add value to customers in a way that is different and communicating it loudly, simply and effectively: 'We are first and different because...'

Leader questions

1 How much time do you spend researching your environment?

2 Are you and your team clear on the difference between strategy and planning?

3 How willing are you to break through perceived truths to disrupt the status quo, both your own and others' current perceived truths?

4 How much do you study competitors' moves and think several steps ahead?

5 What niche can you own that's following a growing trend but your competitors are ignoring?

6 How well do you communicate your differences and how these add value/benefit your customers?

7 What are your customers actually thinking and likely to be thinking?

8 What can you be first in class at?

References

Forbes (2014) The World's Most Valuable Brands. Available from:
www.forbes.com/powerful-brands/list/#tab:rank [Last accessed 26 August 2015]

Procter and Gamble (2015) A Perspective on Precision. Gillette Product Website.
Available from: http://gillette.com/en-us/about-gillette [Last accessed
26 August 2015]

Warman, M (2014) Dyson cleans up as profits rise ahead of robot launch. The
Telegraph Technology, 16/09. Available from: www.telegraph.co.uk/technology/
news/11097738/Dyson-cleans-up-as-profits-rise-ahead-of-robot-launch.html
[Last accessed 26 August 2015]

Leadership not management

03

Introduction

Creating competitive advantage in a business requires effort, and lots of it. However, with the right ideas at the right pressure points it is possible to contribute more tirelessly, effortlessly and effectively to gain advantage. How do you know the right ideas and pressure points? Well, that's the mastery; many leaders are too busy to take the time to find those pressure points, leading to overexertion and inefficiency. In this chapter we look at the key differences between leadership and management with a particular focus on how to enhance the amount and quality of strategic time.

The leadership equation

Leadership today has become synonymous with charisma and magnetism. We tend to think of leaders as inspiring people with an aura and a certain charming presence. As a result, there is a mindset that you either have it or you don't. For example, Timothy Judge and Daniel Cable found that physical height was positively correlated with social esteem, leader emergence and performance (Cable and Judge, 2004). Perhaps it is because taller people have more presence, and/or their presence makes us feel they will protect us better.

The way we think of leadership as being trait driven is unhelpful as it becomes hard to adopt. You are either tall or not! However, in gaining competitive advantage, there is the truer and more original sense of the word to rely on. That is simply to travel ahead, or go first.

The origin of the word 'lead' is believed to come from Middle English leden, Old English lǣdan and Old English līhan, meaning to go first. 'Ship' was added, as in 'captain of the ship' in the 16th and 17th centuries. Journalism cemented the word with 'lead article', again meaning first, that is 'front page' or 'first to the story'. In this context, leaders are simply built from thinking strategically and thus being ahead in their thinking; first or at least out front in ideas with implementation first. In competitive advantage, leadership is also not always a hero (singular) leader, but rather championed by the organization as a whole. Leaders are the people or teams that take people to new places with new and better ideas at the right times. They translate potential into action and (ultimately) reality.

Leadership can be situational, also depending on the zeitgeist of the moment. For example, investing heavily for growth may be the right thing to do but only from solid foundations, so it may be better to fix the foundations first. This may actually require – and often does require – going backwards before going forwards. From my experience with entrepreneur leaders, many just can't see backwards and are therefore typically blind to the benefits of such a strategy. The man many perceive as one of the greatest leaders of all time, Winston Churchill, was not re-elected despite how his vision, strategy and strength took Britain through the Second World War, as he was perceived to be a situational leader. This reminds us that to be truly effective as leaders, we also have to be agile in our approach and mindset, changing our outlooks with the times to ensure sustainability.

Every business owner and CEO wants to be a good leader, but how can you be a good leader if you don't know what leadership really is? Unfortunately, leadership doesn't have a one-size-fits-all definition. We all have our own ideas about what it means to be a good leader. Overall, however, leaders are people who know how to achieve goals and inspire people along the way. A great head start can be gained by thinking strategically ahead in the right way, and thus helping the organization to shape the future, rather than managing the status quo. Looking and thinking ahead, anticipating, generating ideas and building a cause around these are a skill that can be learned, whereas charisma is usually more inherent. Figure 3.1 depicts how your organization's flow and strategy are integral to your results and culture, and how these are underpinned by your business design, which ultimately guides the direction in which you are going.

Leadership versus management

Science fiction shares many tales about humans who can no longer master technology and/or where technology becomes our master, from HAL in Arthur C Clarke's novel *2001: A Space Odyssey* to the Hollywood film *The Matrix*. In 2004, IBM created a supercomputer called Deep Thought to play

FIGURE 3.1 The leadership equation: thinking ahead, ideas and anticipation

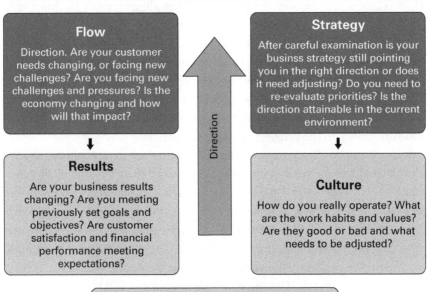

Flow

Direction. Are your customer needs changing, or facing new challenges? Are you facing new challenges and pressures? Is the economy changing and how will that impact?

Strategy

After careful examination is your businss strategy still pointing you in the right direction or does it need adjusting? Do you need to re-evaluate priorities? Is the direction attainable in the current environment?

Direction

Results

Are your business results changing? Are you meeting previously set goals and objectives? Are customer satisfaction and financial performance meeting expectations?

Culture

How do you really operate? What are the work habits and values? Are they good or bad and what needs to be adjusted?

Design elements

What is the business design, and how is it optimized and efficient against the objectives and goals? Does the current structure support delivery of the work tasks? Is the organization staffed accordingly? Are the decision-making processes effective? Are informatin systems supporting the work? Are the recognition and reward programmes reinforcing the desired results?

chess, a game which is both intuitive and logical and therefore intensely difficult to compute. This was the first computer to beat chess grandmasters and today the chess programme on your phone would win. We have become so complex that there is no point in trying to understand everything. We have already discussed how we live in a world of accelerated change; even if you catch up, change will overtake you. Leadership has changed from expertise to harnessing. We no longer need the orchestra's conductor (leader) to be the best musician (operator) but instead the best conductor. As we will discuss later in this chapter, leaders' primary responsibilities lie in strategy, not in management or operations. Leaders – the generalists – create value by bringing the specialists together and harnessing their collective skills and expertise.

Intellectuals who worry about such things suggest that the scientist and polymath Thomas Young was the last man to know everything. He died in 1829. The effort is thus no longer in knowing all, as it can't be done; it is instead in harnessing knowledge. A polymath has expertise that spans a significant number of different subject areas, which enables them to draw on a complex body of knowledge to solve specific problems. I contend that today, in fast-moving markets, the competitive advantage leader is a polymath. They may be specialists in their fields, but they also look far beyond the specialism to all the other components that connect the organization profitably and sustainably to the zeitgeist and market demand.

Many contend that actually being able to do the job or trade the organization conducts is actually a hindrance as opposed to an advantage. The chef that loves to cook is too 'hands on', and fails 'hands off' to design the menu and the overall dining experience, which is much more than the food. Certainly this is a challenge for smaller businesses, where the owners are good at a trade and build a business around that trade, 'hands on' with all roads pointing to them. They scale up and then the business plateaus as they become the bottleneck. The same can also occur for CEOs in both corporates and mid-tier businesses. The leaders get caught in hands-on managing and organizing with (again) all roads and paths pointing to them. This leaves little time, or in some businesses even permission, for strategic exploration and research. Yet how can competitive advantage be achieved unless the leaders aim at this goal with ruthlessness and determination? Management can and should be employed to run the businesses while leaders take the time to harness, conduct and implement an advantage strategy, looking at complexity to solve problems at source. As Figure 3.2 shows, leadership and management are mutually necessary for success.

The contention is that as the world is changing faster, we need to spend more time researching strategy in order to harvest more opportunity. If we are hands on in managing the business, we don't have the time to do this. Managers organize and design the process; leaders creatively develop ideas, inspire and take and manage risks. Organizations need both, but also need to be clear on the different roles to enable more effective growth. Whether someone is good at their job or not is a management question. Decisions as to which new products, strategic alliances, acquisitions or territories an organization needs are the strategic questions.

Companies that require leaders to manage tread a dangerous path, as innovation falters and strategy fails to ride ahead of competitors. McDonald's was innovative in the 1950s and 1960s and has been an absolutely first-class business in its management and processes. Effective processes ahead of

FIGURE 3.2 The interdependence of leadership and management

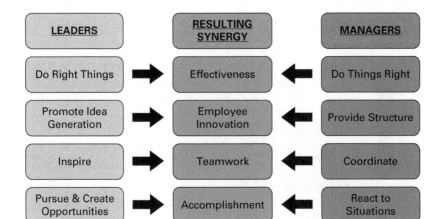

competitors around the early takeaway concept gave it world-class, first-mover advantage, but today it has lost its dominance. There are significant competitors, mainly in the healthy food arena, taking market share. Some observers might feel that McDonald's was arrogant and focused on management as opposed to looking creatively at what consumers were going to want in the future and disrupting themselves to gain advantage. They have left others to disrupt instead. The business is a significant machine, but another factor may well be that the franchisee model makes it harder for them to choose to update. It might be in the corporate's interest to update stores to consider the future, but franchisees may not wish to outlay the capital, depending on the longevity of their outlook.

In the previous chapter I used the chess analogy to bring the strategic idea of thinking more moves ahead. This is important, but as one grandmaster put it, advantage can be won with just one move, the best move. In dynamic markets leaders need more time to invest in securing the best move. Spending too much time in management may prove fatal. Figure 3.3 emphasizes where leaders are (and should be) positioned in an organization, in accordance to their value. This is not to say that managers are of less importance – they are equally crucial to an organization's success, as implied by Figure 3.2. However, what is important is for leaders to not confuse their roles with those of managers.

FIGURE 3.3   The hierarchy of value: leadership versus management

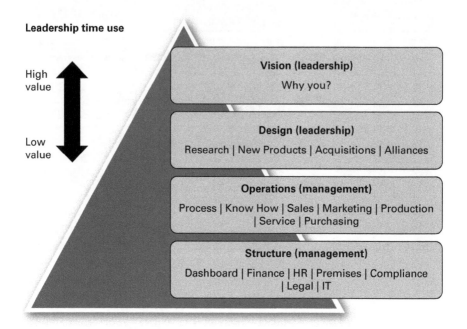

Leadership time use

High value

Low value

Vision (leadership)
Why you?

Design (leadership)
Research | New Products | Acquisitions | Alliances

Operations (management)
Process | Know How | Sales | Marketing | Production | Service | Purchasing

Structure (management)
Dashboard | Finance | HR | Premises | Compliance | Legal | IT

Outlooks and roles

As well as understanding the distinction between management and leadership more effectively, advantage can be gained when leaders consider their mindset more carefully. Most strategy books concentrate wholly on organizational moves for advantage, mainly via marketing niche, product innovation or the business model. However, the leaders that shape organizations are critical; for leaders, understanding their roles better and their organizations' attitudes and permissions to take risks is central. An advantage strategy may require the disruption of existing product lines or research and development, with no absolute guarantee of the outcome.

Leaders may be too conservative or risk averse and the culture may be static. Others may also feel guilty about spending time on strategy, or not really understanding the central role of strategy. Strategy is not busy, meaning it is not 'hands on', and requiring all hours; that is the kind of work most people can relate to. It's not directly related to the production of a good, or the provision of a service. Instead, it's creative, imaginative and insightful. In some respects, to do it well requires the opposite of being busy and many leaders struggle with this, which is why they may have a tendency to revert to management. Management feels like work and can make you feel important. Everyone asks you questions, rather than you asking lots of questions. Strategic advantage actually even requires you to look dumb. Some of the best shifts come from asking the basic and almost childlike question, 'why do we do it this way?'

To create advantage, leaders need to understand where they sit on the spectrum, both in terms of ego, time balance and clarity in their role. They also need to build a second tier that they absolutely trust and empower to manage the business day to day, to implement processes and organize. Leaders also need to trust the second tier, and to leave them to fulfil their roles without interfering. In particular, owner managers used to being the most important cog in the organization have a tendency to interfere with their second tier, out of guilt that they are not feeling busy when working on strategy hands off from the business. The second tier need to understand the leader's role to research the strategy and harness advantage, while leaders need to build a team they can trust and not interfere day to day, to create the slack needed to enable them to look for the new initiatives. Both need trust and permission to operate.

What is surprising in many organizations is how little the distinction between the two roles is understood, or clarified, let alone talked about. The role of the leader, and in this context the managing director or CEO, is:

- With the support of the senior team, to set the ultimate direction of the organization, ahead of and in the zeitgeist to catch and add value to current and future customer demand, sustainably and ethically. Which markets, competitors and products? How do we stand out and gain advantage?

- Researching, to embrace the possibilities and opportunities, investing time and resource into who and what it is we and the organization aspire to become.

- To take more time to look at the market dynamics and competitive moves, to determine where the most sustainable business direction is.

- Creating ideas and a 'give-it-a-go' culture to enable new initiatives to have a chance to grow. Being open about what is holding you back.

- To communicate clearly the direction and set a culture around its achievement, while leaving management to implement the processes and actions.

- Designing the environment to secure and retain top talent and create a cohesive team.

- Building the senior team and setting high standards, enabling effective people performance management.

- Balancing risk and reward in the direction of the organization, while investing in the pursuit of difference from – and advantage over – the competition, anticipating markets.

- Communicating the strategy and listening to ensure it is engaged wholly, continuing to question progress at all times.

- Securing buy-in from stakeholders in conjunction with the senior team, and establishing how the risks are going to be managed and why changes are necessary.

- Putting a cause around the direction. Helping people to understand what they are contributing to the organization and the wider world to make long hours easier.

- Harnessing the components to create results. Not managing the components.

- Financial measures in accelerating both profit and shareholder value and working with the financial team to manage cash flows and capital expenditures, as well as investors and other stakeholders.

- Serving the organization and its customers to make the world a better place, rather than for their own remuneration or ego.

- Being accountable. It is the leader's role to anticipate markets, so blaming markets for poor performance is not an excuse. They additionally hold the responsibility over firing, so blaming resource is again not an excuse. Humility is needed, not arrogance.

- Joining the trends, data and research to develop a coherent and robust strategy and vision, despite the uncertainties when looking to the future as opposed to the now. How do we create competitive advantage?

Time for advantage

Most leaders, particularly entrepreneurs, lack formal training and no one appraises them apart from perhaps ultimately the company's performance. Advantage can be gained with the right leadership time focus, in securing and implementing the right ideas in the right way. If the leader is too entrenched in management or subconsciously avoiding the areas they don't understand or enjoy, the opportunities to seek competitive advantage will be diminished. Leaders may unbeknown have bad habits, particularly in where they spend their time and in being objective about their strengths and weaknesses. Due to this issue, it is likely that whatever is working well or not working well in the business is probably because:

Working well

a) You are good at that aspect
b) You enjoy that aspect
c) You put your time and energy into it

Not working well

a) That aspect is not one of your strengths
b) You do not particularly enjoy that aspect
c) You do not put as much time and energy into it

Furthermore, you may spend more time organizing and managing than on research and strategy. Competitive advantage can be gained therefore when leaders optimize their time and attention effectively, with the right management support beneath them. Time management is about increasing capacity (duration), whereas time optimization is about focusing on what to do (composition). This simplified exercise is designed directly for leaders to explore this concept further.

TABLE 3.1 Activity

Activity	Hours
At work (A)	
Away from work	
Sleeping	
Other activities	
Total	7 x 24 = 168

The above must add up to 168. Try not to make a judgement about this at the moment, but you might like to note your reaction to these figures, as the ratio forms the most basic measure of work–life balance. Then break down the time that you spend at work into some fairly broad categories. Estimate the time you spend.

TABLE 3.2 Activity

Department	Hours
Operations: Actually doing/organizing the work that the business is set up to do	
Finances: Dealing with the finances of the business	
Sales and Marketing: Include customer-related activities, contract tenders, fee activities, etc	
Supplies: Sourcing new supplies, ordering supplies, stock or quality control	
General admin: Any form of general admin that has not been accounted for elsewhere. Include phone calls, e-mails, etc	
Staff: Managing, organizing, recruiting, appraisals, etc	
Governance: Announcements, managing stakeholders and shareholders	
Travelling: If you have not already included this, add it here separately	
Problem solving: Resolving immediate challenges	
General meetings: Not innovation-, research- or strategy-focused	
Total (B) – Hands-on (management work)	
A– B = C Hands-off strategy time to create advantage (leadership)	

While the above is of course a simplification, considering the focus and capability of leaders to drive at advantage is an essential first step to securing it. Building the resource below the leaders, to allow them the space to look ahead at markets and ask where the market is going, and then align the business strategy to take advantage ahead of competitors, is critical. Also crucial to the process is cultural permission to spend more time in the speculative arenas.

The theory here may be new to entrepreneurs but corporate CEOs, particularly those with MBAs, will see the above as basic. Nevertheless, the exercise is still an important check to how much time you actually spend on seeking and creating advantage. Taking the time out to navigate further ahead and design a better business will create a more efficient business, but you can't do all the work alone. Your team has to be involved, trusted and given the space to help drive and deliver the vision. This motivation is best achieved by involvement, careful communication and dramatized ideas; that is, simple ideas and messages that uplift, encapsulate and share the goals well.

Working upstream

Earlier in this chapter, we looked at the idea that it is what leaders spend their time on that makes a difference, not how they increase time capacity. This is essentially about ensuring the direction that leaders face is towards creating change to get ahead, not managing the status quo. In this we can also secure an extra idea. Ultimately, leaders resolve problems internally and externally in how their organizations add value to their clients and customers. It is important that they proactively resolve problems at source, rather than reactively fix problems' symptoms as they surface. It is very easy to spend a lot of time and be very busy in crisis mode, fixing problems and perhaps securing the status 'Hero of the Hour', but in reality this is 'firefighting'. Prevention at source, ie avoiding the fires in the first place, is far more effective, looking more deeply at cause rather than symptom, or context rather than content.

There is a famous river parable that illustrates this. There is a high waterfall, and at the bottom of this waterfall hundreds of people are working frantically trying to save people who are falling down the waterfall, many of them drowning. As the people along the shore are busy rescuing, one individual looks up and sees a seemingly never-ending stream of people falling down the waterfall and begins to run upstream. The rescuers cry, 'Where are you going,? there are people drowning.' To which the individual replies, 'I'm going upstream to find out why so many people are falling into the river.'

> Prevention at source in avoiding the fires in the first place is far more effective, looking more deeply at cause rather than symptom, or context, rather than content.

Competitive advantage is best achieved when new ideas, processes and innovations are secured by leaders who understand the hands-on issues, but have permission or take the decision to resolve them hands off, in context not content. The leader must be a polymath, harnessing all the elements; an astute observer of your world, business or sector. You have to immerse yourself in watching, listening and wondering. Pay attention, ask questions, probe, discuss and gather information, while spotting competitor moves, trends and challenges ahead. Look deep to secure the underlying truths, then reason up from there. This requires more mental energy and abandoning conventional thinking, but it can also yield the greatest results.

Competitive advantage leaders look deeply at the challenges upstream, before building and communicating a simple vision around fundamental solutions, building a cause around resolving those challenges to make the world a better place, inspiring and motivating the organization to work together to achieve.

easyJet is one of Europe's most successful airlines. By working at source with more streamlined bookings, straight talking and cost-effective marketing and stripped-down service, easyJet made 'cost effective' fun and the growth story has been amazing. Many consumers bemoan the lack of niceties such as on-board complimentary meals, but compare the cost to full service and expensive branding, time and time again they opt for low-cost carriers. People want to travel more; and on short-haul, low-cost, fast-turnaround flights, easy booking and a what-you-see-is-what-you-get philosophy works.

Open-mindedness and outlook

> People who are consistently more accurate while generally being more intelligent all share one other vital trait: open-mindedness.

Gaining advantage requires us to be ahead and this requires us to attempt to forecast more accurately. We look at some techniques of how business leaders might achieve that in the next two chapters; however, a leader's outlook will also be as an influencer. Psychological studies, most notably a study in 2015 by Philip Tetlock at the University of Pennsylvania, demonstrated that the people who are consistently more accurate while generally being more intelligent all shared one other vital trait: open-mindedness (Tetlock *et al*, 2015). Open-minded people tend to be able to see problems from all sides, which helps to overcome preconceptions in the light of new evidence, which in turn encourages more accurate forecasts and promotes greater creativity. Open-mindedness allows us to gain the advantage we need to change our minds fast, and more often. Many business leaders see strength and certainty as being the best method to gain advantage. However, these studies, as well as business case history, suggest that flexibility, openness and adaptability are far more important traits in both the leader and the business.

Many leaders are not sufficiently aware of the threats and opportunities that may be present, both internally in the organization and in the external environment. Often this is because the business is successful and therefore perhaps an understandable assumption is made that the business has advantage, but this can lead to complacency. An 'everything is okay, we are making steady progress' mindset is easily overtaken, and the fact that very few firms maintain advantage long term shows how alert, positive and open to change leaders and organizations need to be.

Creating competitive advantage requires understanding and that only comes with research, and lots of questions, as well as active listening: where is the market really going? What do the team and customers truly think? Active listening is not just about silence, as too often in the silence we are thinking of what to say, or reflecting on our views, or judging what has been said. True listening requires a blank canvas to understand what is being said, without external or internal judgement and in particular preconceptions that reduce effectiveness.

The aim is to be clear to the team that there is an achievable, larger goal and maintain a relaxed, natural focus which preserves the quest for competitive advantage. Rarely do innovations and creative change run perfectly. Even when things get tough (and they always will at some point), choose the positive; choose to learn from it and teach your team the same approach. As one leader put it to me, the outlook is always 'I am a believer.'

Things will go wrong, changes will be required and decisions will need to be made; many of these will rest on the leader's shoulders. Too often, however, leaders opt for the obvious choice or make heavy-handed decisions. Great leaders have the ability to quickly step back, listen, watch, and then employ imagination, intuition and creativity. They then use advice, experience, analysis and ultimately their instinct to be decisive with clarity. It's important here to understand that you can't get every decision right, though competitive advantage leaders still usually beat the odds. They know that being decisive and sometimes wrong (after appropriate analysis) is usually better than procrastination.

Self-discipline is an action, thus it is actually stronger than motivation which is an emotion; a source of strength to see something through. The power to deliver large, creative and exceptional undertakings when you say you will is awe-inspiring. Its achievement is overall a learned skill coming from training, breaking the mindset into chunks, managing your energy levels, and patiently building to the end result. Working smart and choosing the right tasks and tools all contribute, but ultimately success is still achieved by tackling things task by task and staying the course to seek the difference. There is no talent to acquiring a competitive advantage mindset; mastery requires effective management of the mind, awareness, focus and practice.

Creativity

How do you transform the ordinary into the extraordinary? The answer lies in design, creativity and ideas. These come through research, collaborative working and allowing the freedom to dream a little. Leaders that encourage innovation and harness a creative workplace environment, as well as allow themselves to be creative, naturally flourish. Creativity is the source of new ideas and inspirations, and these ideas lead to innovations in new products, processes or services, which then ultimately help to drive the organization forward. It is not always essential that the leader is creative, so long as they encourage the trait and provide permission for it in the team, and have the ability to spot the good ideas from the many.

The pace of change has accelerated, which means that innovation is essential just to secure sustainability, let alone long-term success and competitive advantage. If you don't innovate and change, others will and your products and services will become obsolete, probably inside five years (or at best 10). If organizations want to make sure they have the services and products that people are going to want in the future, they need to be thinking about developing them now. There is no one path to creativity – one person or organization's mistake is another's creative work-around.

What can you do to focus your and your employees' creativity, and create a working environment that constantly pushes the creative envelope? Who in your organization or sector deviates positively from the normal or conventional? How can you use them to intentionally destabilize the working environment, foster creative workshops and even sometimes cause the tension that is required to spark innovation?

The leadership remains with the conviction and the communication that change, innovation and creativity are essential to achieve advantage. The purpose is to be creative and to be ahead, but also add value to the organization and the customers, to make the world a better place and receive maximum enjoyment and fulfilment.

What conventional wisdoms today are history and how can you and your team creatively disrupt them? Give the ideas a go; they may fail but you won't find out unless you try. Great products often require initial failure to make them great. Pixar lost over £50 million in the first 10 years trying to be a computer animation hardware business, before they hit the fact that they were better filmmakers. *Toy Story* eventually ensued, followed by a £7.4 billion deal with Disney. If you have not seen *Toy Story*, you should; it changed the game, making 3D computer animation – as opposed to ink 2D animation – a foundation of the global film industry (BBC, 2006).

Open, purposeful, humble, caring and trusting leadership builds, shapes and sustains creative culture, analysis and ideas implementation, against the winds of dynamic complexity, shifting markets and the changing technologies that we face today.

Chapter summary and questions

Competitive advantage is secured by organizations that are run day to day by exceptional managers, who support and allow their leaders the space to create, be different, to research and to ask the more fundamental truths to resolve issues at source. What will tomorrow's common sense be – not today's – and therefore what needs to change? In fast-moving markets, this question is more critical. The status quo today – the way things are – will be wholly different tomorrow. It is in anticipating tomorrow's likelihood that advantage is won, by placing the organization ahead of the moment accordingly. Business, customers and consumers are future focused, therefore organizations that plan for today are already behind the zeitgeist.

Moving from management to leadership takes time and it's painful. It requires more risk and creativity. It's less obvious and perhaps even less busy, so it feels less comfortable in a world where we are told that it's hard work – not working smart – that builds success. On the contrary, it is in the creation of new products, differentiators, alliances and acquisitions, and innovations that sustainable advantage is achieved. If you don't do it, your competitors will. I want to reiterate that securing a culture and ability for this 'creative advantage leadership' to work takes time, but is well worth the investment. We must also recognize that organizations need consistency and reliability to profitably service today's customers. This protects well what already exists, but consistency and reliability are contradictions to creativity. Organizations need to find ways to harness and embrace both. In understanding the difference between leaders and managers and each giving permission for the other to be their very best, we start the work of creativity and bring into existence that which has never been before, gaining difference and competitive advantage.

I mentioned earlier in Chapter 2 how Coca-Cola is a first-class brand and process business, but today they have a problem. That problem is that in the West, fizzy drinks are in fundamental decline. Pepsi-Cola have a snacks business that creates a nice offset. Coca-Cola's purchase of the UK's Innocent Drinks (a health drinks business) and buy-in to Monster (a power drinks business) will help offset the decline (Euromonitor International, 2013). However, these are small purchases and I can't help feeling that Coca-Cola, however well run, has been a sleeping giant in terms of disrupting itself and accepting that its core market is in decline. What products or brands or shifts in customer perception have they achieved for the health-conscious Western consumer? Leadership requires painful choices and the pursuit of the truth. Compare this to the BMW i8 vehicle, which has become almost iconic overnight. It is a plug-in hybrid with the appearance and the breathtaking performance of a sports car, which at the same time exhibits the consumption and emissions of a compact car. The Toyota Prius pioneered the technology, but the i8 convincingly resolves the apparent contradiction between efficiency and dynamics. I have no idea how much BMW spent on R&D to build the i8, but Elon Musk's pioneering Tesla has competition from a mainstream heavyweight that looked ahead and saw the future.

Leader questions

1 How 'hands on' versus 'hands off' are you?

2 How strong and supportive to research and trying new ideas are your second-tier management and what is your culture for innovation?

3 What are your customers' challenges and needs at source and how do you resolve those on a fundamental level?

4 How can you solve these challenges and needs profitably and ethically?

5 How do you put aside your preconceptions when you listen?

6 How clear are the vision and the cause behind that vision, to make the world a better place?

7 Why is your organization genuinely different and better and how do you communicate that?

8 How much clarity do you have on the likely direction of the marketplace, and therefore confidence and determination to make the changes that need to occur in your business, however hard they may be to ultimately realize?

References

BBC (2006) Disney buys Pixar in $7.4bn deal. BBC News, 24/01. Available from: Source: www.news.bbc.co.uk/1/hi/business/4642116.stm [Last accessed 26 August 2015]

Euromonitor International (2013) 'Coca-Cola Co the, SWOT Analysis, in Soft Drinks (World)' [Online] www.euromonitor.com/medialibrary/PDF/Coca-Cola-Co_SWOT_Analysis.pdf [Last accessed 26 August 2015]

Judge, T and Cable, D (2004) The effect of physical height on workplace success and income: preliminary test of a theoretical model. *Journal of Applied Psychology.* Available from: www.ncbi.nlm.nih.gov/pubmed/15161403 [Last accessed 26 August 2015]

Tetlock, P *et al* (2015) The Psychology of Intelligence Analysis: Drivers of Prediction Accuracy in World Politics. *Journal of Experimental Psychology: Applied.* Available from: www.apa.org/pubs/journals/releases/xap-0000040.pdf [Last accessed 26 August 2015]

The line of probability

04

Introduction

Competitive advantage requires leaders, with the support of their senior team, to set the ultimate direction of the organization ahead of the market direction or zeitgeist (current reality). That is, to catch and add value to current and future customer demand, sustainably and ethically. Which markets, territories and products? In this chapter we review how to stand out ahead of others and identify market trends that can be utilized to gain advantage.

Anticipation

Being ahead requires anticipation. What are customers likely to want and why? If your service or product truly anticipates your customers' desires and wishes, you achieve pull, rather than push, with your customers. That is, you influence customers to seek you out rather than needing to persuade them all the time. Influencing is more complex and subtle but far more sustainable than persuading. If you can create a feeling in your customers that they can't, and don't want to, live without you then you have an advantage. Anticipation is well presented in the Ritz-Carlton Hotel Company's ethics in what they call their 'Gold standards': 'The Ritz-Carlton experience ... fulfils even the unexpressed wishes and needs of our guests.'

Anticipation, of course, is not easy and requires a lot of time, understanding and skill. What are the probabilities for your market and likely customer demands? Ultimately it needs leaders who are alert, open and who listen objectively to figure out likelihoods to guide us: understanding the past to build the future. Answering the questions of where are we now and what is likely to happen next can allow us to better understand what could happen in the future, before our competitors do. Predicting singular events is difficult; however, ignoring long-term market trends results in a flawed strategy.

The primary function of prediction is to better define the current reality and present customer need and experience, then build a strategy on the future possibilities. How do you create a vision that drives and empowers the organization and its people, building change around anticipation to constantly attack the status quo ahead of others? The skills can be built and learnt.

Scanning

Beyond intuition and experience, there are two main skills and methods to gain awareness of reality: anticipation insight and strategic perception. Where are we now, and how do we get ahead of others? Both are research orientated. The first method is via analysis of data and direct intelligence; collecting data to 'trend extrapolate'. Trend extrapolation is the most used and understood method, particularly in the big data age, of building a window to the future. It is obvious but not simple. In my experience, data analysis tends to lead to specific and perhaps micro insights. We examine this method in the next chapter.

The second method, which is perhaps underutilized or little understood, is much more intuitive and thus perhaps simpler. The method is environmental scanning to secure the line of probability. This is a technique where leaders seek to look at the whole of the market path: the past, present and the possible which tends, in my view, to lead to the macro or big picture insights. In reviewing the environment, yesterday's history gives us perspective, today's facts tell the story, and tomorrow is a mystery. Scanning and reviewing these elements increase our ability to solve the mystery, by linking the connections between various trends, discoveries, innovations and competitive moves. Scanning increases information which, when absorbed correctly, shows us the current reality and a clearer strategic path to the future possibilities.

The objective of scanning is to look over the widest range of possible factors, events and developments, and identify connections, threats and opportunities to the business and its activities. Scanning aids, provides and develops continuous awareness and evaluation possibilities and probabilities that build better plans, decisions and strategy. It enhances anticipatory action and proactivity, building understanding on the moving elements of the environment that are converging or diverging at a significant pace. When we see these movements we may then perhaps also see the ideas and opportunities that can create advantage.

Scanning might involve observing, studying, researching and examining:

- direct competitors' moves and strategies;
- competitive products (specifications, prices, distribution methods);
- market research and customer surveys;
- details of your market (size, competitors, trends, forecast);
- talking to customers and suppliers;
- analysing specific events such as a competitor product launch;
- parallel sectors with good comparison to your sector (some of the best insights can come from here);
- reviewing social and cultural history, trends and attitudes;
- political climate and legislative environment;
- financial environment review;
- investigating new territories (and countries) and trends in those markets; and
- technological, scientific and infrastructure changes.

The environment

The external environment in which an organization exists consists of a complexity that can appear bewildering. However, by monitoring, scanning and studying the environment, an organization and its leaders can consider the impact of the different factors, events, trends, acts, issues, expectations and specific occurrences in order to make better decisions. This is not just about being informed, it is about thinking contextually to see behind the information to the drivers or causes of the data to understand better what that information might actually mean (see also Chapter 5).

All leaders carry out some form of environmental scanning, whether intentional or unintentional. However, it is rarely focused or observational enough with the intent of specifically trying to anticipate what will happen in a market or customers' likely future needs. We all walk in the park from time to time, but how often do we slow down to observe the shape of the trees or the gentle breeze? We might look at competitors' websites, but we don't often dissect their websites, secure their brochures or carry out a 'mystery shopper' exercise to directly ascertain their approach. It takes much more time and effort to actually be present and connect to where we truly are, and increase observation in our businesses and environment, but when we do this we become alert to many more possibilities. Your business and your environment are complex if you want them to be, but it can be fascinating how much simpler reality is when you strip out the layers of complexity and look at the heart of matters. In my experience, it is surprising when you truly understand the reality and the environment how a few, critically 'right' moves can catapult you and your organization to advantage.

Scanning is really investing in research but with a specific intent of understanding the current environment better on a macro basis as opposed to looking for specific data. As a simple specific example it is quite interesting how many CEOs I meet who admit (on interrogation) that they have never taken out a credit search on their key competitors or looked in any great depth at their websites. How can you beat your opponents' moves unless you study them? It is fascinating just comparing websites and seeing how many of your proud unique selling points actually fail to pass muster when you do a comparison. By the way, if you do this a really good audit test for your company and its website is to also note how many times you list features but don't present the client benefit. Truly understanding your competitors is critical in order to understand where you can stand out and what niche you can own and make yours. Without a more detailed review of competitors and an understanding of the hierarchal environment they and you operate in, strategic understanding is too basic and too exposed to moves from the competitors.

> Our view of history shapes the way we view the present, and therefore it dictates the answers leaders can offer for the future.

A true understanding of today's reality, environment and the likelihoods can be a very powerful way to gain advantage. Our view of history shapes the way we view the present, and therefore it dictates the answers leaders can offer for the future; indeed it has been said that he who controls the past controls the future. Today we live in a time of progress, rapid change and dynamisms. As a result we tend to define ourselves by where we are going, and less where we have come from; however, understanding the past, the environment and present reality better can be the foundation for true strategic understanding and innovation. Can you imagine being operated on by a specialist surgeon who has not seen your medical history? It could be disastrous and the outcome much more uncertain. Environmental scanning creates the medical record.

Mapping the line of probability

A really useful way to visualize, share, collate and build on active scanning is building a probability model. This is a schematic technique where you study and then map the milestones of history, innovation, news, events and key shifts in your sector. In the first chapter I discussed the ultimate macro context of human history and innovation, and below I have pulled this into a mapped line of probability to give you an example of the method. Your model can be a mind-map graph or family tree. The key is a visual that helps you put context to the past in order to assess the likely future.

In my example, the horizontal dotted line denotes the present, below this line is the past and above is the future and we can, using scenarios, trends and supposition take fairly reasoned guesses of innovations in the near future. *Star Trek*'s teleportation is a way off but we already have their communicators in our PDAs (Personal Digital Assistants) or smartphones. I have used this macro example to reinforce a theme of the book that overall the pace of change has increased, as you can see from the sharp line increase in technology evolutions over the last 200 years, virtually in line with population growth and our ability to share knowledge today in an instant.

On this example I have used on the Y axis human population growth, but sector size in sales is useful on the Y axis. The key idea behind the model is that mapping key events helps you see the trends and the pace of change and therefore increases visibility on next steps. The further away from the present, the less the visibility but this is still a powerful technique.

The line enables you to map the key triggers in the past, waymark success, focus on goals and create a trigger for creative solutions. If we can visualize the key influencing events in our sector we may be able to see the pattern and thus understand what we can do, and therefore want, more clearly enabling the focus to be on our *preferred* future. The schematic is meant to provide strategic intelligence to the strategic planning process by identifying changing trends and potential developments, monitoring them, forecasting their future pattern and assessing their impacts. The map creates the engagement in the future and helps people envision and connect better to future thinking. The forecasts may not be right but the work for innovation will be better as you will have more perspective and some lively positive debate.

An interesting case study is Africa: the continent has a population of over a billion; however, today, the vast majority – over 90 per cent – still do not have internet access (Internet World Stats, 2014). However, it is expected that access will reach nearly 50 per cent over the next 5–10 years, which leaves a huge opportunity in telecommunications. This megatrend has the

FIGURE 4.1   An example line of probability:
based on civilization development and future prospects

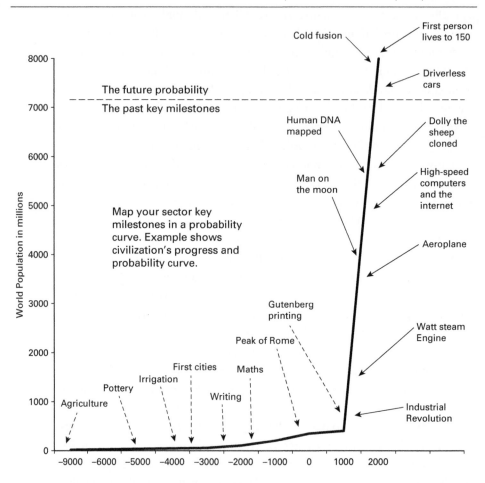

probability and strong potential to mint a new line of internet/telecommunications billionaires over the next decade. But more importantly, with the internet and more open access to information, can we then, as we have seen in other regions, forecast increasingly long-term political accountability and stability for the continent? In 50 years' time will we see a more united Africa and will it be competing directly with China, today's emerging superpower? At the time of writing, its growth is already outstripping Western economies and it has significant labour and natural resource to rest upon. In this, we can see a cause-and-effect relationship established with regard to events and trends for the long and short terms.

Joining the dots

The environmental scanning creates the line of probability and in this picture we can then see how to join the dots. That is, forming scenarios or probabilities from the information and consequent observations and then trying to join them up to create a cohesive and coherent market probability that we can then run against our strategy work. What are the logical inferences from the information and observations? What are the simplest and most likely hypotheses or probabilities for your sector? What are your customers going to need or want and, consequently, how do you plan to take advantage of these likelihoods?

Let me use an example of how we might join the dots to build a probability scenario. Let's examine how the passenger airliner market might be likely to develop in the future. Aircraft have remained fundamentally similar for nearly 50 years. The 1970 Boeing 747 held the passenger capacity record for 37 years, and modern aircraft have had nothing like the step gains achieved in the first 50 years of planes. This is because flying heavy objects take a lot of energy and the jet engine reliant on fossil fuels is the only thing that has managed to get near this output. We use oil to make this fuel and we are running out of oil. Despite all the technological improvements, by 2030 the world output of oil and other liquid fuels from current fields is expected to drop to 43 million barrels per day (mbpd), some 62 million barrels below projected demand of 105 mbpd (Cobb, 2012). The reduction in production from existing fields is about 4 per cent per year. There will be more projects identified in the coming years of course which will offset the decline. Hydraulic fracturing or 'fracking' to extract shale oil will help but forecasts are that it will only add 3 to 4 million barrels of daily production.

To keep us flying in a world without oil, it would be nice to imagine that we will defy the laws of physics and invent an anti-gravity system as depicted in the 2014 film *Interstellar*. However, it seems more probable due to the technical challenge and huge energy required to keep planes in the air, that instead aviation will end up as the last preserve of the oil industry. Today, planes use the oil distillate kerosene. If this supposition is right, for the near future airliner flight developments will be about comfort and fuel efficiency not speed or fundamental shifts in technology. Let's examine the dots that drive my thinking.

Solar planes are encouraging but it is more likely to lead to hybrid planes due to the weight required, therefore the likely line of probability for the near future on aircraft is shifts in business models, increases in fuel efficiency and noise reduction, comfort, interiors and service as opposed to mode of aircraft, type of fuel or faster aircraft (and besides legislation bans sonic booms over land). There are experiments for windowless planes with virtual windows to improve streamlining but fundamentally we have been sitting on the same technology for 50 years. Hydrogen planes have proved a dead end so far with the huge energy cost required to make hydrogen. Biofuels will work if and when oil runs out, but today they require lots of water and in many cases the removal of trees thus increasing CO_2 to create the land mass; then of course with 7 billion people there is the land versus food debate. Concorde, the one supersonic plane, was retired in 2003 as customers favoured cheaper airline tickets and the fuel cost was nearly five times as much as a normal aircraft.

Overall it seems we get amazing technology leaps every now and then. The carbon combustion engine enabled the Wright brothers' first airplane flight of 832ft in 1901. Furthermore, when we know how to do something, we improve inventions well (within 35 years the air-breaking Douglas DC3 could fly 28 passengers a distance of 1,495 miles) and very fast but eventually end up with diminishing gains until the next radical shift comes. In my view, it's going to take a light cold fusion device or something similar to fundamentally change aircraft technology and that is a long way off. If this scenario is right, we can probably plan for the reasonable foreseeable future that incremental gains in aircraft travel will mainly be in comfort and efficiency rather than radical shifts. The line of probability helps us join the dots and see more clearly what is most likely or least likely and in particular looking for the interaction between factors. It is the joining of each of the backgrounds or dots that creates the picture.

So in my interpretation of the dots I imagine it is likely that for the foreseeable future airliners will be mainly about interior, more passengers per fuel load and cleaner engines. Will someone invent a mobile app per flight that tracks my exact departure time, which baggage carousel, notifying me and guiding me to the departure gate and letting me pre-book my preferred lunch? Or, stretching your imagination, picture a robot airport pod seat container that meets me at the airport or even in the city, security bio scans me in and loads me automatically by slotting into the aircraft. I get into the pod, which knows when I will be arriving at the airport and does all the faffing for me, slotting into the aircraft so that I can ignore the whole tedious process in my 3D environment. It could also unload me on destination so all that queuing and shuffling in the aisle goes too! It will be a fuel-efficient aircraft engine that the robot delivers me to but still I suspect for some time a fossil fuel-based jet, unless gravity changes.

By joining the dots we see the whole picture. In this example I have reviewed technology, environment, legislation and current pace of change, customer and economic demands and fused this to create a probability. In my probability supposition I suspect we may well end up banning oil use in all other applications just to preserve our ability to fly. Electric driverless cars are easily in reach but these don't have to fight gravity as much, just friction. Both modes of transport will also have to contend with greenhouse gases and global warming. Electricity still takes energy so we will need to find better renewable sources for generating it with wind and tidal looking more promising than solar. So in my mind, joining the dots if we can win on the ground with renewable electricity we may yet preserve the skies both for flight and environmentally, but unless we achieve a radical shift in engine technology I suspect it will be a carbon-based future. Failing that, we may need *Star Trek*'s 3D holographic deck technology for the majority of our tourist experiences or business meetings.

The chairman of Virgin Atlantic Airlines, Sir Richard Branson, contradicts my suppositions. He believes in, and the company is investing in, engineering companies to develop clean fuels produced from materials such as isobutanol, which interestingly is also algae-based! These biofuels will, he hopes, power our planes without emitting carbon and without eating into our food supply (Branson, 2015).

What are the influences on your sector and customers and how do you fuse or join these to create scenarios? Once you have these, how do you create a plan to catch the direction or place the business ahead of the direction, thus creating advantage?

Seeing from all directions

The information and macro view of the probabilities enable us to predict broad outlines, but we don't know all the ramifications for our businesses. Information travels everywhere and virtually anyone can access everything today as a result of the internet. Consequently, we are driving innovation in every direction, which means faster interconnected change and perhaps, with unlimited combinations, can and will create unforeseen consequences. This is the long way of saying that your suppositions or scenarios may well be wrong but we must continue to try as advantage still lies mainly in anticipation. Increasing our awareness of the skills and techniques is essential with faster change, but it means we must look more and create more time to look in broader directions.

Again, using my airline example and to my mind the biggest threat to my scenario, is today probably not in engine technology, which is plodding. Instead, it is in the possibility that we create artificial intelligence (AI) in computing in combination with Moore's Law of computing power. Gordon Moore, who founded Intel in 1975, forecast from extrapolation that the number of transistors per square inch on integrated circuits would roughly double every two years. This forecast has been accurate, exponentially increasing computing power. I think defeating gravity more efficiently due to the power involved will take humans a very long time to solve but super smart computers set to task may well do it for us. Imagine if we were allowed to devise a mankind solution programme that was able to cross the world's firewalls and join all the relevant information together with the sole aim of creating an answer to more efficient flight. We may then yet resolve the challenge. Artificial intelligence may progress to the point of a greater-than-human intelligence, and that would radically change civilization.

In this comparison we can see that often the biggest disruptions to our probability thinking can come from outside our sphere of thinking or influence. Truly effective business scanning thus needs to be both macro and micro, and it is perhaps, in the attempt at, rather than the actuality of, accurate prediction, that advantage opportunity is created. Several famous scientists have proposed the best way to predict the future is to invent it, but in the scanning we carry out we can ensure better that the new invention, concept, process, service or product is in the likely right direction at the right time. For example, I suspect that algae-grown bio-snack food is 30 years too soon to sell. The algae spirulina is about 25 times more efficient per square foot than any other plant and it contains all of the amino acids and is a complete protein (Instructables.com, 2015). With pressure on land mass its use is compellingly logical and sound but the market demand is not yet mature; too many psychological and historical barriers need breaking down at this point.

> The future of advantage leadership lies in our ability to understand both our business environment and to see in all directions the broader world.

In this context, the future of advantage leadership lies in our ability to understand both our business environment and to see in all directions the broader world around us, and how we and our organizations fit into it.

The specific market developments that occur may well be a surprise, but by scanning the probabilities it is more likely that we will lead the surprise, or at least better understand the important market shifts.

Often leadership quite rightly has high standards, often seeking perfection. Attention to detail like this can make the moment exceptional to customers; however, the flaw can be that we are so busy micro-managing the detail that we lose sight of the bigger picture and fail to see the implications of our environment. Perfectionism can also waste energy. This is akin to the artist never finishing or the report writer agonizing over the minute details, yet the improvements of the finalization are often not appreciated by the customer and, worse, take far too many resources. Perfection could be spent on researching the environment and consequent probabilities, innovation and strategy. One certainly suspects this is, for example, Microsoft's product roll-out strategy and while we bemoan the bugs on product launches one must concede that they are successful and manage to quickly fix the big issues. Love or hate them – and that does seem to be the divide – Microsoft still dominate the PC operating system market today, after nearly 40 years, and with the purchase of Nokia aim to fight back in the mobile arena. Time will tell if they are too late. We should seek exceptional service but also know where to draw the line so we can have the time and resource for innovation, and to look strategically at our environments from all directions.

When considering the macro environment and the probabilities, leaders may also need to consider how they and their teams think. While we may be seeking answers to specific challenges, it may also be helpful to look at and give better consideration to the numerous variables and how they link, whether that be customers, employees, capacity, competitors, cost structures, sector developments or regulatory environment. If we can do this we can capture the multidirectional relationships between all of these variables in our minds and are therefore usually better able to see the challenges and the opportunities. Leaders who look for advantage in their environment in all directions tend to:

- consider more variables to a problem;
- seek out alternative views and contradictory data;
- avoid simplification and accept complexity to avoid limited thinking;
- maintain open minds deliberately;
- keep the whole picture in mind;
- accept and seek tension; and
- strive for creative solutions.

Good teams will actually have all types of thinking and exist in embraced unresolved tension and it is the tension that creates the better understanding and strategy. To simplify this I am reminded of an old business joke:

> There was a balloonist who realized he was lost. He lowered his altitude and spotted a man in a boat.
>
> 'Excuse me, can you help me? I don't know where I am,' the balloonist asked.
>
> The boat man consulted his portable GPS. 'You are in a hot air balloon approximately 30ft in the air, 31 degrees north latitude and 49.09 west longitude.'
>
> The man in the balloon rolled his eyes and said: 'You must be a finance director.'
>
> 'I am,' replied the boater. 'How did you know?'
>
> 'Well,' said the balloonist, 'everything you told me is technically correct but I have no idea what to do with the information and I am still lost.'
>
> The man in the boat replied: 'And you must be a managing director – your head is floating in the clouds and you have no idea where you are going. Worst of all, you are in exactly the same position you were in when you started but somehow it is now my fault!'

Forgive the joke but in this we have the perfect example of how finance directors tend to be very specific in their micro attention to detail and managing directors very broad or big picture as business jargon affords. The polar opposite usually creates tension that many fight but the key is to absolutely embrace the difference, which beyond the debate is far more likely to lead to new ideas.

Looking at things from all directions as well as specifically solving challenges creates positive tension, which leads to more questions and in questions lies the opportunity to think differently, and being different is where advantage usually lies.

Mapping parallel sectors

Environmental scanning that considers overall wider market trends increases anticipation but it can also help to map out comparable sectors or parallel sectors. Done correctly there will be comparables and indeed you may also find new customers. For example, many keen skiers are also cyclists. Many cyclists use a CamelBak (a rucksack with an inbuilt hydration pack so you can carry your drink with you and access it via a long tube which reaches your mouth). Such cyclists also use them for skiing but ski shops don't tend to stock them. Why? How many skiers who don't cycle would buy them but are simply unaware of the product?

Overall, if we are researching the trends and future probabilities in our sector that path may be a little too predetermined by our own mindset and thinking about the sector. Parallel sectors may actually be a better place to reinterpret our strategy by constructively questioning the normal practices that have been so established in our own environments. Or, put simply, it's amazing how many *new* ideas are repackaged ideas from other territories or sectors. How many business ideas have been inspired by travel and holidays? Look at how travel has influenced architecture. If we only look at the world through the lens of our own sector or probabilities we fail to see the trends in other arenas. For example, at the time of writing, digital print companies are, with cloud solutions, scanning and the paperless office, facing declining volumes and margin. The solution is to start offering the new products.

If we don't look across sectors we miss things. Malthus, one of the world's early and great tacticians and thinkers, blundered famously and quite loudly when, at the end of the 18th century, he mapped population and birth rate and, against trends, forecast that the world's population would outgrow resources, thus predicting looming disaster. The population is now seven times the number at the time of the prediction and still growing – so what went so badly wrong with the Malthus forecast? Although the growth trend was accurate, there were two other directions that he didn't account for. Firstly, he failed to understand the readily available, albeit emerging, economic theory that demand stimulates its own supply, and that this principle could also be applied to food products as much as any other. Secondly he failed to map agricultural technology development which was, and has been thus far, as fast as population growth.

Today, with genetically modified food on the horizon and the ability to develop super foods including algae-based products it remains likely that we actually have the landmass to increase population further, and substantially. As opposed to food source, the bigger cap to population growth is probably our ability to create enough energy for consumption in sustainable ways without damaging our environment beyond repair.

In 1913, Henry Ford is credited with revolutionizing mass production and batch production with his Ford Model T. Certainly the work he carried out was extraordinary and changed the world, reducing the time it took to build a car from more than 12 hours to 2 hours and 30 minutes (Ford, 2015). However, the most significant piece of Ford's efficiency crusade was the assembly line, which was inspired by the continuous-flow production methods used by flour mills, breweries and industrial bakeries, along with the disassembly of animal carcasses in Chicago's meat-packing plants. Ford installed moving lines for bits and pieces of the manufacturing process. Manufacturers now understand to look cross sector when designing factories, but at the time who would have thought that the food sector would show us how to make cars more efficiently? Interestingly, one Mr John Penn, an early English manufacturer in the time of the Crimean war, carried out one of the first pieces of batch production for the British admiralty. Given just 90 days to create 120 gunboats he had a pair of engines on hand of the exact size. He took them to pieces and he distributed the parts among the best machine shops in the country, telling each to make 90 sets exactly in all respects to the sample. The orders were executed with unfailing regularity (in part because of Joseph Whitworth's pre-work in standardizing screw thread sizing), and he actually completed 90 sets of engines of 60 horsepower in 90 days – a feat which made the great continental powers stare with wonder. How much did Henry Ford look at shipbuilding? In this example, we can also see there are very few big new ideas – mainly borrowed ones repackaged, and repackaging the right idea can create significant competitive advantage.

By the 17th century London had over 600 independent coffee shops. Corporate chains, however, dominate today's market with Starbucks in the lead. Starbucks took the McDonald's model of reliable format, fast delivery, marketing and consistency, adding volume and buying power and it is very hard for independents to compete. Starbucks first arrived in London in 1990. There are, according to the company's own website, 246 Starbucks cafes in Greater London and nearly half of these, 119, are in the central Zone One (Starbucks, 2015). This is far more than any other European city predominantly because the English moved on from a coffee culture in the 20th century to tea, leaving the gap wide open to the corporate coffee machine and the US roll-out concept. How much did the hugely popular TV show *Friends* and its coffee culture establish the trend in London? Starbucks have not, however, had free reign. Costa started in London in 1971 and opened their first coffee store in Vauxhall in 1978. How much did the coffee sector learn from food takeaway chains?

In this context we can see that mapping parallel probabilities also means defining your competitors broadly. Your competition might include anything that could draw potential customers or clients away from your business. For example, cinemas might compete not only with other cinemas, but also with bowling alleys, restaurants, live music, and movie downloads. Try to see the choice from the perspective of your client or customer rather than your organization. What motivates you to go in one direction or another? What impediments today or tomorrow stand in the way of customers choosing your business?

To secure advantage we must create the future by intercepting old, negative thoughts and strategies and instead insert new ideas and expectations. Inspiration and new business models that deliver and capture value are more often gained from outside rather than from directly within the environment.

Competitor probabilities and scanning

Securing competitive advantage usually requires both defining the competition better and mapping out the environment to create better understanding. Researching the competition enables us to both identify and potentially exploit strategic moves against the competition. Such research is broadly ongoing and while it is important that leaders ensure they have continuous research support, the final responsibility to deeply understand objectively the competition's marketing, model, strategy, position, pricing and services should always sits with leadership. Table 4.1 is a grid which shows the type of comparisons your organization can conduct. The approach might include:

Research as a customer. Visit, call and ask a lot of questions and take notes. If you can't, find someone who can. First-hand knowledge of their approach is critical. How do they pitch, what is their sales approach, how clear are they on their compelling propositions, what is their pricing model and why?

Compare your customers. Meet, talk to and research the customers of your competitors. When you lose a customer ask why and objectively how was the competitor better? Why do they buy from your competitors? Is it because of the quality of the product or service, the price, the location, the customer support, or just habit?

Use the internet. Facebook, LinkedIn, Duedil, Dun & Bradstreet, Dow Jones interactive, Twitter feeds all allow you to find out more truly what your competitors are doing. Make sure you are on their mailing lists. Carry out a detailed internet audit: what search terms are in use and why? Who is optimizing these on both a paid basis and an organic search word basis; how are the competition capturing and using data versus your approach? What demographic is being targeted and focused on and why? What products are being promoted heavily and what are the buying patterns?

Company filings and Companies House. Many of those filings are public record and contain information about the company's goals, strategies and technologies. Disclosures are required to Companies House, public offerings, shareholders (consider buying shares in plc competitors) patents or trademarks, and more.

TABLE 4.1 Competitor scanning example

Company names	Mid to premium range category			Low-cost category		
	Mercedes	BMW	Volvo	Daewoo	Nissan	Renault
Key for success	Engineering	Driving	Safety			
Product quality						
Technology						
Product differentiation						
Key financials						
Market share						
Quality of service						
Unique selling points						
Quality of management						
Sales force/ distribution method						
Brand name recognition						
Advertising/ promotion						
Internet positioning						

Industry conferences and trade shows. Attending carefully selected
events is one of the best ways to get to know your competition and
the nature of your environment. What are competitors focusing on
and what have they stopped promoting? What are customers
interested in that's new?

Research resource

Mapping the line of probability and scanning the environment take time,
and require a team approach. In the previous chapter, we discussed that with
faster changes in markets, leaders need to secure more time for this work by
building driven management teams to take care of the day-to-day running
of the business while leaders look ahead. In this sense I am clear that many
leaders delegate and even abdicate market research and keeping up with
their competitors to the marketing department. This does not make sense. It
is too important to strategy. What is right is that a team approach and
resource can be built and added into the equation on an ongoing basis. For
example, Tesco, one of the world's largest retailers, employs over 50 data
and market analysers. If you are a small business perhaps consider each year
the employment of a summer business graduate intern to carry out a market
and competitor review. Technology and medical companies have long
invested heavily in research and development with dedicated teams built
wholly around these functions. In both service and retail or leisure environments we need to adopt some of the mindset of continuous research resource
to maintain and create advantage.

Beyond building an internal research team we can also consider outsourcing
– via market research organizations perhaps for primary research, or utiliz-
ing specially trained business librarians who can help you with your research by providing assistance with market research and lists, competitive
intelligence, and industry trends for established businesses. For example in
the UK, for a low-cost membership fee, all Institute of Directors members
can have up to 25 secondary research enquiries per year, each up to 30 minutes
long and pulling on significant resources: electronic databases, journals and
press release information. If you are looking at new countries or export, UK
Trade & Investment (UKTI) offers research resource and trade fairs for
nearly every country in the world, again at very low-cost access. Most other
countries have similar services and bodies. Investigating how you can
research more systematically, effectively and continuously need not be high

cost and the return from spotting opportunities will nearly always offset the investment.

Leaders and organizations can obtain information from different sources, but it should be ensured that the information is correct and in the correct chronological order. The correct source should be tapped for specific information for more accuracy. Information received from secondary sources may sometimes misguide, hence it is important that information should be verified for accuracy before it is processed and decisions are taken based on it. The various sources from where information can be gathered might include:

- internal (see also next chapter on data) files, records, management information systems, employees;

- internet, television, radio news, etc;

- trade publications, magazines, newspapers, books, e-shots, newsletters, annual reports of companies, case studies, etc;

- external customers, suppliers, marketing intermediaries, advertisers, dealers, trade bodies, regulators, government agencies, shareholders, competitors, etc;

- market research reports, consultants, educational institutions, testing laboratories, etc; and

- customer surveys, mystery shopper analysis.

Chapter summary and questions

Before you can plan where you are going to gain advantage you need to have a clear idea of where you are, and also where the market is likely to go. This means reviewing your current market and parallel sectors situation – identifying trends within the economy and society that may affect you, as well as building a better understanding of markets, customers and competitors, and where you fit within this framework. This can be a fairly lengthy process, but it is invaluable.

The line of probability is a mapping tool that enables you to collate and present the environmental scanning date in one place and to then start predicting the flow of future events. The idea for me was inspired by the great sci-fi author Isaac Asimov and his 1950s Foundation series set around an idea known as psychohistory. Psychohistory depends on the idea that, while one cannot foresee the actions of a particular individual, sufficient social behavioural patterns and trends (see next chapter) in large groups of people could broadly predict the general flow of future events. I liken this to steam coming out of a kettle. You can predict the movements of a mass of gas near the funnel but as it gets further from the funnel the units spread out and become more individual and thus wholly unpredictable; physicists actually call this movement of gas 'kinetic theory'. With the right information on human behaviour and trends the near future for most sectors is foreseeable and can be planned for.

Competitive advantage requires leaders, with the support of the senior team, to set the ultimate direction of the organization, ahead of and in the zeitgeist to catch and add value to current and future customer demand, sustainably and ethically. Ultimately the further from the funnel (now) you go, the less forecastable life can be, particularly in an accelerated world without boundaries. However, it is actually the act of asking the right questions of the future, and thus generating ideas that enable competitive advantage leaders to write the future.

Leader questions

1 What are customers likely to want and why?

2 Which markets, territories and products?

3 How can you stand out ahead of others and market trends to gain advantage?

4 What probabilities does your organization face and how can you anticipate them better?

5 How much time have you and your team spent on research seeking the right questions?

6 What strategies could you employ now, ahead of the competition?

References

Branson, R (2015) Making Sustainable Fuel a Commercial Reality [Blog] www.virgin.com. Available from: www.virgin.com/richard-branson/making-sustainable-fuel-a-commercial-reality [Last accessed 27 August 2015]

Cobb, K (2012) Long term oil forecasts – merely guesses. Oilprice.com 12/12. Available from: http://oilprice.com/Energy/Crude-Oil/Long-Term-Oil-Forecasts-Merely-Guesses.html [Last accessed 27 August 2015]

Ford (2015) The evolution of mass production. Available from: www.ford.co.uk/experience-ford/Heritage/EvolutionOfMassProduction [Last accessed 27 August 2015]

Instructables.com (2015) Food of the Future: Window DIY Spirulina Superfood. Available from: www.instructables.com/id/Food-of-the-Future-Window-DIY-Spirulina-Superfood/ [Last accessed 27 August 2015]

Internet World Stats (2014) Internet users and population statistics for Africa. Available from: www.internetworldstats.com/stats1.htm [Last accessed: 26 August 2015]

Starbucks (2015) Store Locator. Available from: www.starbucks.co.uk/store-locator/search/location/london [Last accessed 27 August 2015]

Trends, systems and big data

05

Introduction

A key theme of this book is strategy in fast-changing markets. Strategy requires us to anticipate likelihoods in the future. However, in a dynamic global economy with a boundless 24-hour culture, this is much more difficult than in previous ages. Consequently, many people have argued that strategy is dead in favour of agility. Essentially the idea is that if you can't plan to steer around the choppy seas (market movements), then you can ride them (the waves). There is a basis for this argument and I have therefore included a chapter on agility, but as I have said already, it is in the attempt at anticipation and looking ahead that the strategy ideas come, not necessarily the accuracy of the predictions. Surfing (agility) works but rarely results in a planned leading competitive advantage. For this we must understand and lead with the 'current'. Therefore, with the theme of changing markets, we continue in this chapter with the question 'How do we anticipate better?' and thus improve strategy and advantage.

Predictions

In the previous chapter we examined how environmental scanning can create an essentially intuitive approach and a macro window and view to anticipation and the future. However, there is the analytical approach, which today sits in the arena of what's now referred to as big data. The ability to extrapolate trends from the data enables us to foresee the future with greater efficieny. What trends can we see against the data and key performance indicators (KPIs) that help us understand what is happening in our businesses better; which markets, territories and products should we pursue? What are customers doing today, and what does this tell us about what they are likely to want and why? Trend analysis of data and business intelligence can help us gain both macro and micro insights. In order to carry out this work, we need to understand how we gather, collate and display the information to then improve our interpretation of that information. With the right data feed we might identify, for example, a long-term trend that our customers are getting older. This of course creates a finite problem, so the question becomes: how do we engage with a younger audience?

The reason it is described as big data is that today there is a lot of it. From social media and marketing journeys to financial data, the key is to link all the elements together. The aim is to transform our awareness of the way customers are thinking, to be able to see the patterns and trends. The data is useful if it's accurate and when you are able to understand and communicate it, relate to it and share it to improve strategic awareness. The more everyone sees the data trends and bigger picture, the better the awareness of how to take advantage. However, collecting and analysing the data take time, process, investment and systems across diverse arenas. It also takes clarity, efficiency and focus. Building systems can be complex; if garbage is put into the system, garbage will necessarily come out. For example, do your salespeople really understand the importance of the metrics they input to the customer relationship management (CRM) database?

Intelligence is dangerous if it is unreliable and unfocused. In the first chapter I suggested that the key to managing big data is the question of what do we *really* need to know, and not what can we collect. I also reminded you of Douglas Adams's *The Hitchhiker's Guide to the Galaxy*. In the book, a group of hyper-intelligent pan-dimensional beings (this is probably your IT department or if you are a corporate, your data scientists) demand to learn the answer to the ultimate question of 'life, the universe, and everything'. They build a supercomputer, Deep Thought, to tackle the challenge. It takes Deep Thought 7½ million years to return with the answer 42. Deep Thought points out that the answer seems meaningless because the beings who instructed it never actually knew what the question was. How do you turn intelligence into something manageable and translate it into better decisions?

The process of capturing, managing and analysing large and complex data sets can have profound benefits for organizations. The process can allow organizations to better understand their customers and therefore significantly improve their decision-making and business practices.

Business planning based on big data and predictive analytics is still uncharted territory for many executives. Many feel it is too complicated, risk inherent and the preserve of data scientists or information technology, leaving them to fall back on intuitive decision-making. Often this is ego driven, the justification being that 'my' experience is better than the data feeds which are too complex. The contradiction, however, is that the data is there to reduce the fear in decision-making, and improve intuition. Using data to only examine results is also dangerous, as the data displayed may already be obsolete, therefore we must also look at the lead or trend indicators.

Data analytics – the process of capturing, managing and analysing large and complex data sets – can have profound benefits for organizations. The process can allow organizations to better understand their customers and therefore significantly improve their decision-making and business practices. Data analytics can also support the development of tailored products and services in many different industries and fields. Effective data analytics creates major advantage if prioritized correctly in the right systems that join the dots; see Figure 5.1 for a basic depiction of this process. As an example, fusing marketing data more effectively with financial data is very helpful; if we can truly understand how much a customer costs to win against their average sale, we can use these metrics to both drive that cost down and programme better marketing campaigns ahead, with clearer returns on investment. It amazes me when I ask leaders how few know these metrics; surely they are fundamental to understanding how to drive growth?

FIGURE 5.1   Using data feeds and interactive dashboards to create advantage

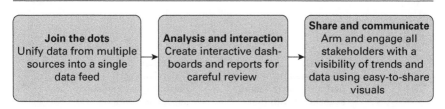

The idea of unifying financial and non-financial indicators is not new. It is one of the underpinning characteristics of the widely used Balanced Scorecard (BSC) performance report, first introduced in the early 1990s by Dr Robert S Kaplan and Dr David P Norton (Kaplan and Norton, 2005). The BSC measurement concept suggests we develop and collect analytics and models that link four main data sets and perspectives. These are 'learning and growth', 'internal processes', 'customer' and 'financial'. The goal is that increased learning will lead to improved processes and customer satisfaction; financial results are merely the result of these perspectives and should not be the sole focus. The aim is to align a business's operations to these perspectives and as a consequence convert vague goals such as 'increase customer satisfaction', into actionable targets, such as 'reduce complaints by X', perhaps by 'reducing staff errors by Y', which could be 'balanced' and addressed by 'increasing training hours per employee to Z'.

The BSC seeks to translate strategy into measurable and operational goals, by focusing on both financial and non-financial indicators. The system then encourages aligning all employees' incentives to these goals, adjusting future strategy in accordance with the results obtained. The BSC has been a

FIGURE 5.2   Using data feeds and interactive dashboards to create advantage

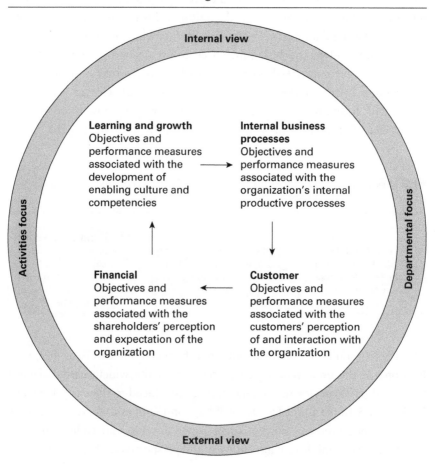

popular area of study in academia and the system has been adopted by various organizations, including DuPont, ExxonMobil, Lloyds TSB and even the UK Ministry of Defence. The BSC's holistic approach could be integrated into an organization's data analytics efforts, to build a deeper competitive advantage. By focusing heavily on the indicators that are most relevant to your organization's long-term strategy, you are more likely to make better, more strategic decisions and receive more actionable feedback. Financial data on its own is inadequate; investment in customers, suppliers, employees, processes, technology and innovation also needs to be monitored.

The dashboard

Many business leaders are not numbers or data people. Leaders tend to be creative and charismatic, but numbers and data are critical as indicators of both where you are and where you may be heading. They are essential to building knowledge, visibility, insight, better decisions and consequently competitive advantage. Imagine a dashboard in a modern car. Much like a business, a car is a highly complex, evolved machine, but the system manages to take complexity and turn it into data. The system then feeds the key information into a simple picture that helps the driver make better decisions about both the road ahead and how to manage their vehicle. The dashboard today tells us whether we are safe, need to fasten our seatbelt, or if the road is icy. Our cars can even interpret panic stops by both scanning the road ahead and assessing the rate at which a brake pedal is activated, automatically braking for us if need be. In other words, the dashboard can not only identify challenges but also – if it is sophisticated enough – help us resolve challenges. Many companies, often without really realizing it, actually look at Key Results Indicators (KRIs) that show only results and not progression – indicators that look at the past rather than prepare for the present and the future.

The business dashboard analogy is well used and understood. There are even specialist companies that have software designed around turning your data feeds into a visual dashboard. As an example, a fuel gauge predicts when you will run out of fuel. A cash flow forecast predicts when you will run out of cash. However we arrive at the dashboard, having a clear and manageable window to your key performance and trends indicators is critical. Ideally we will also then have a system that enables you to interrogate the data in more depth. The dashboard is the feed from the business engine. When we see data that's curious, we will want to stop, open the bonnet and see what is really happening. This may be by trend analysis, review of anomalies or extrapolation. I will review data interrogation and how we can actually create better reports later, but what might be the key reports required?

Key performance indicators

Before even thinking about key report and technology, an enterprise must ensure they understand the key drivers for their business. The key reports will depend on the organization and their trade; however, as a steer, avoid the traditional year-to-year reports. The problem is that year-to-year reports can take six months or more to show performance or trends. Adopt trailing trackers instead. These are rolling reports, typically showing the last 24 months or more. The effort is the same to create a tracker, but they help you to see seasonality and continuous trends more effectively. Table 5.1 provides some examples of key performance indicators, or KPIs.

Once KPIs are defined, they give a clear idea of both trends and performance. This enables you to not only set goals and targets, but to also change course if a particular trend shows something is clearly not working. In retail, 'sales per square metre' can help us both improve the ratio and spot when things are not working: is the trend up or down and in what product arenas are customers showing most interest? Another great example would be lead generation in business-to-business services. Historically mailshotting was highly cost-effective, but today post is rarely opened, so marketing activities have moved to Google and e-mail shots. Salespeople used to be effective at lead generation via telesales, but today, the phone is less answered. Google is also cheaper than having a salesman open the door. These trends seem to be continuing, and have strong implications for those organizations that are not yet fully adept with the changing times.

The use of KPIs should also not be limited to executives and senior managers. By displaying the data on the shop, sales desk or factory floor, employees have a better sense of performance levels and therefore tend to strive for higher performance. Visual management also provides actionable information that allows supervisors to better monitor performance and determine, in real time, areas that may need improvement. The overall result helps to drive productivity throughout the organization by increasing efficiency and quality.

The list of reports you can generate is endless. It is important to decide what is critical for your business. Design a simple tracker dashboard for measurement over longer periods than just year to year, then monitor the results. Through this activity we can assess trends, set targets and proactively

TABLE 5.1　key performance indicators

Financial dials	Marketing dials	Production
A daily cash report	Number of leads	Cost per unit
Weekly cash forecast	Source of lead per campaign	Waste reduction
Aged debtor creditor analysis	Cost of return on investment per campaign	Capacity utilization
Fixed costs / gross margin percentage	Number of prospect meetings	Quality assurance
Turnover	Cost per click	Yields
Operating expenses and profit	Click-through rate	Machine output
Profit/capital employed (return on capital)	Conversion rate	Downtime to operating time
Sales split per product and territory	Number of clients	Production length
Average operating profit as a % of sales	Average sale	Task time, or cycle time
Sales per employee or per square metre	Items per sale	Work-in-progress inventory
Current assets / current liabilities	Complaints	Stock inventory

manage performance. If we know both the cost of winning a client and their current life cycle, we have much better foundations for growing a business.

Using the indicators

However familiar you are with reporting and data feeds, it is worth looking at a few examples of how they can help. By measuring the return on investment and cost per acquisition of a client, you can select which campaigns to keep, and drop the lower-performing ones. You can then use the freed-up budget to trial new campaigns. Understanding how much it costs you to win a client enables you to catalyse growth via marketing programming. 'If we run a campaign and scale it up, we will win X new clients which in turn generates Y.' It's amazing how many leaders see marketing as a 'soft creative-led skill'. In reality, marketing should be driven by the maths first – the 'hard analytics skill' – with the soft aspects following. If you are engaged in branding, such as sponsorship, PR or exhibitions, be wary as these are areas where it is notoriously difficult to track response. Of course, your marketing team should also be monitoring all the subsets, such as internet or e-mail campaign clicks, speed of response to clicks.

The tracker concept also allows us to identify trends over long periods of time. As an example, the Google pay click landscape has become more heavily populated, so the general trend in many sectors is for the average cost per click to go up as a consequence of demand (Gunelius, 2014). Figure 5.3 shows an example of how trackers can be used to identify long-term business trends. In this case, you can see a clear, positive correlation between the 12-month moving averages of employee training, employee satisfaction, customer satisfaction and sales. Perhaps from these findings we can hypothesize that each of these four elements is sequentially causative, and that we should therefore encourage further employee training in the future. Rolling averages, or trackers, help organizations proactively identify trends as they develop, rather than only becoming aware of such trends in hindsight.

In respect of finances, beyond cash, the most insightful measure on trends is looking at the margins. The main way to grow businesses organically is by generating additional profit that you reinvest – either partly or wholly – back into that growth. This means you need sufficient margins for reinvestment, which could also mean that you will need to look at all your lower-margin customers, products and services. You may need to drop them or find better ways to justify and put through sufficient price hikes. With very few exceptions, the way you gain competitive advantage is by generating more profit to then reinvest.

Anyone in the know will actually see I am merging the concepts of tracking KPIs with big data. For experts this is probably sacrilege, but this book is for leaders and I believe we should start with the dashboard or indicators, before working backwards to the data fuel. Without the dashboard, we end up with systems that have hidden answers and limited ability. We then have to settle on individually and manually opening the bonnet to see how the business engine is performing and assess any trends that might be developing.

FIGURE 5.3   Using trailing monthly trackers to identify long-term business trends

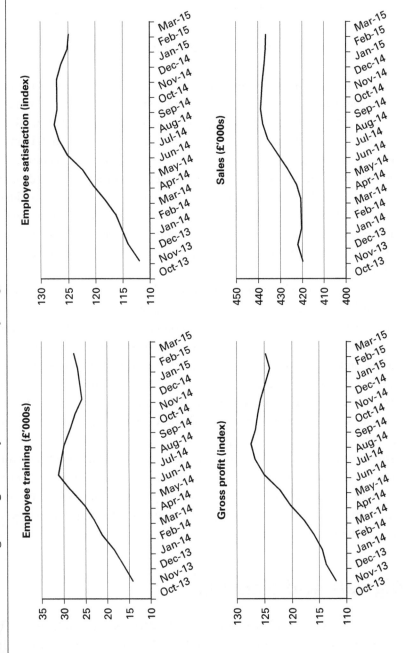

A manual process is inefficient and may not work, as it assumes the right data is being collected and can be found. Put simply: however fancy or powerful your IT people can make the data engine, it is pointless unless you have the right convergent feed to the right dashboard for the driver to analyse. If you like, we must engage the data engine as efficiently as we can with the driver in order to get maximum output and traction on the road. Perhaps then we can finally see the route ahead.

Many leaders see messy, disorganized data as a major hurdle to effective strategy and anticipation. They also have a common misconception that it is best used to confirm decisions they have already made. However, with the right questions, systems and dashboard, predictive analysis and data mining for behavioural patterns and future trends in themselves can become a competitive advantage. We can create a far clearer view of the road ahead and any mission we might be contemplating, and we can do this more confidently than our competitors. Creating this view and visibility effectively takes time. Although a data-driven competitive advantage cannot be built overnight, the next time you review your systems, tools and technology, start with the end in mind.

Company-wide adoption of business intelligence can also call for a shift in company culture, one that will ultimately create a new company environment that is more agile and ready to act with confidence. This needs promotion of high standards in both data input and system best business practices so that people understand the need for visibility and the dashboards. The 'road ahead' analogy can be useful for this promotion. It is obvious if the driver next to you can tell what his engine is doing and you can't. Furthermore, if they can see the patterns on the road ahead more quickly and with more data then again advantage is typically secured. Robust tracker and trend key performance indicators on good conjoined platforms take the heavy lifting from the decision process. Figure 5.4 shows an example of how significant key data can be layered on few pages. If you are using Microsoft Excel rather than a specific dashboard system, **www.chandoo.org** is a great source of Excel template examples.

Big data and planning

Big data, as the current business jargon affords, is as you would expect: big. However, what makes it interesting is the ability to turn the intelligence into something manageable and translate it into better decisions.

FIGURE 5.4a   Leader review dashboard

Curr Qtr WW Data	
Avg Proj.	135.8
WW Sup	156.6
WW Req	160.8
QTD Order	102.9

K units			
QTD order	WW req	WW supp	Avg Proj
102.9	160.8	156.6	135.8

1Q 2011 WW

Product	WW Req	WW CtC Changes	WW Supply	WW Add Supply	WW Supply to Req
Product 1	1700	[100]	2000	0	300
Product 2	1000	50	1200	0	200
Product 3	50	0	70	0	20
Product 4	37000	1000	35000	0	[2000]
Product 5	3000	[200]	2900	100	0
Product 6	2200	0	2000	0	[200]
Product 7	0	0	0	0	0
Product 8	15	0	0	20	5
Product 9	150	20	0	83	[67]

Last 4 Qtrs + CQ 2009 order load by product					
Product	1Q09	1Q10	2Q10	3Q10	4Q10
Prod 1	2.6	1.6	1.8	2.1	2.2
Prod 2	1.9	1.8	2.1	2.2	2.3
Prod 3	2.1	2.1	2.2	2.3	2.9
Prod 4	2.2	2.2	2.3	2.9	3.1
Prod 5	1.6	2.3	2.9	3.1	3.3
Prod 6	1.8	2.9	3.1	3.3	3.5
Prod 7	2.1	3.1	3.3	3.5	2.2
Prod 8	2.2	3.3	3.5	2.2	2.4
Prod 9	2.3	3.5	2.2	2.4	2.2
Prod 10	2.9	2.2	2.4	2.2	2.5
Prod 11	3.1	2.4	2.2	2.5	2.6
Prod 12	3.3	2.2	2.5	2.6	2.8
Prod 13	3.5	2.5	2.6	2.8	2.7
Prod 14	2.2	2.6	2.8	2.7	2.9
Prod 15	2.4	2.8	2.7	2.9	2.8
Prod 16	2.2	2.7	2.9	2.8	3.3
Prod 17	2.5	2.9	2.8	3.3	3.1
Prod 18	2.6	2.8	3.3	3.1	3.2
Prod 19	2.8	3.3	3.1	3.2	2.6

As previously discussed, business planning based on big data and predictive analytics is still uncharted territory for many executives. The main reason is likely to be that executives have a natural bias to look to their own 'reliable' experience, rather than complex data feeds. The contradiction, however, is that the data is there to help them reduce risk and uncertainty in their decision-making, and to improve intuition. On the other hand, data can also be relied upon too much to justify decisions or examine results. However, this is a retrospective use, which can be dangerous for the reason mentioned before that the data displayed may already be obsolete. We must therefore combine the current view with lead or trend indicators.

FIGURE 5.4b *continued*

2Q 2011 WW					
Product	WW UBF	WW CtC Delta	WW SOP	WW Chase	WW SOP to UBF Delta
Product 1	1700	[100]	2000	0	300
Product 2	1000	50	1200	0	200
Product 3	50	0	70	0	20
Product 4	37000	1000	35000	0	[2000]
Product 5	3000	[200]	2900	100	0
Product 6	2200	0	2000	0	[200]
Product 7	0	0	0	0	0
Product 8	15	0	0	20	5
Product 9	150	20	0	83	[67]

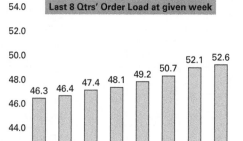

Good business intelligence platforms and dashboards transmit accurate information in real time and thus make data easy to analyse, even for non-technical executives. Further, many systems have the ability to make adjustments and searches based on different purposes, without the need for technical programming each time. With practice, today's executives can get direct and hands on with the data, which helps build both trust and deeper understanding of the lead trends and indications. The right systems also reduce the classic Excel (spreadsheet) challenge of manual entry, which can result in poor accuracy. Soon, we will look lightly at how to create the right systems.

FIGURE 5.4c *continued*

QTD Order Load cob 6 Feb level	
Product	**K units QTD Load**
Prod 1	10.0
Prod 2	9.0
Prod 3	5.0
Prod 4	4.0
Prod 5	1.0
Prod 6	3.0
Prod 7	2.5
Prod 8	1.6
Prod 9	2.0
Prod 10	2.3
Prod 11	2.5
Prod 12	5.3
Prod 13	2.7
Prod 14	8.0
Prod 15	9.0
Prod 16	10.1
Prod 17	7.3
Prod 18	6.4
Prod 19	11.2
Total	**102.9**

The specific lead or trend indications enable decisions based on fact as well as intuition. Combine this with the macro picture created by environmental scanning and we improve visibility on what is likely to occur in both our organizations and the market, without suffering from paralysis by analysis. The ability to capture, manage and analyse large and complex data sets allows for improved decision-making and business practices, as well as tailored products and services in many different industries and fields. With the trends in hand, the market ahead unfolds and the road becomes more obvious.

By tracking the data over longer periods, it is possible to better define the customer relationship and provide a stronger opportunity to engage with the customer more effectively. In predictive analytics, the other main concept is to try to corroborate the data to create a profile of your customers; this can prove particularly insightful during the process of trying to differentiate the good ones from the bad ones. Who do you need to focus on, and recommend more to, and who is wasting your time? Understanding this today helps reduce inefficient operations and increases conversion rates, but it also provides the future opportunity of knowing who the real customers are today, so that we can plan better products for them tomorrow.

The following tips should help you and your organization plan and construct systems for the future:

- Create dashboards that show the data simply and aim at capturing results over longer periods than the traditional year-to-year model. See trackers and dashboard above.

- Ensure your data systems are dashboard generative, ie show good clear reporting capability. Simple extraction is as important as collection otherwise the cost of 'mining' to find answers is prohibitive.

- Your big data road approach needs to not only reflect what your company wants to achieve, but also take into consideration ongoing initiatives and existing technology investments.

- Before even thinking about technology, an enterprise must have an understanding of the key drivers of its business.

- Ideally move the organization beyond a technology-led view of big data to a business-wide view, taking the jargon out. Translate the 'technology' language into English and share it.

- Big data is not about IT. Instead, it's about listening. For example, if we record reception enquiries in a hotel more effectively, and we find that more customers are asking for an iron, we can determine that irons in hotel rooms might be useful and furthermore that perhaps more business travellers are using the hotel.

- There is no single big data technology, nor is there a single big data starting point, so take your time to understand how to conjoin systems and avoid expensive silos. There are good products out there that are poorly set up to conjoin with other systems.

- Make sure your systems and dashboards are agile, scalable, future-proof and upgradeable. A great example of a system like this today is Salesforce. It operates on an app basis, so as well as a first-class sales CRM, Salesforce allows you to bolt on applications as and when you need them.

- Be clear on which are the most important questions you need to answer with big data and why, and remember to prioritize.

- Big data techniques and technologies can (and should) be leveraged by any part of the organization or executives.

When we are considering how we use data and trend awareness to be more competitive, the platform in itself can also revolutionize business functions. For example, imagine being able to use historical data as well as predictive analytics to respond to changes in the supply chain. Infrastructure and applications might then speed response by operating semi-autonomously, creating a more responsive and resilient supply chain, to meet customers' orders faster and more accurately.

Trend extrapolation

The right systems and dashboards will track results and indicate trends. However, to better predict likely market and customer movements, we may need to speculate as to the extensions and likely futures of those trends. What patterns can we see in the trends and therefore forecast forward? For example, the trend for increased life expectancy is directly correlated with the trends of increasing wealth, greater access to high-technology medical support and improved diet habits. All three have moved up on a similar curve over the decades, so we can reasonably extrapolate continued life expectancy increases. The trend for obesity is creating drag on the 'increase' trend but at this time is insufficient to reduce it. The scanning tells us the pattern and in this case, the actuarial big data more than supports the trend.

In mathematics, extrapolation is the process of estimating beyond the current observation range, based on the current range and trends within that range. Extrapolation results in conjecture-based knowledge extending on the current position in that it is not fact but a probability. Trend extrapolation is the process applied against already established trend patterns. For example, climate change forecasts are traditionally based on the last 30 years' collected historical data extrapolated forward. At this time the trend clearly shows 'warming' as a result of 'greenhouse gas emissions' with a likely global temperature increase of 2 to 4 per cent over the next 50 years, assuming that business is as usual for emissions (Intergovernmental Panel of Climate Change, 2015). The impact of such a rise on our planet is more extreme weather conditions and likely sea-level rises as the polar ice caps melt. There are many variables, not least of which is whether green (solar, wind, hydro) technology can dramatically reduce greenhouse (CO_2, methane, nitrous oxide, ozone) emissions and can we adopt and develop these technologies fast enough in line with human population growth? Despite the 'green technology revolution' nearly every extrapolation shows further warming. However, we don't know exactly – if you will forgive the pun – to what final degree.

Trend extrapolation is the most straightforward and objective component of trend analysis. Extrapolation essentially consists of taking historical data, fitting a curve to the data, and extending the curve into the future. Trend extrapolation assumes that things will keep changing in the future in the way they have been changing in the past. One simply extends the line or the curve forward to predict where things will be at a certain future time.

It may be too complex to analyse whole sets of big data and in this case, we can instead use sampling. Probability samples allow us to take smaller subsets of records or data and make probability statements about the sample statistics. We can estimate the extent to which sample data and statistics drive trends and the trends themselves may tell us where things are heading. For example, is the average sale increasing or decreasing and why? What key variables does the data suggest are driving this trend?

We can also use trend analysis to anticipate cycles. Many phenomena and trends appear to operate in cycles. The fashion sector is well known for cycles, perhaps because whatever was fashionable when we were kids can be nostalgic when we hit our late 20s and have more money to spend. Recently iPod first editions have been selling for twice their original purchase price despite being old electronics. The business cycle is probably the best known example of cycles, in which a recession is followed by recovery, which eventually then leads to overexpansion of capacity, which in turn leads back to recession, and so the cycle begins again. The path is well trodden and economic statistics and data can show the overexpansion time and time again. Figure 5.5 exhibits the UK economy's annual real GDP growth rate over the 1949–2011 period; needless to stay, economic growth has not been consistent (Office for National Statistics, 2011).

Creating platforms and data infrastructures

The key with 'big' data is to actually think 'small'. There are very few important numbers needed to understand the possibilities and probabilities. The IT sector sometimes – in its complexities – loses sight of the reason why we want and need the data, disappearing in information overload.

FIGURE 5.5 Percentage real GDP growth (annual) of the UK economy, 1949 to 2011

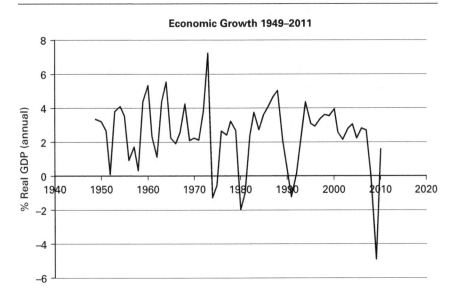

Every organization's needs are different and you will also have legacy systems to consider. However, a 'fresh look' stripping aside the vested interests is usually fruitful. Assuming platform changes are needed to create and conjoin better dashboards, platforms and reporting, leaders should state clear business objectives and then invest carefully in research to find the right partners and teams to deliver. Often in this exercise, the biggest mistake is in seeing the systems in silos and rushing the design, as leaders panic in the jargon and consequently choose the wrong partners, platforms and/or software. If a proposal has jargon in it, ask the naïve questions: it's a lot cheaper in the long run – don't be rushed.

Creating a data infrastructure is a complex arena, but leaders can help by thinking ahead about what their company's organizational strategy and business model will be in the future, without silos. For example, retailers might think about intelligent shopping applications that advise customers about the product suitability based on previous buying habits, the presence of certain ingredients, or allergic components or expiry dates. Some applications can also gather feedback, allowing you to further analyse the buying trends. This means joining point-of-sale to stock ordering to average sale and then back again; no silos and a loop. The potential application of conjoined systems across every sector of industry and the public sector is endless, although increasingly in the cloud era we need to be mindful of the hidden costs of licensing across multiple user devices.

The fresh look should start with a full and detailed audit of the current infrastructure which may not be conjoined or integrated. To report and trend extract on a broad front with this set-up, you would have to dip in and out of each system and have some very skilled people make the connections between the various information sets. This is not very effective and increases the chances of inaccuracy. Furthermore, there may well be subtle indicators of trend activity that simply can't be pursued because of the inability of staff and leaders to be able to simply play with the data and there is no genuine, single all-seeing real worldview of the customer, to look at the commonalities.

Here are some tips on how you and your organization can approach and support the process of creating new platforms, systems and data infrastructures:

- Strip out the information technology jargon, however naive your questions may appear.
- Remove silo thinking to join the dots.
- Only use partners or vendors who understand your business's overall objectives and see their solution as part of the question, not the saviour.
- Identify what works well in your legacy systems; these elements might be used as a base for a conjoined system.
- Research what your competitors are doing, visit trade shows and read trade press.
- Use the latest data warehousing technology and analysis tools and be clear from the outset of the reporting and data extraction requirements.
- Put together a group made up of people from all departments to review, steer and help drive change and implementation.
- Analyse the software options on the market before approaching vendors.
- Think about the ongoing costs of managing the systems and the hidden costs of getting stuck in both silos (systems that don't join) and corridors (technology that proves hard to upgrade over time).
- Scalable, upgradeable and flexible are the mantras.
- Build in asset registers and licence tracking as you go and ensure there are no intellectual software infringements.
- Choose your priority of data: amount, velocity or variety.

- Conduct a pilot phase and begin with the end in mind, but start small as overly ambitious projects can struggle.

- Research and look at the commonalities and technology that link your platforms together.

- Seek a system that can get not only a single view of the customer but also incorporate a wide range of data from other sources. Departmental data at one end of the spectrum; commercial bought-in information at the other.

One of the hardest aspects of creating new infrastructure is that it is subjective. There are so many possible routes to take and so many vendors offering solutions, but don't rush the process. Design the whole architecture from top to bottom, showing how you will conjoin the set-up. The great news is that today virtualization makes this accessible to more companies without expensive hardware infrastructure, which reduces complexity, increases future flexibility and creates more vendor choice.

Most successful organizations – small and large – will either hire or outsource to experts to help with the data specialism. Specialists can like tech for the sake of tech, and forget that it's a tool with a very specific endgame. As ever, objectivity is crucial. Above all, you should be looking for enthusiastic partners with past evidence of proactive, collaborative work with other partners. Good interdisciplinary vendors are likely to be open-minded, willing to learn from other disciplines and have a broad appreciation of the objective for conjoined systems and better reporting, taking reactive systems to proactive and predictive. Leaders that take the time to listen to the technical team will gradually increase their awareness of the opportunities and change the culture of their organizations. Transformations take time, but don't let jargon be the excuse.

Managing collection privacy

Some companies are already far ahead of the curve in both system set-up and data analytics. Typically these tend to be digital economy businesses, such as Google or Amazon. Netflix is using survey data, not just purchase history, to ask its customers to rate movies. They then take this data so that they can train their systems to make more precise recommendations; they are forming impressive predictive capabilities. There must, however, be a word of responsibility; as users' digital footprints become louder, privacy becomes a bigger issue. How much should our phones, for example, transmit about ourselves? I can soon see the day when a shop assistant greets me by name and refers to the purchase I made last month. Just because we can track pretty much everything, does not mean we should be allowed to. Leaders need responsibility to be firmly in their mind when privacy is considered. With highly personalized data exchanges and conjoined systems, some corporations and governments know us literally better than we know ourselves, in our behaviours and inclinations. This can create value and competitive advantage for those organizations, but raises ethical issues for leadership.

Chapter summary and questions

Although today's leading-edge technologies – cloud, mobility, social, analytics and others – are enabling important new business capabilities, they are also straining companies' IT infrastructures to the breaking point. Most organizations struggle with an existing IT infrastructure that is inflexible, layer-caked and often underpowered. The business consequences of this situation are significant. Teams may struggle to collaborate and important trends are missed, leading to the loss of business. The components of better systems are known; the challenge now is to integrate and manage them effectively. Developing intelligent big data infrastructure services and better dashboards can give companies significant competitive advantage, as part of their overall digital strategy, and help leaders build more effective long-term, holistic strategies.

Trends reporting and analysis are a well-trodden path to securing advantage. They can tell us more accurately what is going on in the business today and consequently we can extrapolate future possibilities more effectively. Building the right platforms and reporting against the right data questions, with the right data infrastructure and culture, usually lead to inherent competitive advantage. I know achieving the right infrastructure is complex and fraught with delivery difficulties. Nevertheless, imagine if instead of conjecture we can speed decision-making up and increase its accuracy; we can then collaborate and innovate more effectively. In this synopsis, leaders getting more hands on in the reporting, systems and data over time will pay dividends. Even if it's just an hour a day – for instance helping the data team, partners or vendors build better platforms and reports or reviewing them with trends in mind. Try to look at the world from your customers' viewpoint. What do they need (but bear in mind they don't always know what they want)? What are the trends telling us what our customers' 'pain' or 'trigggger' points are? Answer those questions and you may find your own fountain of innovation and advantage and be able to serve customers better. Before concluding this chapter, here is a selection of tips that should help you and your organization build a data-centric competitive advantage more effectively:

- Work out your aims for the data analysis, your existing assumptions and how accurate data will help you make decisions.

- Consider bringing in external expertise by pairing up with experts and vendors that understand your business priorities and the concept of conjoined systems.

- It is in the attempt at understanding the future, rather than the accuracy of the probabilities forecast, that the ideas and opportunities lie.

- Virtualization reduces complexity, costs and increases sustainability.

- Fully understand the data already in your company's systems or surveys. Bring it together so comparisons can be made across the business.

- Consider the additional sources of data available.

- Investigate what different tools and ways of collecting data are out there and how they fit with your needs.

- Access as broad a pool of data as possible, to minimize the risk of bias or reading false conclusions and continue collection and analysis over time.

- Be transparent. Draw up guidelines with key employees governing proper use of data and how it will be incorporated into the business operations.

- Keep an open mind. The data may disprove long-held unchallenged assumptions.

- Don't be blindly led by data. Use it in conjunction with your usual decision-making.

- Take the time to check the data and your subsequent conclusions. Forecasts will be incomplete and the future will always have surprises.

Data and trend analysis creates a clear window to organizational and customer behaviour. This window, combined with quality environmental scanning, thus affords informed leadership with secure foundations and better anticipation, supporting strategic innovation and helping to secure positive disruption, ultimately supporting the creation of competitive advantage. Figure 5.6 provides a holistic, visual summary of the key ideas discussed throughout this chapter. The approach to data analytics should represent a perpetual cycle of continuous improvement, in which vendors, business analysts, IT managers and leaders all play their part.

FIGURE 5.6   Big data and platforms: a holistic, visual summary

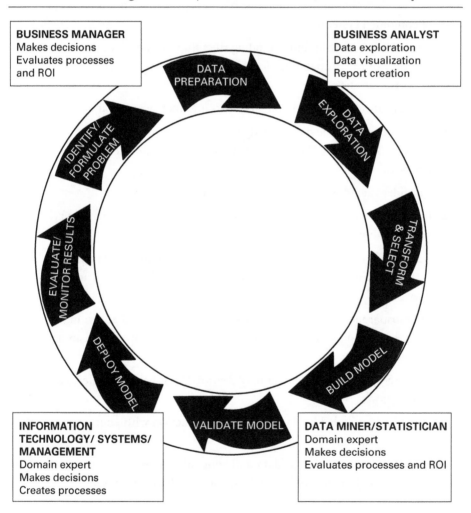

Leader questions

1 How much do your analytics and systems conjoin?

2 How much importance do you place on analysis to drive strategy?

3 What work has been done to understand the real key performance drivers specific to your business and strategy?

4 How visual and easy to understand are your dashboards?

5 How automated is your reporting, and does it tell you what you really need to know?

6 How simple, accurate and timely is your reporting?

7 From the data, what can you extrapolate forward: what are your customers actually thinking and likely to be thinking?

8 What can your organization be first in class at?

References

Gunelius, S (2014) 5 Statistics that Define the Digital Marketing Landscape in 2014 [Blog] Corporate Eye. 29/01. Available from: www.corporate-eye.com/main/5-statistics-that-define-the-digital-marketing-landscape-in-2014/ [Last accessed 27 August 2015]

Intergovernmental Panel on Climate Change (2015) Future Climate Changes, Risks and Impacts. Available from: http://ar5-syr.ipcc.ch/topic_futurechanges.php [Last accessed 7 September 2015]

Kaplan, RS and Norton, DP (2005) The Balanced Scorecard: Measures that Drive Performance. *Harvard Business Review*. Available from: https://hbr.org/2005/07/the-balanced-scorecard-measures-that-drive-performance [Last accessed 27 August 2015]

Office for National Statistics (2011) Data on Economic Growth in UK. Available from: www.economicshelp.org/blog/2688/economics/data-on-economic-growth-in-uk/ [Last accessed 7 September 2015]

Strategic planning and scenarios

06

Introduction

With more time to spend on leadership and better management support, leaders should have increased permission to research and strategically look for opportunities. The work in the last two chapters in creating a probability line and also improving the analytics gives us both a broad view of potentially changing markets and a narrow view of the specifics occurring directly in our businesses, particularly customer-driven trends. With these two pictures overlaying we are far more likely to be able to see and anticipate where things are going. However, as will be examined in this chapter, we may need to do some work to join the views, dots and clues up.

Increased visibility

Overall, the goal is better anticipation and increased visibility, enabling us to put the organization strategically ahead of the market current, and thus gain competitive advantage.

It may be obvious from your and your team's work where things are going and consequently, what to do. However, assumption against anticipation is inherent in risk and while we may risk some procrastination in analysis, it is worth taking stock. Probably the best way to do this is by creating models and scenarios in combination with expert opinion and the senior team. The big picture line of probability and the micro data analytics overlay each other to create a focused picture, then we can use models and scenario planning to put this more focused picture under the microscope. We can then better see the products, services and strategies that are game changers,

FIGURE 6.1   Strategic goals: iterative loop

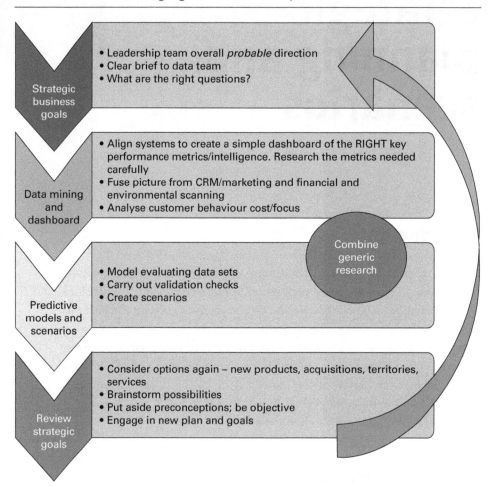

Strategic business goals
- Leadership team overall *probable* direction
- Clear brief to data team
- What are the right questions?

Data mining and dashboard
- Align systems to create a simple dashboard of the RIGHT key performance metrics/intelligence. Research the metrics needed carefully
- Fuse picture from CRM/marketing and financial and environmental scanning
- Analyse customer behaviour cost/focus

Predictive models and scenarios
- Model evaluating data sets
- Carry out validation checks
- Create scenarios

Combine generic research

Review strategic goals
- Consider options again – new products, acquisitions, territories, services
- Brainstorm possibilities
- Put aside preconceptions; be objective
- Engage in new plan and goals

enhancing the decision-making process at your organization to support any major initiatives.

Ultimately, with our review and enhanced picture of the market direction, we are seeking new ideas that build higher value, more purposeful and sustainable organizations. We can play out the market scenarios to create a better understanding of both customers and our environment, then use these to guide the overarching strategic direction and plan. The plan should, with increased anticipation, take more account of the inherent threats, trends and opportunities.

By playing with models and scenarios supported by good research, we can strategically explore, with an increasingly blank canvas, more possible organizational futures, and challenge the conventional thinking. This thinking is typically driven by history, the vested interests of senior management, and the need for reliability and process as opposed to competitive strategy. If you like, we become more entrepreneurial, creative, strategic and imaginative, yet are anchored in a clearly thought-through method of arrival. The method gives us more permission to be disruptive and increasingly helps us answer *why* a business should move towards a direction or goal rather than *what* direction or goal. The combination of research in the line of probability and better data metrics improves the validity and strength of our scenarios, which presents us with a much clearer understanding of why a direction or strategy needs to be taken. This enables us to see more strategic moves ahead and the method of arrival actually gives more permission and authority to create change, perhaps in less obvious directions. The approach can be shared, continuous and iterative; we then back this up with the plans that detail the actions required to create change.

> By playing with models and scenarios supported by good research, we can strategically explore, with an increasingly blank canvas, more possible organizational futures, and challenge the conventional thinking.

In my previous book, *Navigating the Rivers of Cash*, I used the analogy of fitness interval training for elements of strategic thinking. In interval training the idea is that you can train and build endurance strength far better by speeding up, and then slowing down, so the heart rate fluctuates more. Constant endurance 'the old way' training would seem the better route to fitness and a fast-slow approach seems counterintuitive; however, the research and tested science create the evidence of the strategy. The technique was first employed with long-distance running and hill training which create the effect naturally. Without the data and the science we would continue with the obvious 'old way'.

Overall, our approach of combining research, data and scenarios brings strategic thinking methods usually associated only with the intuitive and maverick entrepreneur who instinctively knows why a direction needs to be taken and typically achieves it only via sheer strength of will and persuasion, which can be both exhausting and ineffective. It also becomes more difficult for larger businesses, typically those with over 50 employees, which are far more valuable when market- and employee-driven as opposed to leader-driven.

Scenario planning

Scenario planning is perhaps out of fashion today in favour of agility. The argument being why waste your time analysing and mapping out events that *might* happen when you can focus on being lean, poised, agile and reactive to actual events that *do* occur? It seems to me that surely seeking both is a better way; scenarios may or may not predict the future, but being more formal in the work can reduce the 'educated guess' approach combined with the 'if it is working it must be right' approach that many leaders seem to rely on.

Furthermore, they avoid assumption that today's current trend is the only trend and that it will operate in a straight line. How many times have we made an argument for the status quo or today's trend only to find a better way later, or indeed find that one of our competitors has? Scenario planning helps increase objectivity, set expectations and establish assumptions to allow leaders to manage the future of organizations.

The aim of scenario planning is to gain understanding from the environment to seek understanding and explanation. Each scenario developed creates a picture and a story about an alternative possibility and is then used to encourage exploration on consequential strategies to develop perspective and decisions against a broader range of possibilities. Ironically, with formal scenario planning, we become more prepared and better placed to challenge assumptions and complacency, and can therefore actually increase agility.

Many organizations and leaders struggle with such planning simply because it is speculative and takes time which, at executive level, means significant cost. They might also justifiably ask for proof that this work actually helps. The response might be 'Prove it doesn't, suggest alternative methods, please, and surely it's better than luck, instinct or guess.' However, the solution is probably to carry out scenario planning in context, and in a concise and lean way. Be clear who needs to be involved and why. It is imperative to ensure we have both the macro picture via environmental scanning and the data analytics to hand. When we go into scenario planning these create a strong and informed base for the discussion. Returning to cost, the return on investment of being ahead of your competitors surely far outstrips the time invested in creating better strategy.

The 'educated guess' or intuitive style of decision-making is, I suspect in reality, based on similar methods and scenarios but packaged into the knowledge of the leadership. In other words, we map out scenarios inherently and perhaps subconsciously. A process approach should create a stronger platform, both shared, more thorough and considered, even if ultimately we still need the final 'educated guess'. Too many leaders perhaps bet on just one future scenario; this is actually linear and over-predictive and thus unlikely, whereas a scenarios exercise helps an organization to take account of the truer likelihood of multiple possibilities and future directions.

As with most management tools there are misconceptions and doubters with scenario planning, although the reality is that leaders carry it out every day consciously or subconsciously. One common misconception is that scenarios are about risk and event management, that is, only 'How do we react if there is a fire in the plant or a catastrophic event, or an oil spill?' This is contingency or resilience planning as much as it is scenarios. The emphasis is on learning how to avoid, manage and/or exploit the single future event.

> It is unlikely that we will identify all of the forces and interactions in play, and the future will twist and turn but we may gain some better visibility and knowledge, which in turn leads to strategic insight.

Instead, with better data via environmental scanning and data analysis, we can use scenarios as key executive tools to describe possible futures in broad terms, enabling us to seek increased anticipation with regard to technology, products and services, competitive strategy and supply chain. The consequent strategies are within leaders' and organizations' direct control. They are essentially proactive and reflect a long-term planning horizon. In one recent example we examined the demographic data of an exclusive travel company which showed that its clients were spending more but getting older. There was concern about whether the next generation, with a lack of savings and a 'spend today' mindset, would have access to the future capital to maintain such exclusivity and what could the organization do about it. In this case, no significant action was being taken as the challenge was felt to be more than 10 years ahead, although strategic alignment is being sought with an investment organization focused on the next generation to better identify the new but fewer next generation.

It is unlikely that we will identify all of the forces and interactions in play, and the future will twist and turn but we may gain some better visibility and knowledge, which in turn lead to strategic insight.

How to manage scenario planning

1 Agree a timeframe and scope. How far out do you want to try and model? This might typically be five years plus. Are the trends compatible within the timeframe in question?

What specific objectives do you have? As well as seeking advantage are there small challenges you would like to solve or consider on the way?

2 Identify an objective team representing key interests and divisions in the business. Consider using external facilitation to aid objectivity.

3 Create early scenarios against the line of probability, research, your dashboards and big data analysis. Extrapolate and map basic trends and driving forces. Do the forces describe uncertainties that can construct probable scenarios?

4 Brainstorming is commonly utilized to broaden the narrow early scenarios, where all trends that can be thought of are presented before they are assessed, and create a team view.

5 Prioritize important over unimportant views of the possibilities and link scenarios if appropriate.

6 Identify any extreme elements or anomalies and consider possible outcomes of these.

7 Continue objectivity: many scenarios will disturb the team inherent in the exercise and vested interest, therefore the status quo may create drag. It is essential that this is managed correctly.

8 In the end, usually two or three scenarios are arrived at with a particular eye on market direction and strategic plans. Ideally create short, one-page visuals on each prospect, and try to assess positives and negatives of the possible scenarios.

9 Typically the scenarios identify additional research needs.

10 Conjoin your scenarios with your traditional existing business plans and budgets. How do they fit?

Once research is conducted and the review is fused with current plans, new strategy and actions can be engaged upon and decisions made to address the fundamental issues facing the organization. Be cautious of betting on one future. Multiple changes in direction are more likely.

FIGURE 6.2 Scenarios process

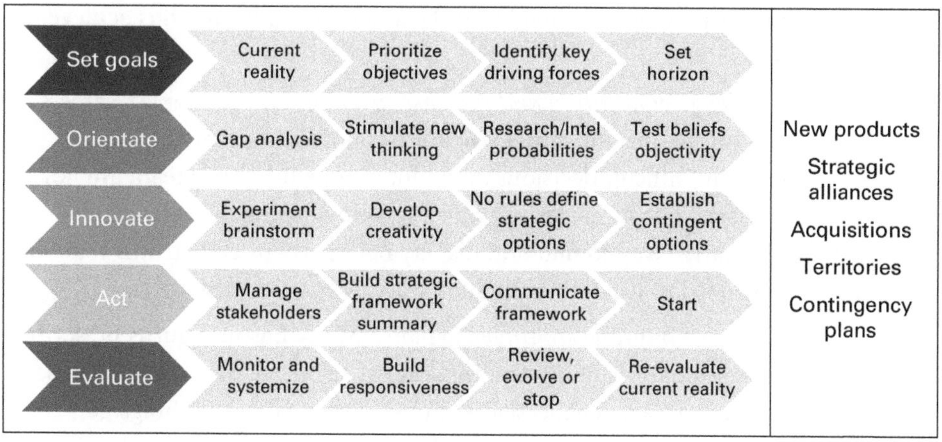

Set goals	Current reality	Prioritize objectives	Identify key driving forces	Set horizon	
Orientate	Gap analysis	Stimulate new thinking	Research/Intel probabilities	Test beliefs objectivity	New products
Innovate	Experiment brainstorm	Develop creativity	No rules define strategic options	Establish contingent options	Strategic alliances / Acquisitions
Act	Manage stakeholders	Build strategic framework summary	Communicate framework	Start	Territories / Contingency plans
Evaluate	Monitor and systemize	Build responsiveness	Review, evolve or stop	Re-evaluate current reality	

The advantage in scenarios

There is a significant amount of literature on both strategic thinking and scenarios planning: from military originations to Shell adopting a global and embedded formal process in the 1970s that is still ongoing today. The main benefit is visibility on:

- *Predetermination.* In some scenarios we can discover almost inevitable consequences of events that have already happened, or of trends that are already well developed. In scenario planning these are the ripple or domino effects. Population demographics, the boom and bust of economic cycles, supply and demand reactions and consequential price changes all fall into this virtually inevitable predetermination category.

- *Scenarios expand your thinking.* By nature most of us are conservative; we live today so we broadly assume the future will not be that dissimilar and we miss change. Consider the tree or child you have not seen for many years. We are always surprised by how much they grow yet when we live with them day to day we don't see it. We think of listed markets as very stable for example, yet a full one-third of the companies listed in the 1970 Fortune 500, for instance, had vanished by 1983 – having been acquired, merged or broken up. At the time of writing, there are only two FTSE 100 companies that were listed 50 years ago: a revolution. By demonstrating variable market directions we increase anticipation, and can better see why the past and present might not be a helpful guide and thus achieve new answers.

- *Challenge convention and increase listening.* Many people's careers rely on the current strategy or status quo, and further change can result in difficult decisions and a lot more work. Your team are not unbiased but scenarios provide a less threatening, objective and alternative way to find and display new, perhaps clear truths that we may need to listen to, thus subsequently turn towards or face.

- *Scenarios improve contingency plans.* Many business gurus prescribe only positive visioning and thinking as the route to success. This is false advantage. Leaders accept that in the real world things go wrong and they plan accordingly, putting in place the appropriate back-up systems and plans.

- *Take the politics out of challenges.* Putting a process to scenario planning is simple and the research and data that feed the process give it legitimacy, which in turn increases the free flow of debate allowing leaders to be open and challenged. Many people think it is their job to agree with leaders but the more valuable people are prepared to correctly challenge leaders, who may need reminding from time to time that their ideas are not always the best. Scenario work also creates permission for the introverted personality type to be more influential. Introverts don't operate well in workshops as they are never the loudest but with better research and data they can create the best scenario models with genuine fresh insight from the desktop.

Advantage in the unknowns

An interesting aspect of both strategic thinking and scenario work is that much of the effort executives employ is focused on creating reliability, and certainty, out of current known possibilities. However, there are also un-known variables, that is scenarios, trends and options that we have not even considered. It's hard to digest but often the best advantage can be found when there are no rules. That is, when we are objective and go back to zero, when, as leaders, we put aside what we know as that creates clutter and engage playfully and creatively ask more effectively what problems we can solve for our clients. The analysis and scenarios create the picture and options but the intuition writes the story; creativity leading to originality leading to new ideas, innovations and competitive advantage.

Essentially we are exploring how we secure eureka moments, so what supports this thesis? There are of course many examples of eureka from Isaac Newton's falling apple to Paul McCartney of The Beatles waking from a dream with the tune 'Yesterday', the most recorded song in history, in his head, or to the origination of the word eureka itself and Archimedes's apparent first use of the word relating to finally understanding how to calculate the purity of metal.

Eureka discoveries such as Newton's may literally look as though they have fallen upon us but they are actually the culmination of significant past thinking, knowledge and exploration even if they are not formal. It was a French astronomer, Ismael Bouillon, who first suggested that the sun was pulling us with a force directly related to how far away it was and Newton who subsequently enhanced this idea with a realization of the current truth about gravity. Perhaps as importantly, his ideas came at a time when others could recognize it was right or the current truth. Consider instead that Galileo was put under house arrest in 1633 for supporting Nicolaus Copernicus's 1543 heliocentric model positioning the sun at the centre of the universe, motionless, with earth and the other planets rotating around it in circular paths. How long did it take for that current truth to erode? In a business context we have already mentioned Sir Clive Sinclair's C5 as having been brilliant but too early, and how McDonald's were too slow to get involved in the green and health food debates. By comparison, how long will it take food manufacturers to stop putting so much sugar in our processed food? As a species this is unethical and causes rises in obesity. Laypeople, however good the labels are, cannot all be expected to be nutritionists.

Perhaps because it remains in the US education system to teach creationism, over 42 per cent of the population believe in an earth and species created by God whereas 87 per cent of scientists wholly accept Darwin's theories that nature evolved from simplicity to complexity as it consistently competed in its habitat to survive (Newport, 2014). This not only shows us that current thinking varies from environment to background and education but that it also changes. Darwin's ideas are taking a long time to change beliefs rightly or wrongly. Some 'right' strategic business ideas may be before their time or come at the wrong time.

The creative process of these eureka moments of discovery and insight from the unknowns actually develops gradually as we explore them repeatedly in our thinking, both consciously and unconsciously. Essentially, we build new knowledge about that concept and ideas layer on layer until we secure the insight that may lead to new strategy and advantage.

In the previous chapter we looked at how big data can play a role in both understanding trends and triggering insight. However, we can use this as further support to the thesis that advantage can perhaps best be found in the unknowns. It is interesting that the greater insights can often be found from the silent anomalies or variances rather than from the trends. Simply put, it is perhaps the data that stands out as wrong that can give us the biggest clues to the unknowns that stimulate these eureka moments. Leaders that notice and follow up on surprising data often do well. To look for anomalies, ask questions such as: Is your market share or revenue abnormally low or high in a geographical market? We might, for example, see a trend for customers on cruise ships getting older but also start seeing a pattern of a few but regular younger people booking which could be an indicator that a new group are joining in on a retro or nostalgia basis, thus an opportunity arises.

Consider an anomaly in global e-commerce. One might think that in Russia, with 100 million middle-class consumers and the majority having access to the internet, e-commerce, as with elsewhere in the world, would be a growing market (EY, 2015). However, a poor postal system and credit card infrastructure leave online only accounting for 1.5 per cent of total retail. Recognizing the anomaly, the Russian entrepreneur Niels Tonsen created a very successful online clothing store, Lamoda. The business model employs couriers directly to deliver purchases, collect cash payments and even offer customers fashion advice in their own homes. The opportunity lay in the anomaly.

Interestingly, 96 per cent of the mass of the universe is actually unknown to science (Moskowitz, 2011). Maths, analysis and models compellingly tell us it's there, but today we just can't see it and we don't know what it is. This mass is called 'dark matter'. The portion of the universe that we can't see holds perhaps more answers than the moon, sun, stars, asteroids, etc that we can see and do understand their composition. We can certainly see this impact in customers. How many quietly cease to deal with you and give you no reason as to why they just gently go elsewhere? If we could find these probably reasonable yet quiet customers and ascertain why they have gone elsewhere, we would no doubt have more ideas and opportunities rather than strategically reacting to the noisy unreasonable customers who are probably dissatisfied whatever you do.

Where are your salespeople winning more often, or what surprise comment is being made? Where is productivity unusually high? These variances may point at opportunity to create advantage.

FIGURE 6.3 Big data anomalies

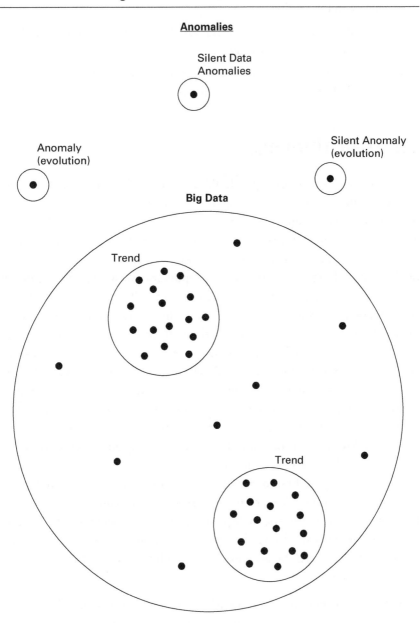

- Big data – the all-encapsulating data which encompasses all information.
- Trend – groupings within big data that clearly correlate with each other and allow you to understand where your current strengths lie.

- Anomaly (evolution) – a reported anomaly that has arisen due to a change in the market.

- Silent data anomalies – occur but aren't reported. This could be the key to unlocking new strategy.

- Silent anomaly (evolution) – a change in the market has caused the anomaly but it hasn't been captured.

Strategic thinking

I have already defined strategic thinking as the ability to think more than one move ahead using the analogy of the game of chess. Overall, we can perceive strategic business thinking as being a systematic and enlightened approach to seeking future opportunity by being both creative and analytical in order to advance and succeed. In thinking strategically we take account of the past and present, as part of the inputs for considering the future. It requires both the macro and micro pictures to be effective and encompasses broader possibilities than simply plans. It seems to me that plans can only be internally focused, whereas strategic thinking will always take account of and seek to react to and anticipate the other players: in business terms, the environment and the competition. Plans might also be specific, and often have budgets associated with them whereas a strategy might well draw on a number of plans to achieve overall ambitions and competitive advantage.

It may seem semantic but it is important to be clear on the type of thinking we are employing at any one time. For example, many business improvement protagonists also insist that successful businesses have a vision. This is an overarching simplified big picture that motivates, often with an audacious goal attached. Business leaders and experts can get too hung up on the title, but strategy-specific realistic multiple plans that anticipate both market and competitor movements are vital to achieve a vision. I risk being thrown out of the business experts' 'magic circle' for simplifying to this extent, but let's try and summarize:

- Vision: the big dream. An audacious and aspirational aim that inspires to create a common goal. The classic example was a Microsoft PC on every person's desk in the world.

- Plans: specific, usually linear, with budgets associated.

- Strategy: a number of interactive plans that anticipate competitive and market environment, and consequently result in clear decisions.

The aim is a cohesive series of moves, goals and actions created with insight, research, data and realism to gain competitive advantage.

When working in groups and organizations, strategic thinking is the collaborative method through which individual insights and ideas are shared to create a common cohesive view. Leadership's role is to bring all the experiences and insights together into focus and perspective. The approach should draw on all areas and expertise levels within the organization, across all divisions. Furthermore, to be effective, diversity in age and sex is also critical. The eventual aim is to make decisions that lead to engaged and coordinated actions.

We all have the ability to think strategically and, contrary to popular opinion, there is no magic. It requires awareness of the elements that build to the moves and actions ahead and the time to study them. These elements combine with experience to secure better traction. It is important to recognize that you don't always, in the end, need panels of people and lots of decision-makers to set out a strategy. Indeed, how many great businesses have been born from notes on the back of an envelope (to use the famous English colloquialism)? Figure 6.4 sets out the core questions behind business strategy.

Stimulation for strategy

In our scenario and strategic thinking for competitive advantage, there are a number of key areas where we can stimulate our creativity for improvement ideas, innovation and change.

Convention and the status quo. Doing the same thing each day but expecting different results has been defined as madness. In business, the phrase 'if it isn't broken don't fix it' is an oxymoron; and we must always assume that the competition are 'fixing' it. The majority of leaders look for what is broken and concentrate on change there but very often the break is actually the symptom caused by something that appears to be working. We discussed this in Chapter 3, in Working upstream. The idea is that opportunity can lie in studying what works well and how to make it better. There are many protagonists who suggest that as individuals we should play to our strengths and worry less about our weaknesses and the same advice may apply for businesses. More effort may be required to consider what we can do to challenge convention and enhance what is already good. For example, historically, companies have been nervous of working mothers with childcare commitments. A temporary worker employment agency I have worked with

FIGURE 6.4 Strategic thinking for competitive advantage

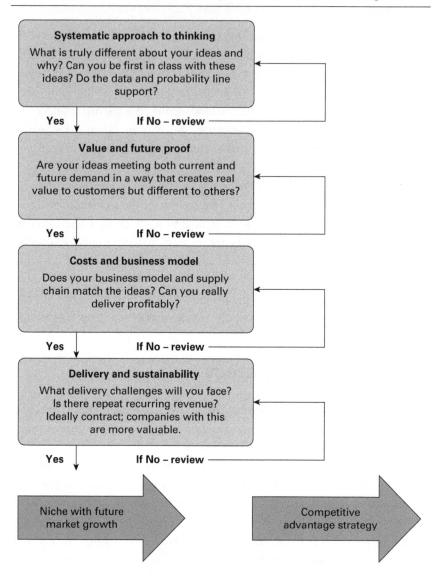

challenged convention and instead of seeing this as a negative, they have built a great business around employing mothers as legal interims. The nature of interims suits mums and their time commitments and firms get great, high-powered individuals with more flexibility and less cost. A changing world constantly throws up new possibilities; often the biggest obstacle to seizing them is letting go of the old.

Crossroads. When trends or technologies cross over it can be a signpost to new products or business ideas. Netflix have succeeded by securing exclusive content as cult TV shows have become mainstream while taking market share from satellite and cable by being on demand. The internet has been fruitful for new models and products but crossroad innovations might include the advent of global positioning technology and smartphone apps such as Tinder or Uber. It is, however, not just the big successes that count. In the marketing of our professional practices we use a fast-tracking start-up called Infinity, which uses the crossroads to combine with search engines enabling internet marketers to track which calls came from which searches.

The ideas presented in Chapter 4, The line of probability, can be particularly useful when seeking clues that signpost what innovations might fit together and interact. Ask yourself: What are the major economic, demographic and technological trends affecting my organization, industry or market, and how might those trends cross over?

Frustrations. Have you ever got annoyed about an experience as a customer or owner? Unless you are unreasonable with your expectations, your irritation is potentially a signpost to strategic advantage. What is causing the frustration, and what could be changed about it? Are you someone who just complains or are you actually in a position to do something about it?

It was Anita Roddick's passion for the environment and irritation at how we abuse the world around us that propelled her to launch the Body Shop global shopping brand. In line with this, for years many consumers have been frustrated by the automated answering and call-waiting facilities in bank services. To counter this, one of the banks has launched a marketing initiative promising real people answering calls quickly. However efficient call waiting might make a company, it is poor for the consumer and reversing the approach has created an opportunity for a bank to encourage new customers. A great example for me personally involves one of my clients who was employed as a driver in a small removal company. He became a manager and eventually agreed a deal to buy the business. However, as soon as he became the owner he got so irritated by small-minded homeowners, claiming for damages that his company weren't responsible for and squeezing prices to the point that residential jobs were not worthwhile that he decided to concentrate on commercial removals. The company now has facilities removals' contracts with recurring revenue worth six figures and a robust business valued at over £5 million.

What bothers you personally about your business? Where do you get the most complaints, and what just seems to never work, take too long and why?

Comparisons. We have already discussed comparisons by mapping progress in other sectors. This creates cross-sector and territory innovations. Look for analogies, processes and innovations in your own experience as a customer. The attention to detail in some sectors, for example top hotels, can be inspiring. What are they doing that you could borrow from, even if it's in the layout of your office to make a more relaxed atmosphere?

As an example, on noticing the demand trend for healthy eating in restaurants and at home, brothers Greg and Jamie Combs compared this to the 'on the move' snack food market and found opportunity away from sugary snacks and chocolate. They set up Natural Balance Foods in 2004. Its Trek energy bars, which contain oats, fruit and nuts, are designed as an alternative to sugary sports nutrition products and its compressed fruit and nut Naked bars a substitute for chocolate and other snacks, thus providing wholefood alternatives to processed foods. The business has grown by 57 per cent in the last three years alone, with sales now approaching £15 million. Similarly in London and the United Kingdom, Itsu is also taking on the fast food sector, such as McDonald's and even the predominant sandwich store Pret a Manger, with its new stores dedicated to lower fat, lower calorie, delicious food. Interestingly, Itsu is run by the original founders of Pret a Manger.

What trends in other sectors can be applied to your business? What do other sectors do better than your sector and why? Consequently, what models and processes can be applied within your organization?

Creatives and rebels. A really interesting area for accessing innovation is to embrace the deviants in our organizations. Because we like reliability and 'one voice' businesses, we actually supress the alternatives, or if you like the anti-establishment – but some of the best changes, whether process or product, can come from these players. When someone is behaving badly or does not seem to fit the corporate mould do you fight or embrace them?

There are many examples of rebel entrepreneurs. Consider the British-born and based entrepreneur Dale Vince who founded the £100 million value firm Ecotricity. He actually started as an alternative New Age traveller in the 1990s and his first wind turbine powered his old army truck and caravan on a hill in Gloucestershire. The opportunity lay in the alternative. The question for firms is can they identify and unleash the power in their own internal organizational rebels, or more simply, is your next appraisal actually suppressing innovation?

What can we learn from those who are most intense in their complaints or enthusiasm that we could apply to our company or our role?

Customers. What are your customers saying? How can you see, meet and ask them more about what they think or perhaps, as we mentioned earlier, what they are not saying? How can you get them to be vocal? Social media can both aid and break customers in this respect. How much damage is done by poor ratings reviews but could these reviews be managed better? The customers that complain may instinctively know that an improvement is needed perhaps in comparison to their experiences elsewhere and consequently these complaints are not only an opportunity to win clients back but also to understand where your competitors are winning.

Learn how your stakeholders live, work and behave. Ask yourself: What are the social, cultural and environmental factors that affect their preferences and behaviours? How can we create solutions that respond to those factors?

Be sure to encourage regular personal calls and data collection, thus eliminating the silence and learning more about your customers. Deliberately seek out negative criticism – if you are constantly responding to the needs of customers, your competitors (that aren't doing so) should have a hard time competing... plus your customers are likely to be more loyal; if you listen to their problems and respond to/address those problems, they will have little reason to go elsewhere and may actually move to advocate stage, that is customers who actively recommend you as a consequence of the extra help you have given to get over a challenge. Customers are expensive to win and working out how to keep them, even if it means being generous, is much cheaper than winning new ones.

Loyal customers are also more likely to point out the improvement opportunities to you and this feedback can be built into the strategic thinking. Advantage companies assess the risks rather than take them, and go beyond cost reduction to seek out new revenue ideas and opportunities.

FIGURE 6.5 Contended or questioning thinking

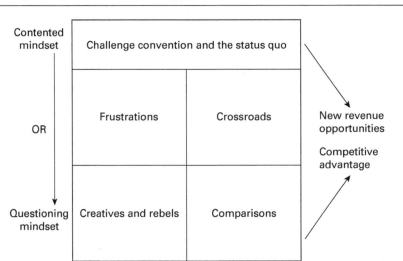

Chapter summary and leader questions

The scenarios pull on both the probabilities and analytics to show likely market direction and consequently we can see and think further ahead to drive improvements and advantage despite dynamic markets. We combine this with being clearer on the difference between management and leadership, which then gives leaders more permission and time to explore the strategy ahead of the competition. The scenarios enable us to carry out this exploration with visuals, tools and models to build strategic insight and thinking. In combination, an effective route is to look more moves ahead, with increased confidence even perhaps if those moves are the less obvious ones. The scenarios develop insight into both internal and external opportunity and ideas to create new products, strategic alliances, and acquisitions or add new territories as well as improve processes and efficiency ahead of our competitors and thus gain advantage.

Strategic planning and scenario work are not so much about precisely predicting the future as they are about understanding the business environment and the nature of the trends, opportunities and risks in the market environment. Strategy and insights gained from scenario planning help leaders anticipate better how to respond to change in order to build agility, listen to customers, challenge convention and spot opportunity to secure competitive advantage. Many people arrive at great ideas more or less serendipitously – but it is possible to approach innovation in a more systematic way.

The process is collaborative, requiring a broad set of skills and a hybrid of both intuition and analytics. Training can enhance awareness and focus on the process to help people understand the difference between planning and strategy and also the benefits of strategy. Leadership awareness, for instance, that selecting just one view of the future is usually flawed.

Whether corporate or small enterprises, companies can still thrive, and build sustainable growth regardless of dynamic changing markets through strategy. Agility is a complement not a replacement and by employing both, organizations and leaders can change the game in the marketplace.

Leader questions

1 What scenarios do we envisage and how can we narrow these down?

2 What works well and can be improved as opposed to what doesn't work?

3 What needs to be challenged?

4 What needs to be improved?

5 What are both your vocal and your silent customers saying?

6 What is the greatest risk?

7 Where is the market going and what can we do to take advantage of it?

8 What time do you really dedicate to strategic thinking?

9 How much do you look at your competition to ensure you are ahead?

References

EY (2015) Making it Work in Russia: Middle Class Consumer Profile. EY.com. Available from: www.ey.com/GL/en/Industries/Consumer-Products/Making-it-work-in-Russia---Middle-class-consumer-profile [Last accessed 27 August 2015]

Moskowitz, C (2011) What's 96 Percent of the Universe Made of? Astronomers Don't Know. Space.com 12/05. Available from: www.space.com/11642-dark-matter-dark-energy-4-percent-universe-panek.html [Last accessed 27 August 2015]

Newport, F (2014) In US, 42% Believe Creationist View of Human Origins

Uphill, K (2015) *Navigating the Rivers of Cash*, Thorogood Publishing, London

Elementary decisions

07

Introduction

I have borrowed the idea for the introduction to this chapter from Sherlock Holmes. The detective is known for his brilliance in spotting clues others have missed, in combination with deductive reasoning, to create elementary conclusions. Elementary refers to the simple, easy facts or parts of a subject that must necessarily be learned in order to understand subsequent ones. Leadership for competitive advantage ultimately requires simple shared conclusions achieved from complexity. Advantage can seem remarkable because the competition has been less effective in understanding the critical movements of the zeitgeist and/or market age and consequently failed to engage in the appropriate strategic action. To me this is the encapsulation of great business leaders and entrepreneurs. In this chapter we examine how advantage leaders assess the options, spot the elements others have missed, assess the risks, then make decisions and drive the business against these decisions. We see how they are not risk takers but highly observational and ultimately decisive assessors of risk and market direction.

Elementary

People reach decisions in very different ways and there is no one right way; there are both tools and traits involved. Tools might include traditional methods such as weighing up pros and cons or SWOT analysis of strengths, weaknesses, opportunities and threats while styles might be the differences between an intuitive and instinctive approach versus an analytical approach. Styles might also recognize that some leaders make decisions in an inclusive executive way and others in a commanding way; again neither is necessarily right or wrong. Indeed it can be argued that it perhaps depends on the circumstances. Britain's greatest prime minister, Sir Winston Churchill, was generally considered to have too commanding a decision-making style to be effective in peacetime, but in wartime shone with brilliance. Whatever the style, conclusions must be arrived at and acted upon. Inaction is also legitimate but only as a result of the decision specifically not to act, not of fateful indecision.

Good strategic decision-making requires a mixture of skills: clarity of judgement, creative development, identification of options, timeliness, firmness of decision and, ultimately, effective implementation. This is easier to say and harder to do. Beyond the skills we must also combine experience and awareness; it may, for example, be that we are faced with decisions that we are not necessarily best qualified to make. Recognizing our limitations is also inherent in the final decisions we make. Some decisions have to be made when you are not ready, others are not as urgent as they first seem or indeed may be unnecessary, and awareness of these elements is again critical to the effectiveness of great leaders.

> Many leaders are chosen for their ability to persuade and in this trait we often assume talk, but it is research and listening that are more critical to spot the elements others have missed at the right time and to act upon those elements.

Fast-changing markets can increase the perception of chaos and there is increased uncertainty. This has changed decision-making; the complexity and speed require leaders to be more reflective in order to assess the elements. Many leaders are chosen for their ability to persuade and in this trait we often assume talk, but it is research and listening that are more critical to spot the elements others have missed at the right time and to act upon those elements.

In the idea of elementary we also have basic truth or simple truth. How many great businesses struggle because their leaders missed the basic truth, very often because their egos ignored the facts?

CASE STUDY

For me, one of the most fascinating examples of an elementary or basic truth being missed by its leaders led to the virtual collapse of the Royal Bank of Scotland (RBS), one of the world's biggest banks, in 2008. This was only narrowly averted by a huge taxpayers' bailout. Fred Goodwin brilliantly spearheaded the RBS takeover of the mundane, yet significant, UK bank NatWest in 2000 and as a result, became

CEO of the group in early 2001 (despite having a very limited banking background, having spent his early career as an accountant for Deloitte). Sir Fred's (his knighthood has now been removed) leadership came at a time when the corporate and UK plc's maxim was to virtually expand at any cost. RBS lived the dream of growth relatively successfully, in particular pursuing growth in investment banking.

Inevitably, with fast growth comes high leverage and the balance is always tricky. In 2007, Goodwin and RBS hatched an audacious plan to extend their reach. Competing against Barclays, RBS won the bid to purchase the Dutch bank ABN Amro but at a price that was too high against the quality of the assets. Furthermore, the bid was won just as markets appeared to be turning from growth. Liquidity was starting to dry up in banking as banks started to worry increasingly about the collectability of many of the loans issued in the sub-prime market. To be fair, RBS realized this and tried to renegotiate but the law firm, Linklaters, advised that a general market downturn could not be used to renegotiate the agreed bid. ABN Amro issued an earnings update stating that it would beat its forecasts, which made it impossible for RBS to use poor financial performance as a get-out clause. Even without the problems in the credit markets, funding such a large balance sheet would have been a major challenge for RBS but as ABN Amro's wholesale business combined with RBS so the bank began to breach the risk limits of many of its corporate savers. This resulted in an outflow of corporate deposits and increasingly scarce funds. Despite various late attempts to raise capital, cash remained king and the government bailout ensued.

In review, history has revealed worrying elements in the RBS decision-making process after the NatWest purchase. There was a lack of internal governance, an over-persuasive chief executive who was not held to account by the board and directors who were afraid to speak up. This, combined with a 'grow at all costs' mentality and regulatory oversight, allowed overtrading. A few basic truths, poor ego-driven decision-making and a failure to understand the current times almost led to RBS destroying itself and in so doing it nearly took down the entire banking system. Some might even say that capitalism itself was at risk. Government intervention on such a scale rather contradicts the dream of free capital markets and Goodwin's is a classic case of arrogance, an exceptional track record and ego leading to basic truths being ignored. Despite advice that the assets of ABN Amro were not good enough, and the price possibly being too high, the strategy was led by self-belief and ambition rather than fact, with potentially catastrophic consequences for us all. However, in defence of Goodwin, he was a product of the times, and perhaps if it wasn't RBS, another would have led the charge. His board and his chairman were equally complicit. Goodwin still receives a lifetime RBS pension of £342,000, some 15 times the average national salary.

Reality

Advantage decisions are made when we seek, without ego or personal agenda, the clues others have missed that lead to insight others have failed to secure. In order to see the elements of truth that create advantage we need to remove all the filters and actually enhance objectivity. Exceptional leaders might rely on their own experience but they will also recognize that that experience creates a filter that can detrimentally only let in the information with which they already agree. To be philosophical, our own experiences define us but how we see the world is not reality; it is our perspective of reality. If we define reality as the sum of all the things that exist and the moments at a given point, a balance sheet sum of life and everything, if you like, no one can have a true snapshot of the reality balance sheet and we can only hope to access components of it. Furthermore, even if you could take a snapshot of all the elements of reality, the second you have the shot, in fast-changing times it would be out of date. Therefore, be open. You never know what's around the corner and be aware of how your own perspective can skew the truth. Advantage leaders assess more clues and elements to better see the state of things as they truly are and thus to make better decisions.

An ivory tower is an English and French (tour d'ivoire) metaphor for not knowing about or wanting to avoid the ordinary and unpleasant things that happen. The phrase was coined in an 1837 poem by Charles Augustin Sainte-Beuve, where it was used to describe the poetical attitude of Alfred de Vigny as contrasted with the more socially engaged Victor Hugo. Today, the colloquialism is much used in business leadership jargon as something to strongly avoid. For me, the main context of the phrase is that ivory is expensive and hard, and the tower is lofty. Leaders and executives in the tower are too high up and too expensive to see the reality on the ground and, even worse, people are dazzled by the beauty of the tower and tell them what they want to hear.

Decisions are much better when based on reality, as far as we can perceive it; therefore, leaders need to discreetly talk regularly to customers, staff and suppliers but as the common man. I have heard this called 'walking the shop floor' or 'touching the corners'. However we disguise it, it is critical to find ways to secure reality. I recall a visit to one client's factory where he walked the floor every day, which is commendable; however, when I joined him one day, he greeted a member of staff and asked if they were busy. Now, what are you going to say to your boss when asked that question? You may need to go out of your way to become part of the equation rather than just reviewing the equation.

Earlier in this chapter, I wrote about Fred Goodwin. An ex-RBS colleague told me that whenever Sir Fred visited a branch he insisted on it being redecorated before he arrived and he never bothered to learn the names of the team as he arrived in his limousine. How on earth can the leaders see what needs to be improved in this situation so far removed from reality?

A good example of how ivory towers can be demolished is from the much-celebrated US police chief (and notable businessman) William Bratton. Bratton has been highly influential in reducing crime and in one of his commissioner appointments he was horrified when his board decided to purchase small squad cars that would be cheaper to buy and run. His strategy needed officers to be relaxed with space to think. He could have tried (probably unsuccessfully) to insist on an increased budget but instead he invited the board's general manager for a tour of his unit and its district in one of the new cars. William Bratton ensured he was loaded with his baton, gun and handcuffs. He also wedged the seats forward to show the manager how little space there was if a criminal was in the back. Several potholes later, the manager wanted out and on his own volition reversed the small car policy. This demonstrates that it is possible to both see and assail the ivory tower.

Serendipity

I debated about using this word as it is often misconstrued as meaning luck. To an extent there is an element of luck, as it can be defined as having a talent for making fortunate discoveries while looking for other things. This is exactly what is needed when securing competitive advantage. I have already mentioned that more time needs to be spent on research, and convention put aside, in order to be more free thinking and objective. If, as leaders, you do this without ego then opportunity becomes more apparent as you consider all your options in order to create advantage. Simply put: with serendipity you may seek advantage and believe it to lie in a certain direction yet through fortune you may discover other opportunities that are better.

The word 'serendipity' was first used in English by the author Horace Walpole in 1754. Walpole formed the word from an old name for the country of Sri Lanka: Serendip, which is based on a fairytale: *The Three Princes of Serendip*. As Their Highnesses travelled, they were always making discoveries, by accidents and sagacity, of things that they were not looking for. While travelling, the three princes hear of a lost camel. Although they have never seen the camel, they describe it so perfectly, as being lame, blind in one eye, missing a tooth, bearing honey on one side and butter on the other that when they meet the merchant who has lost the camel they actually get accused of stealing it. The merchant takes them to the emperor, Beramo, where he demands punishment.

Beramo asks how they are able to give such an accurate description of the camel if they have never seen it. The princes describe the clues. Grass had been eaten from the side of the road where it was less green, so the princes concluded that the camel was blind on the other side. There were lumps of chewed grass on the road that were the size of a camel's tooth so they deduced that they had fallen through a gap where the tooth was missing. The tracks showed that a foot was being dragged, indicating that the animal was lame, butter had obviously been carried on one side of the camel and honey on the other because ants had been attracted to melted butter on one side of the road and flies to spilt honey on the other.

At that moment a traveller enters the scene to say that he has just found a missing camel wandering in the desert. Beramo spares the lives of the three princes, lavishes rich rewards on them and appoints them to be his advisers. This is a tale of fortune being secured by enlightened observation and openness and we can apply the same to business strategy for competitive advantage. Despite appearances, sustainable advantage is rarely secured by luck and usually by greater observation and awareness of all the elements in strategy. Jack Dorsey, the founder of Twitter, actually discovered the technology when he was designing technology for despatching ambulances and taxis. Why track ambulances when you can track friends?

Risk

Risk simply means a chance of danger. The word is from the French word 'risqué', which means tending towards impropriety. Impropriety suggests that actually it is our approach that makes a situation risky, which is useful because it reminds us we can manage risk to a large extent. We can see this clearly if we look at the example of road traffic fatalities. Risk is being eroded from driving as safety takes precedence in car and road management. In the United Kingdom in 2013, 1,713 people were killed in reported road traffic accidents, 2 per cent (41) fewer than in 2012. This is the lowest number of fatalities since national records began in 1926. The total number of people killed in 2013 was 39 per cent lower than the 2005–09 baseline average (UK Department for Transport, 2014). With practice, we have got much better at taking out the risks. We have airbags, seat belts, seat belt laws, speed restrictions, automatic braking, ABS brakes, soft bumpers, crumple systems, traction control and head restraints. All of these, together with clearer road systems such as speed cameras have revolutionized safety. Good design and market demand have actually led legislation, not the other way round. Overall, this is exciting because it shows that we can embrace safety or risk while still embracing change. Today there are more vehicles on the road than ever.

Creating competitive advantage will usually require us to make changes, and this often means doing untested and new things. By nature, practice makes perfect and therefore we will have greater risks in those new activities than perhaps in the old. The question for executives is whether they can improve, enhance and accelerate safety in the new service, product or activity faster than they can offset decline in the old as markets change around them. We know that old design is always surpassed by new design and it is the management of risk that we must consider. We also know that while the old may be tried and tested it will diminish; therefore, there may be as many risks of being outclassed as there are of getting it wrong on the new. How do we coordinate and practically apply our knowledge and resources to minimize, monitor and control the probability of unfortunate events while we maximize advantage? By using design, system and approach how can we address uncertainty to ensure we reach our ambitions? As already mentioned, good leaders are usually risk assessors not risk takers.

Leaders assess risk

Risk management could be a topic by itself. Advantage leaders understand and question strategic plans at a base level and further analyse the underlying assumptions within the plans. They design and implement in ways that achieve the goals but as safely as possible while vigorously asking 'what if?' scenario questions that determine whether alternative plans and actions to mitigate risk are in place. They ask what if an objective of a plan is not met, or what if something or someone goes wrong, and how do we better monitor for failure? Good design will usually reduce risk and increase the chances of strategic success. Invariably there will be acceptable risks, ie risks that are understood and tolerated usually because the gain is large and the cost of reducing the accepted vulnerability exceeds the expectation of loss. Risks might be legal, financial or commercial such as supply or cost base, resource absence or failures including staffing, technology, project failure, environmental or competitive. Advantage risk assessment requires:

- *Identification.* Identify the scenario and determine the potential adverse consequences and any knock-on effects. The classic what happens if we run out of money or do the advantages of the new, if we pull it off, outweigh the disadvantage of failure and by what factor? What is the return on investment over what period against potential loss?

- *Exposure*. Consider the likelihood of the scenario and any other influences. What happens if we get a high number of customer complaints while we try something new and how does this impact on our reputation? Also consider what happens if you don't disrupt and pioneer and how this may balance.

- *Response analysis*. Consider the actions or systems, and the cost of them, versus the consequences. Carefully determine the relationship between the scenario and the potential responses.

However well designed your initiative is, remember that things can go wrong and for me understanding it is usually a series of events, not one that causes difficulties. Much risk assessment assumes one failure and this is flawed. By comparison, for example, in 1912 the Titanic, the world's largest and most advanced liner at the time, sank on her maiden voyage after hitting an iceberg which resulted in the death of more than 1,500 of the 2,200 passengers on board. The liner spanned 883 feet from stern to bow, and its hull was divided into 16 compartments that were presumed to be watertight. The Titanic was considered unsinkable because four of these compartments could be flooded without causing a critical loss of buoyancy, yet she sank within three hours of hitting the iceberg and the gash caused by the iceberg took out six compartments. Despite seven iceberg warnings, the captain (Captain Smith) was believed to be going too fast under pressure from his White Star Line owners to set new records. Fog obscured the iceberg so the lookouts could not spot it soon enough. Added to this, there were not enough lifeboats for all of the passengers onboard. When assessing or managing the risks inherent in our new strategic initiatives assume nothing is unsinkable and assess risk against a series of failures rather than one event – and make sure you have enough lifeboats!

In Chapter 3, we suggested that leaders need to be more hands off in order to spend more time on research. In this model, risk thus sits more with the middle-tier managers, but managers tend to look after their silos, so one of the keys in 'advantage business design' is to get managers to look further across the division's organization. Finance should better understand marketing operations, for example. When I worked as a trainee in retail banking before the investment world took the limelight it was not possible to become a manager unless you had worked in every department. While I earlier bemoaned slow promotion in banking leading to talent drain this is the one very positive experience I took with me – Fred Goodwin did not have this background! How can you support and guide your managers to become directors so that they look beyond their silos to the whole organization and how it interacts, while understanding their fiduciary duties to protect the overall organization, even if that means asking difficult questions? How can we develop managers to ask appropriate, substantive questions as well as develop appropriate risk mitigation strategies? The UK's Institute of Directors runs some excellent courses to help leaders and managers understand the essential differences between direction, management and ownership as well as best practice in corporate governance, sustainability, risk management and disclosure when running boards. These courses can be excellent for reducing silo 'my division' thinking, as can involving non-executive directors or mentors.

Financial risk

A new client we work with recently shared a tale of woe: during the 1990s and 2000s he built up a successful facilities contracting and management business; feeling empowered, he delegated the day-to-day running of the business to senior staff – but this is where the story turns sour. Financial performance became spasmodic, particularly as contracting became exposed to a high risk of debt default and construction margins eroded. His managers, whose jobs relied on the status quo, carried on doing the same things, but the business model needed changing. Instead of doing this, increasingly better ways of keeping the numbers looking good were introduced. The balance sheet was slowly dressed with work in progress extending out, for example, and the accountants who failed to understand the business were complicit. Our client was a trusting soul and not financially savvy in any way so he took the numbers on faith. Of course, eventually, with cash being king, an overdressed balance sheet and a few bad debts later the inevitable collapse came. The business was rescued by investors but at what cost, and perhaps, unnecessarily. It seems the mistake that was made was in the assumption that what you are being told in the numbers is absolute and that numbers people are competent and cohesive and, further, that they are looking after you. For me, the risks in the business were built because the right key performance indicators had not been employed and my client had not learnt to be financially aware despite running a good-sized business.

Non-financial people often assume that numbers are numbers, but accountants can manipulate numbers in ways that you cannot imagine.

Accountants can be complicit in manipulation by ignorance of the business model. Would you really expect an accountant trained in maths to understand a contracting business with retentions and work in payment deferred payments? Let's take the example of the mighty Enron's ability to overstate its numbers: Enron chose to report the entire value of each of its trades as revenue (Ackman, 2002). While this was legal, it enabled subjectivity, which was missed by Arthur Anderson, one of the top accounting firms at the time. Key managers brought trades forward to conclusion to meet Wall Street expectations in maintaining the stratospheric share value. Again, it was the accountants not understanding the business, together with the vested interests of the status quo and in this case the share packages, which led to disaster.

Numbers can lie and it is the story behind the numbers that you need to question. This is the single biggest and greatest risk inherent in any business. Leaders need to learn how to interrogate the numbers in depth, and ultimately in plain English; further, we link back to the dashboard concept discussed in Chapter 5 where we need the right information. An important de-risk for leaders is not to trust 'suits' (numbers people) while at the same time learning how to become a 'suit' (a numbers person). If you can run a business, learning these numbers is not as hard as you may imagine and there are some great finance for non-finance people courses and books available.

What if?

Directors should participate in a discussion that is both respectful and challenging. 'What if?' questions are a really engaging way to examine each strategic plan at foundation and test it for weaknesses. Another great approach is from the famous US TV series *Colombo*: 'I am probably being confused and slow minded, but...'. Some ideas are not as sensible or as exciting as they first appear and people very often become lost in the complexities. The 'I am dumb' approach again takes matters to their foundation, which is often where the flaws are. You may remember that in Chapter 3 we discussed how advantage leaders solve problems at source upstream – the same can perhaps be said of how we can manage risk more effectively. Removing the risk or changing the game can be better than resolving the challenge. If we look at car design, we will very soon have computer locking systems that create road trains of cars on our motorways which will take human error out of the equation.

Good leaders become competent at asking the right questions to express their intelligence and good judgement. Advantage organizations will build boards that create an effective balance of challenge and change. It is also important to measure and document the risk between the management and the directors, thus creating an effective oversight of the company's strategy and a safer culture of 'what if?'. Many leaders are enthusiasts and optimists and it is easy to tell them what they want to hear. A good board, where challenge is accepted, the numbers are tested and open and 'what if?' stupid questions are actively encouraged and listened to, both creates new ideas and diminishes risk in seeking advantage. The real key to risk management is to encourage and embrace challenge rather than to fight it. The oak tree will always fall in high winds as it's inflexible whereas the pine tree blows with the wind. Flexibility with challenge better manages risk and the organizational tone is set by the leaders.

Competitive advantage may require us to try new things but we can do so in a better prepared way. In my last book, *Navigating the Rivers of Cash*, I used the example of the 1970s Formula 1 racing driver, James Hunt, who was all talent and flair versus the measured and calculating Niki Lauda. The 2013 film *Rush* gives a really accurate comparison between the two. Hunt was probably the more talented driver but his success never got near Lauda as Lauda relied on micro-planning as well as talent. We can follow the line of probability ahead of the market with great new ideas but we must robustly micro-test to enhance and tune them, thus ensuring credible effective change.

Experts

There may be times when a decision is beyond the leader's expertise and this is the time for expert help; however, people have a tendency to place too much emphasis on what experts say. Experts can have their own set of biases and prejudices based on their own experience and they don't know your business as well as you do. Never employ consultants to tell you what your strategy should be; employ them to create a better picture of the market, the options, threats and opportunities and to help *coach* you objectively in building a strategy but not *tell* you the strategy. Leaders can both over- and underestimate the value of the information they receive from others, so as well as thoroughly checking the methods and credentials of experts there is a need to keep the opinions of others in perspective. In the end, not listening to your own analysis and intuition can be one of the biggest mistakes that can be made during the decision-making process. Figure 7.1 follows the common risk stress points in seeking advantage.

FIGURE 7.1   Risk stress points when seeking advantage

Risk stress points when seeking advantage		
Concept		**Risk**
Review the line of probability and data	↓	Research flaws and failures
Scenario analysis	↓	Planning and visibility risks
Disrupt and look to the future demand	↓	Scale, uncertainty and untested
Focus on organizational direction	↓	Business model versus product category
Decision-making	↓	Lack of data leading to hesitancy
Implementation and execution	↓	Management risk

Tools

There are many executive tools and models that can be used to help make decisions. The simplest and most used is a weighting model. Many organizations have complex variants of these but fundamentally they sit around a base method. The idea is that you examine all the options in front of you. You then 'chunk' or 'group' these together to reduce options. Many issues are facets of the same cause. One might say we have a poor IT system but actually we have poor organization so we might chunk this into what investment is required in processes and systems rather than seeing them as isolated. Once you have fewer options you can see singular decisions and score them in order of importance; once you have the most important you can apply pros and cons to your ideas and weight them. Don't worry if this sounds complicated; I have shown a simple example of weighting around a research decision in Figure 7.2. Of course this would be more complicated

FIGURE 7.2   Decision weighting method

Should we outsource or recruit our research resource?

Pros	Score	Cons	Score
better flexibility	3	less continuity	5
lower desk cost	3	desk space and service liability	3
lower service liability	4	less reliability	2
better holiday cover	3	less internal expertise	2
better scalability	5	reduced accountability	4
more prestige	2		
Total 6 pros	**20**	**Total 5 cons**	**16**

if you were deciding on which country to base a new plant in. Use whatever scoring method makes good sense to you for your situation. This example shows a low score method.

In the above example, on the basis of the pros and cons and the weighting applied, there seems to be a clear overall and calculated advantage in the decision to go ahead and outsource. For bigger, complex decisions where there are several options, create a template that enables measurements according to different strategic factors and also use other tools such as SWOT (Strengths, Weaknesses, Opportunities, Threats) analysis and PEST (Political, Economic, Social Trends) analysis. There are lots of decision tools using many methods available online and these are worth a look.

Analytical intuition

Logic and analysis can create a better picture of now but they can suppress creativity by filling the mind with how things are rather than how they might be. On the other hand, intuition and dreaming can lack practicality and can result in crucial steps being missed. If we don't know how things are, how can we hope to change them, and we need to know how they are beyond superficiality. In my mind, most of the great leaps in advantage require a hybrid approach to both thinking and decision-making. A hybrid of intuition and logic, analysis and creativity, a fusion of the big macro picture and the micro details, whether this is in one person or in teams creating better shifts. This is of course logical as combining detail and carefully crafted analysis with leaps in imagination and jumps in the steps will help us both spot the gaps others have left and leap to clearer and new conclusions. The process of thinking is more holistic and therefore deeper, even if it can appear confusing.

To use one example of a great intuitive leap, the Victorian Charles Babbage's difference machine was the first calculating machine but in 1936, Alan Turing described the first computer. A universal machine which, with tables of behaviour complex enough to read the tables of other machines. Such a machine might thus handle variables (Copeland and Proudfoot, 2012). If this seems strange, note the modern parallel that any computer can be simulated by software on another computer. Turing's early ideas intuitively go to the heart of the modern computer, whereby it is essential that programs are themselves data that can be manipulated. Turing even understood that to be effective the machine needed to be simple and thus a learning machine is digital as opposed to just electronic. Turing was a mathematician but also a philosopher and spent many hours debating the importance of answering variable questions such as the classical liar's paradox. If a liar states he or she is lying, the paradox is that if they are lying they are telling the truth; ergo a classical binary truth value leads to a contradiction. Don't worry – this threw me too! The point, however, is that he combined maths with philosophy and it was this binary thinking that led to the universal idea. He used logic and intuition across disciplines to envisage new ways of doing things and consequently, since 1936, with digital computers and the internet we can virtually access the sum of human knowledge with our fingertips. Throughout his life, in every sphere, Turing made unexpected connections between apparently unrelated areas.

Einstein also stands out: his intuition forced him to think contrary to the quantum theories at the time. Although hugely successful, the maths behind them was increasingly being distorted. Despite not having a respected academic post, Einstein felt that there was something wrong for this level of manipulation and set out to seek a more basic truth, culminating in the theory of relativity and in particular that space and time should be considered together and in relation to each other, including demonstrating the maths behind this, showing us a new, simpler truth (for now!). Einstein himself accepted that intuition could play with ideas at a looser level, leaving the conceptual framework that the status quo leaves us trapped in. Without knowing the details, intuition can match patterns and see where connections are possible in a different framework. The process is more error prone than an analytical narrow approach but for many problems it is the only possible approach.

The contention is that the truly best and ground-breaking ideas and decisions or competitive advantage come when truly expert knowledge of the current 'how and now' says 'Hang that, let's play' and then creates a new game with the simplicity of a child's mind. A beautifully woven and controlled interplay and balance of analysis and intuition, logic and creation, gut feeling and fact, assessment and pioneering, the dream and the practical. A highly balanced tapestry that gives us the freedom to know our strategy both with and without specific reason, freedom to create and understand new futures. Figure 7.3 summarizes this thinking.

Society teaches us that we should not blend logic and emotion, and academic work leans towards ignoring feeling and sticking to the facts. Additionally, the left- and right-hand brain thinkers and protagonists tell us we have tendencies that are dictated by which side of the brain we naturally lean on. For example, a person who is left-brained is often said to be more logical, analytical and objective, while a person who is right-brained is said to be more intuitive, thoughtful and subjective. The right brain–left brain

FIGURE 7.3   Analytical intuition

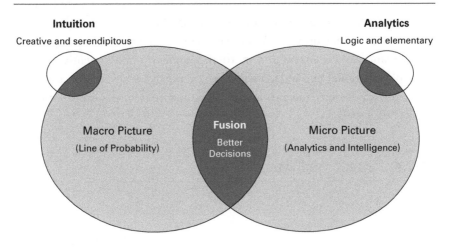

theory originated in the work of Roger W Sperry. While studying the effects of epilepsy, Sperry discovered that by cutting the corpus callosum (the structure that connects the two hemispheres of the brain) you could reduce or eliminate seizures (Cherry, 2014). This built on previous thinking that the brain is made up of two halves; however, today there is absolutely no scientific basis that one type of thinking is on one side as opposed to the other; indeed it is a convenient myth that helps us understand the differences we have in style. After decades of experiments, particularly on language, science has proved categorically that while there are some functional asymmetries, the two brain hemispheres do not work in isolation but rather together, in every signature cognitive task. We can test the unhelpful belief that logical people can't be intuitive and vice versa to create a more blended style of both rational and emotional decision-making. We can combine fluidity and hunches with plan and structure to see the differences and the similarities to solve problems better.

Expertise and intuition

The further paradox in decision-making is that 'know-it-alls' are often so constrained by the walls of their knowledge or expertise that they really struggle to access intuition. Interestingly, naivety can lead to innovation, as can mastery, but the middle cycle which many leaders arrive at when we are accumulating or believe we have full expertise can actually suppress innovation. This is well summarized in the famous saying: 'The day you think you are a master is the day you cease to be a master.' Shakespeare's quote, 'The fool doth think he is wise, but the wise man knows himself to be a fool', also sums the point up well. When we become truly expert, we appreciate every nuance in a scenario and its total complexity, consequently become more observational and indeed with the complexity, embrace our ability to be surprised, thereby increasing openness and thus, intuition. Figure 7.4 shows this cycle.

FIGURE 7.4   Stages of intuition

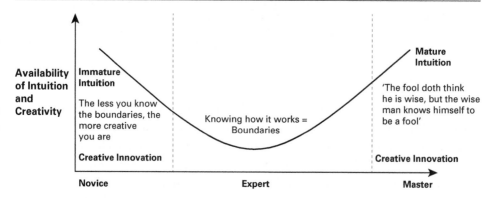

Understanding the cycle we are in when we are accessing our gut feeling or intuition helps us use the intuition tool more effectively in decision-making, and further understanding its inherent importance. We have better confidence to trust our gut instincts beyond the logic, the feeling that something is right, and better, if we can be clear of the disparity between our intuitive and our analytical minds, our scorecard if you like. We create better alignment between the 'I just know' and the 'tingly vibe' we inherently feel when making decisions; this is typically an alignment of the conscious and the unconscious mind. The best analogy I can give you to understand the unconscious mind is this: do you ever drive home and think you can't remember how you got here? The process of driving and finding home has become subconscious while you ponder other matters. The subconscious sum of our experience is what I suspect drives the intuition and very often the 'call' is right because we are not exerting the effort to decide. I know people who deliberately take a big problem to bed in their minds with the explicit choice that they will run it overnight and see what the conclusion is in the morning. This is known as 'I will sleep on it' and is as legitimate as any other decision style.

Advantage does not directly come from the analytical or intuitive mind but instead the decisions we make as a result of the scenarios secured from looking at the environment and our dashboards. What can we do that is beyond the value a market delivers today to be ahead of the value it might deliver tomorrow?

Workshops and the board decide

In this chapter I have used the phrase leadership but elementary decision-making may of course, depending on the organization, be singular or collective. Much may also apply to collective thinking but group decisions are of course different. We must foster an environment of appropriate questions, freedom to think and be aware of what can and can't be decided by a group. For example, design can really struggle when carried out by a committee. Can you imagine what Frank Lloyd Wright's inspirational Guggenheim Museum in New York, with its wonderful spirals, would be like if a committee had been involved? Committees generally function on compromise and design *can* be lost if artists compromise.

The decisions the company board should help with and why are subjective. Managing and running boards are also an entire topic, as is facilitating group decisions. As a general synopsis the main view is that boards should be involved in areas where they have direct control and liability. Additionally, there is a view that they should help with anything strategic. We could define this as substantial changes in plans that are long term not short term. They should also have a say in areas such as regulatory changes, competitor moves and significant technical, reputational or legal problems.

It is typically the managing director or chief executive who decides how often the boards sit and what the agenda is. Larger companies will, depending on which country you are in, have a chairperson and there may be a regulatory requirement for non-executive board members, that is board members who are not involved with any management role and therefore bring better objectivity to decisions. The chairperson ensures that the board is effective in its tasks of setting and implementing the company's direction and strategy. This would mean helping the CEO with the board's composition and leading discussions towards the emergence of a consensus view and summing up discussions so that everyone understands what has been agreed. Some smaller companies combine the managing director and chairperson role. When directors have the opportunity and resources to carefully vet the underlying issues, the board can bring valuable ideas and insight, resulting in a better company decision than management would have made on its own.

In Chapter 3 we discussed leadership not management and the balance of time spent in delivering versus thinking always being critical to any venture. It could be argued that small companies are too biased towards action and don't see far enough ahead whereas larger companies can be inertia-led due to their sheer size, and may need to be broken down into a more divisional model to be leaner and more entrepreneurial when it comes to decision-making.

Boards need to act purposefully to create advantage. Capitalism can lead to short-term-gain thinking, particularly if actions create short-term wealth for the directors; this can in turn lead to poor decision-making. Many strategies take time and inherently have longer returns. Sustainable competitive advantage requires the balance of purposefulness and quality with elegance, as well as financial gain. Boards need the vision and determination to create something better beyond the immediate. Careful objective evaluation, risk management and a cohesive yet entrepreneurial mindset should enhance decisions. Figure 7.5 sets out a foundation for the balance that might be required in boards.

FIGURE 7.5   Board decision-making influencers

Board decision-making influencers		
	What we see	**What we do**
Analytical intuition	The line of probability and data input	Risk of indecision greater than decision
Listening and evaluation Objectivity and cohesiveness balance	Scenarios Opportunities Change	Shareholder alignment Long term vs short term
Identify your biases	Trying new things	Reward vs risk

Hakuna matata – no problem

Seeking advantage will have its risks inherent in trying new things. It requires us to be more pioneering and, as already discussed, you can counter this with better risk assessment and risk management. Ultimately, however, we make the decisions and some will succeed and some will fail. If you are competitive, and you probably are, in order to become a leader or executive then you won't like failure. This means that you probably worry about the decisions you make and worry about the consequences. It is inherent that we want to get it right, but part of leadership is also learning to accept and live with our decisions and failures. Ideally of course, learn from them, but most of all accept them and move on.

On a visit to Kenya, I learnt the phrase 'hakuna matata'. In Swahili this means 'There isn't a problem' and 'Don't worry, be happy.' You might also recall its use in the famous Disney film *The Lion King*. In the end, when making decisions we must keep perspective. I am sure that as a seasoned executive you know this but there are times when we need to be reminded. One way I help owners who are, as we might call it 'sweating an issue', is to reframe it. I remind them they are not freezing to death in a failed polar exploration or being shot at in a futile war and I hope the comparison pulls them back into perspective. I have always been horrified by the trench warfare that the First World War resulted in. This was largely driven by the nations involved completely underestimating the power that machine guns brought to war. This resulted in the total number of British Empire casualties from a mobilized force of 8,904,467 broken down as follows: 908,371 killed, 2,090,212 wounded; 191,652 taken prisoner and missing (PBS, 2015). To reframe your issue, is it as bad as being in the trenches?

The decision process

1 Identify, define and clarify the decision: Is the decision important, urgent or actually necessary? Is the timing right to decide? Remember that what appears to be the loudest is not always the most important. Work upstream and make decisions that impact at source.

2 Research and gather the key information: What are the data and our probability research telling us? What other information do you need for a decision? We may also look internally in our minds for experience and insight as well as research. Gather all the facts and understand their causes.

3 Seek qualified expert advice: Do you need expert support and if so, how can you ensure that you get the right experts? Seek input but eventually hold your own counsel.

4 Seek difference: What clues and elements can you spot that others have not? If you are being forced into a decision, what alternatives have you missed?

5 Identify alternatives and scenarios: Through the process of collecting information you will probably identify several possible paths of action, or alternatives. What clues have others missed?

6 Weigh evidence and risks: Reflect on the information, scenarios and perspectives to imagine what it would be like if you carried out each of the alternatives to the end. There will always be risks – how do you minimize them and are they acceptable? Run your pros and cons model and weighting tool.

7 Ensure measured objectivity: What false filters are you overlaying to the information and are your feet grounded in reality? What past experiences might over-influence you or hold you back?

8 Involve others: Bringing others into decision-making early rather than presenting foregone conclusions aids their implementation. Incorporate teamwork. What checks and balances exist, particularly in risk management?

9 Choose, communicate and take action: After effective consideration, select the choice that seems to be best suited to you and your organization, communicate precisely and act. In complexity a bias towards action taken will help avoid paralysis by analysis.

10 Review your decision, actions and consequences: If it's working how could you improve it? If your decision or actions are not working, do you need to change? Evaluate, review and tune.

11 Hold the line: Inherent in many decisions come compromises. It may sound hard but compromising, particularly when trying to please everyone, especially in the vested interest arena, rarely creates advantage. Advantage can require difficult and tough decisions to do the right thing. Stay the course, have a vision and stick with it.

12 Permission to fail: Organizations build themselves on reliability; this is the opposite of failure yet trying new things will always be riskier simply because we have not had the chance to learn from what worked and what did not work. We can evaluate but we must accept risk if we are to gain advantage and this means accepting and indeed embracing failure. Each failure is feedback towards how to succeed. Fast-changing markets actively increase the need for 'try it small, ditch it fast or change it' initiatives.

Figure 7.6 summarizes these points.

Chapter summary and leader questions

In dynamic markets we face increased complexity and risks we can't easily analyse; yet ultimately, advantage requires deciding what to believe and how

FIGURE 7.6 Decision-making process

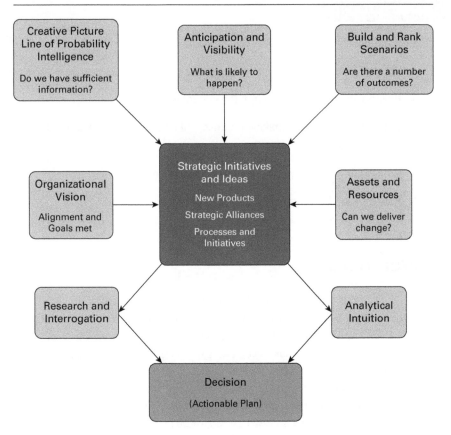

to act on it. In the idea of 'elementary' we seek clues others have left behind and combine this with step-by-step reasoning to aid decision-making. In the idea of 'reality' we remove ego, and filters, to see more clearly and truly things as they are and might be, and then better decisions arise. In 'serendipity' we identify better opportunities that we were not seeking solutions for but are nonetheless salient. In analytical intuition we increase the awareness of our styles and seek congruence in different styles to help us apply our whole minds to the challenge of deciding.

Good strategic decision-making, particularly when faced with creating new futures, requires a mixture of skills: clarity of judgement, creative development and identification of options, timeliness, firmness of decision, risk management, good board governance and ultimately, effective implementation.

> ### Leader questions
>
> 1 What have you spotted that others may have missed?
>
> 2 What are the risks of the market overtaking you?
>
> 3 How do you best decide where the market is going?
>
> 4 What is your decision-making process and what checks and support exist to help?
>
> 5 What tools and methods can aid decision-making?
>
> 6 How can you better manage the risks inherent in change?

References

Ackman, D (2002) Enron The Incredible. Forbes.com 1/15. Available from: www.forbes.com/2002/01/15/0115enron.html [Last accessed: 27 August 2015]

Cherry, K (2014) Left Brain vs Right Brain. About Education. Available from: http://psychology.about.com/od/cognitivepsychology/a/left-brain-right-brain.htm [Last accessed 27 August 2015]

Copeland, B J and Proudfoot, D (2012) Alan Turing: Father of the Modern Computer. *Rutherford Journal*. Available from: http://rutherfordjournal.org/article040101.html [Last accessed 27 August 2015]

PBS (2015) WW1 Casualty and Death Tables. Available from: www.pbs.org/greatwar/resources/casdeath_pop.html [Last accessed 27 August 2015]

UK Department for Transport (2014) Annual road fatalities. Available from: www.gov.uk/government/publications/annual-road-fatalities [Last accessed: 27 August 2015]

Changing the game

08

Introduction

From our conversation so far, and given the line of probability and better analytics, we should now have a far greater understanding of which direction the market is moving and from our work on scenarios, we should have ideas as to how to define the rules in our favour. We are clear how to decide on the direction and now in this chapter we examine finding the courage we need to 'change the game' – this phrase comes from the idea that to win we might need to write new rules, to create new games where we naturally have advantage.

Game changing

I recently worked with an ambitious professional services business under a new leadership regime. Our brief was to increase cost-efficiency by streamlining headcount and to help them join up the marketing, sales and IT silos to create both efficiency and a more coordinated approach. The business was seeking a 35 per cent increase year on year on a £20 million fee income and they were also looking at their brand. I asked them what they thought their advantage to customers was and why they were better than their competitors. Their response was: 'Our senior people...' STOP! I have been there, and so has every professional services firm. I have no doubt that their people are good, and do not question whether they are critical and central to growth, but the simple question asked was 'Why are they better?' Almost every professional services firm I know sells itself as having the most experienced team and the best track record. The strategy they presented did not have a 'game changer' and with every other firm using the same message would actually take a fair number of the competition head on. Furthermore, as leaders, we are always biased and our tribe will always be the best!

What did they have that could make them stand out from their competitors? Did they have a niche or service, with potentially recurring revenue that we might focus on? I want to reiterate that I have no doubt that their people were indeed better than those of the competition but as a potential customer I would have to meet them to judge this, so straight away there is a limited door opener. When I do meet the people as a customer, everyone is very professional so it is hard to decide or differentiate in a one-hour meeting. Maybe there is no game changer for such a firm, or maybe it is too risky or troublesome to develop one but we should take time out to look and see what else is different. In particular, there is significant scope in the brand arena.

Creating a brand can create pull; customers want to deal with you because of what you stand for, so they are influenced, whereas selling people requires a 'persuade' approach and you have to be in the door already in order to get this approach across. The word 'brand' historically comes from the mark stamped on livestock to ensure it is easy to identify its owner. Today a brand is the design and image that identify an organization to its customers and crucially also differentiate us from our competitors, by giving quality and satisfaction. A brand stands for benefits and value.

In order to create 'game changers', identify 'why are you really different?' in a way that is fast to articulate, that no one else is using well and how you can better communicate this to demonstrate benefit and value. The ideal is 'pull': customers seek you out (this is low cost) because you offer better value (this does not mean cheap) and you deliver that value more efficiently. Game changing is usually perceived as innovative, or disruptive, and typically we think of it as being high tech. This is true, but it can also be achieved by ordinary companies in a very quiet and simple way if the elements of pull, value and cost are kept at the fore and at the heart of the leadership's strategy. Advantage perhaps best comes to those who are patient and keep it simple.

Many people struggle to find the 'game changers'. I argue that this is probably because they don't spend long enough looking for them and probably don't believe they are possible. In Chapter 3, we discussed the concept of leadership versus management. If you can move to this role you have more time to complete the quest to find the disruptive ideas that truly are game changers but we have to become more observational and listen more, particularly when we are operating in fast-changing environments.

I have been asked on numerous occasions how you spot the ideas that are game changers and again we must put the classic analytical business management school of thought aside. When you look at organizations, the game changers are usually the hidden areas of the business that no one has, as yet, thought too hard about. They are quietly doing well but have not been prioritized. Interestingly, on research, they are often the products or services that the people who are offering them are most passionate about. I worked with a manufacturer in the water industry, which was quite spread out across sectors and products. We asked which area was the easiest, with good margins, and had the largest potential growth and the lowest competitive pressures; we then narrowed the sales and marketing drive to this arena and thus secured strong growth. We have come back to the idea that in a specialist world it is those who think really hard about where to focus that win.

> When you look at organizations, the game changers are usually the hidden areas of the business that no one has, as yet, thought too hard about.

Business strategy can learn much from military strategy. A great historical example of focus and surprise was the D-Day landings in Northern France to regain German-occupied Western Europe during the Second World War. A second front was desperately needed as Russia could not defend itself for much longer and might have been forced to reach a compromise with Germany. The Germans had taken almost four years to create exceptional fortifications yet there was no alternative way for the Allies to make an invasion by land. Operation Overlord was hatched, enhanced by Churchill and Eisenhower's unwavering belief that victory could be secured, against the odds. They chose Normandy to base the invasion instead of the more obvious beachheads of Dieppe or Calais which were closer so would have been technically much easier. Special technology was developed to meet the conditions expected on the Normandy beachhead, including two artificial ports known as Mulberry harbours and an array of specialized tanks nicknamed Hobart's Funnies. In the months leading up to the invasion, the Allies conducted a substantial military deception even down to creating fake field armies to divert attention from where an invasion would be launched from. The landings of the first ever amphibious operation were successful. They were focused over a narrow area that was heavily and very well defended but because the Germans had been misled they lacked the crucial reinforcements required to push back an Allied offensive.

Overlord opened a second front and the highly effective German military machine eventually failed. Despite the success of Overlord, we must remember that it was probably the German decision to invade Russia and fight on too many fronts that stretched them to the point where an invasion became possible. In business terms it was the competition's attempt to fight in too many territories across too many areas that allowed a focused surprise to secure advantage.

The Overlord strategy is a great example of changing the game; new ideas were employed and technology developed quietly over a two-year period to ensure the best chance of success. Analysis was carried out to determine where the surprise would be most effective. Deception was engaged to wrong-foot the competition and finally, focus was applied at a weak spot. Leaders who look to challenge the status quo and identify where to really focus will be on track to truly change the game. Breakthroughs in business don't follow set formulas but from continually exploring options, testing and modifying our assumptions based on results, listening and feedback. The 'game change' might be as simple as Ben and Jerry's, who first added their trademark chunks to ice cream in the early 1980s, or Tesla's electric cars or John Lewis in the United Kingdom, who took an original, and highly innovative for its time, approach to partnership in its stores. This partnership approach was implemented in 1920 because it was felt that staff had no incentive to serve. The partnership led to a revival and today, nearly 100 years later, the John Lewis Partnership remains a flagship in retail advantage.

I am aware that there is a real trend towards 'hyperbole' business books. They seek to inspire with big-name case studies and breathless, churned-out rhetoric that tells us nothing new. We need practical approaches and while not a business example, Operation Overlord shows us that more often than not it is the sum of a combination of approaches that secures the competitive advantage, including thorough preparation, not just the innovative maverick-led ideas or ground-breaking innovation boards that create advantage. When we see the big-name game changers we rack our brains and stare in envy, yet there is hope for business leaders who are not creative geniuses to find and secure game changing simply by teamwork, awareness, technique and wisdom. It is a question of quietly and strategically out-thinking the competition, combined with determination, that ends in advantage.

Category and value

Category is a widely understood marketing term. It defines a product sector. The phrase can be broad or narrow. Motor vehicles are a broad category whereas 4×4 sports cars are a narrow category. Many businesses attempt to sell in broad categories for fear of narrowing market share too much. This actually undermines advantage as the messages of difference become too weak for customers to hear them. Much like the Germans above, we end up fighting on too many fronts (the West and the East) and ultimately lose. In category thinking, we can see that large markets are actually sub-sectors batched together. Market on too many fronts and we have weak offerings that appear highly diluted and confusing to customers and thus fail to gain advantage.

A proven game-changing tactic is to identify growing narrow categories in broad categories then choosing to focus and specialize in this growing yet still narrow arena. By doing this we can significantly turn up the volume in our difference and furthermore, we can then aim to be first in the narrow arena. You might note that this has not meant that our product is materially different or better, it just appears so, as the quality of conversation in the narrow category has leapt forward. If you are not a marketer this might all appear rather complex but the strategic question for leaders is this: is it better to gain 50 per cent of a narrow and even new category, than have 2 per cent of the whole market? Audi realized this when it first produced its legendary Quattro model in the 1980s. It was a niche 4×4 yet it could seat four adults while still remaining sporty. A new concept that is still mentioned with reverence by motoring enthusiasts today. The new category or subcategory that Audi found was defined with a set of associations that delivered a real value proposition. It was practical, fast and safer. The conversation became easy especially as the car won rally after rally when it was first launched. It created an alternative that appealed to customers yet in reality there was no new technology, just a combination of other ideas that appeared new.

> The strategic question for leaders is this: is it better to gain 50 per cent of a narrow and even new category, than have 2 per cent of the whole market?

Retailers are great at understanding category. You can't sell fashion easily to a 20-year-old that also appeals to a 50-year-old. Good retailers set out their stall. They decide on the niche they want to target and then design the stores to target that niche. The apparel they sell may not be better than that of their competitors, but in the environment they sell it, it appears different. A Savile Row (a street in London renowned for its bespoke tailoring) suit shop will not blare out loud rock music whereas a fashion shop might. One is discreet and discerning while the other is loud yet to its customer each appears fit for purpose. What about the concept of 'Rock Star Suits', where you combine exceptional tailoring with 'super cool' and take the best from both: bespoke tailoring but in an ultra-cool environment? Retro Pac-Man games and some very cool staff might pull suit buyers back off the internet.

CASE STUDY

A good example of a company that gained advantage when old categories combined in a new way is the Rainforest Café, founded in 1994 by Steve Schussler. The business differentiates itself by providing high quality, fresh food and retail merchandise in a themed environment; the categories of restaurants, retail and theme park merged. Today, the business has over £100 million in annual sales and over 25 locations in the United States and internationally (Encyclopedia.com, 2015). Each café is situated in a prominent high traffic location and simulates a rainforest environment featuring a visually and audibly exciting atmosphere which usually includes a variety of live tropical birds, large custom-designed aquariums, animated robotic animals and trees that create a canopy of foliage. The company's distinctive concept, combined with high-quality food and retail merchandise, makes the Rainforest Café appealing to children, teenagers, adults, and senior citizens. It attracts both tourists and destination customers. Each Rainforest Café has an animatronic tree, which entertains guests every five minutes, educating them about the rainforest. As well as combining categories to create difference, the business educates about environmental issues and is highly supportive of charities including the World Land Trust, which was established to protect tropical land forest. Ethics, purposefulness and making a difference also sit on the strategic agenda.

Identify weakness, attack and broaden out

In the category concept the quest is not always for better products but for narrower or new subcategories where we can gain advantage early on, gain rapid market share and possibly get to dominate the new arena. Later, with a very secure foundation, we can consider line extensions to broaden the offerings, growing outwards from the subcategory with the benefit of being known for clear value propositions. Range Rover is a great example of this.

In 1970, they took the ability and dependability of the Land Rover and added refinement and performance to create a new and narrow category: luxury all-terrain vehicles. Robust, aspirational and highly practical, the idea grabbed sales with many other manufacturers following later. Range Rover is still considered to be the best luxury 4×4 (probably because it was the first) and even today with its smaller 'Sport' and 'Evoque' line extensions they are growing outwards from the subcategory but sticking with the original value proposition. Advantage can be secured by choosing and owning a subcategory and once you have dominated this, with clear value propositions in the mind of your customers, then consider broadening out.

You rarely win by following the pack so figure out where the incumbents are vulnerable and exploit that as the basis for taking market leadership. For example, in the world of property search agencies in the United Kingdom, Zoopla used the presentation of open pricing statistics to secure property search traffic thus breaking the virtual monopoly that Rightmove had secured to shift the market to a duopoly. Despite now operating in a duopoly, Rightmove remains a privately-owned company and made profits of 73 per cent on £167 million in 2014 (Gallivan, 2015). The site has massive traffic content and an excellent tech platform so why not now launch Rightcar and take on Autotrader, the leader in that sector?

What business is our brand really in, and what differentiates our products and services from our competitors? How do customers see us and how do we want to be seen? In summary and using our military analogy, attack in a focused, highly planned specialist way by finding a weak point in your sector or creating a new subcategory and once you have broken through behind enemy lines scale up and cause havoc to create advantage. What is your D-Day or Operation Overlord strategy?

Lose in order to gain

Categories are really batches of subcategories – address too many and you have to shout far too loudly into the wind. Find the right sub-niche and you can whisper yet still be heard and once you successfully have the eyes and ears of those customers you whisper directly to, you can then broaden out to create advantage. This, however, requires one of the bravest and yet most crucial business decisions. It requires saying no to customers – losing to gain. It requires profiling and being clear as to who you really want your customers to be and deliberately choosing to say no in as efficient a way as possible so you can concentrate on those you do actually want to attract.

The more you help those customers you want, if you have chosen the right subcategory, the more that type of customer will see what you have done for others and come to you as the specialist. Your brand is starting to have pull as opposed to push.

This means advantage leaders take a long hard look at where the market is, which direction it's going and decide what to stop doing and who to say no to as much as they decide what to do. The line of probability and our data analysis, in combination with the scenarios, should give us much better insight into where to focus, but once we have this we might also need to look at where we should no longer be operating. 3M, the Post-it notes and adhesive company, has over £1 billion in revenue. The company started as a paper mills business but realized that success lay in innovative products and took the brave decision to sell off the original core mills business so it could focus. Today the business still spends over 6 per cent of its revenue on research and development and a fifth of this is invested in basic research or pursuits that have no immediate practicality (Clough, 2015.) Even my local fish and chip shop (it's a British thing) has got in on the act. Previously it was a traditional takeaway appealing to snack food consumers such as builders and students. Having been empty for some years, it was refurbished by new owners to a light restaurant style with open bi-fold doors and a 'bring your own bottle' licence, together with much higher quality ingredients and as a result the business has thrived. The restaurant prices are twice as much as before but by saying no to the original customers through positioning it has gained a much more affluent repeat trade.

Creating a category

The point of creating a category and choosing to say 'no' to customers is to make sure you and your most desired customers understand what your key differentiations are. Which customers are unprofitable and distracting? Which of your star products are starting to decline and which of your new hidden ones could become stars? How much time do you spend on identifying these, and how can you better communicate why they are different? Remember, it is not always about being better, but being different. It is interesting, however, that on review, even when you start out on a new path you may not be better, yet practice makes perfect and so you end up better. Figure 8.1 below sets out an overview of the category and value concept.

1 Think that your business has an identity and a personality that need to be managed.

FIGURE 8.1   Category, value and innovation

Create 'pull'

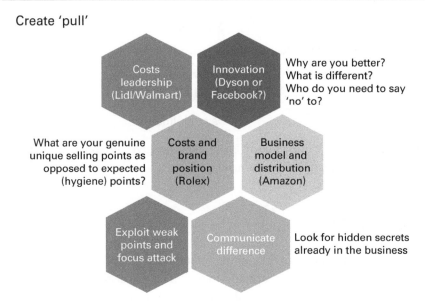

2 Focus on what your company enables people to do, not what you do.

3 Choose relevant differentiators, not hygiene (expected to have) points.

4 Communicate the relevant differences effectively at every step and level, throughout the organization, and to customers – in that order; many businesses tell their customers but forget to tell their staff.

5 Develop an image, logo and strapline that communicate your dream and differentiator.

6 Align your businesses, procedures, training, recruitment, PR and approach around what your business really does and why it is so different.

There are many ways to be different and game changing, for example:

Speedier service: Amazon, FedEx

More quality: Harrods, Cadbury

Value for money: McDonald's

Cheap, no frills: easyJet, Walmart

Fun: Virgin

No-fuss replacement policy:	Marks & Spencer
Driving machine:	BMW
Build quality:	Mercedes
Most supported product:	Microsoft
Creative and innovative:	Disney
Prestige in ownership:	Rolex
Mature	Saga Holidays

These associations are subjective but they do give difference and this is powerful when matched with a market need.

Saying 'no'

Some clients are a delight – I call these symbiotic. Others are not and I call them parasitic – harsh perhaps and they don't do it deliberately but this is where they end up and remember that a parasite can be symbiotic to another host. The parasites use you but don't value you, and thus live off you, always demanding, complaining and undervaluing what you do, consciously or subconsciously, thus making it almost impossible to make a profit from them. The parasites make it impossible to find more of the symbiotic 'delights' because you are too busy carrying or curing the parasites. Again, this is similar to the work upstream concept we used earlier and flows from the 'lose in order to gain' concept. By defining and then selecting who we want and who we don't, over time we can create the organizations and brands we want.

In 1896, the Italian economist Vilfredo Pareto published his first paper, '*Cours d'économie politique*', in which he showed that approximately 80 per cent of the land in Italy was owned by 20 per cent of the population (Wikipedia, 2015). He first developed the principle by observing that 20 per cent of the pea pods in his garden produced 80 per cent of the peas. As it is now known, the 80:20 rule or Pareto principle is a generalization but it is interesting to see how the rule applies to so many things in life. It means that only a fraction of what you do is responsible for the rewards you enjoy. Only 20 per cent of the things we do are really important, or worse, in the internet age of social networking, 20 per cent of our friends are really friends and the rest are mere acquaintances. Look at your products, customers and marketing campaigns and you will see that only about 20 per cent will contribute to about 80 per cent of your revenue. It won't be exact – you might see a 64:36 or even a 99:1 relationship – but you can dramatically increase your effectiveness by focusing on the minority that are quality and saying 'no' to the less productive parts over time. This means more time and more profit.

In your analysis, research which customers, markets or products comprise that delightful 20 per cent then seek out and focus on others like them, and over the long run feel free and confident to replace the less productive and rewarding customers who, realize it or not, are distracting you.

Disruptive innovation

Like 'category', 'disruption' is a known marketing term for new ideas and products that change or transform an existing market and supply chain by reducing other technologies or services. The ideas are often considered to be unexpected but history tells us that they should be expected. The digital camera was an innovation but it was not completely disruptive as most camera manufacturers still made them. Next came the smartphone, with its immediacy, convenience and the ability to post and share photographs online, relegating cameras, digital or otherwise, to a niche.

New technology can be ignored in favour of what is currently popular with today's best and mainstream customer as opposed to tomorrow's potential customer. New ideas often also require evolution before they can become disruptive. Karl Benz invented the first car in 1886 but it took Ford's mass production before traditional transportation became disrupted. This is important because it means you don't necessarily have to be the first to innovate a new product; advantage is often more about spotting and executing the new concept or trend ahead of others and implementing a strategy more effectively around it. It can also, as with category, be about saying 'yes' to the new sales and 'no' to the old, and in this way we can see that disruption and the 'lose in order to gain' concept above are closely linked.

We need analysis to work out where we are but we need creativity unbounded by the status quo to change to where we need to be. Our creativity can be bound by the status quo. Managers will worry if their department is no longer seen as critical or needs downsizing and competitors may deride new competitive advantage trends to discourage them. The horse and cart operators versus the motor car and today, the petrol operators versus electric cars. The electric car will be resisted by the oil companies in the same way that automated teller machines (ATMs) were resisted by bank tellers. Technology in itself does not restructure or disrupt; it requires management to change the strategy and business model around the technology and it can also take courage, in particular when it may mean you have to directly compete with your core business. Many retailers are struggling with this as their online sales are forcing their retail estates into retreat.

Competitive advantage can require disruptive adoption, but it does not always mean investing heavily in research and development to achieve game-changing technology breakthrough. It can instead be about being quietly more alert, spotting and embracing the new trend, adapting the business model around the new trend more quickly, not fearing competition with yourself and just saying 'no' to the old and 'yes' to the new.

CASE STUDY

Remember it is not always technology that is disruptive. Hamdi Ulukaya identified the lack of an all-natural Greek yoghurt ahead of the market and, with a government loan, bought a struggling yoghurt factory from Kraft in 2005 thus creating 'Chobani'. His product is high in protein, low in fat, tastes good and the company now has an annual turnover of over $1 billion (Gruley, 2013). Ulukaya disrupted a space that was previously dominated by corporates by offering a product in clean, simple packaging that perfectly matched the interests of increasingly health-conscious consumers.

We now live in times of rapid change. Many strategic approaches are at best simply too incremental, and our focus on reliability actually favours the status quo. More time and an unbounded mindset are required to design our points of difference, unique value and uncover disruptive hidden categories and value no other organization is addressing in your sector. Figure 8.2 below summarizes the steps in 'changing the game' to competitive advantage.

Innovation

In the above, I have argued that disruption is not always research and development to create ground-breaking ideas but instead early adopters that change the model quickly around the new, and perhaps better understand the value of the new innovation. They find the weak spots, identify the new categories and attack.

FIGURE 8.2   Game-change thinking

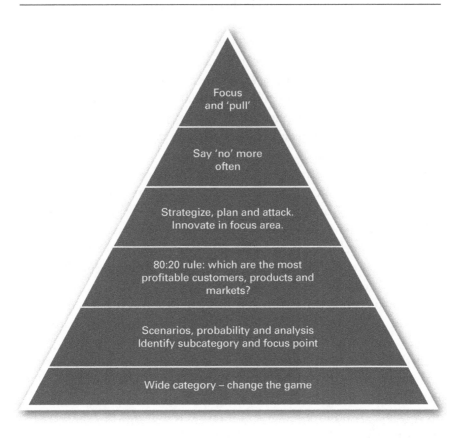

Nonetheless, innovation may also play a crucial role. There are many inventions, or ideas, that dramatically change a market, especially products. This means it is still legitimate, particularly for product businesses and technical businesses, to place a strong emphasis and cultural focus on research and development to both secure incremental improvement and ensure market competitiveness. We may also need to devote some investment into the more radical ideas that will create new markets or shift existing ones in a more sustainable direction. It would be marvellous if we could all create a game-changer new product. However, in the above work of identifying competitors' weak points and general market direction we can also focus on innovation. If we broaden the focus on research and development too much, the costs will spiral very quickly. Developing new products can be an expensive game to play, despite the tax breaks usually involved.

Leadership must set the direction and investment in research and development, and provide permission for investing speculatively to achieve breakthroughs, by articulating how sustainability issues affect the future. This must combine with structures that protect research and development and ensure that the needy child of day-to-day business does not drag time and resources. A balance needs to be found between research and development on an incremental basis versus the more radical, difficult and risky areas.

There are numerous big-name examples of companies that failed to spot the new opportunity perhaps because their innovation thinking or culture had flaws. IBM at one stage led the PC market but they saw it as a *niche* rather than *the* market, maintaining at the time the belief that mainframe computers were the future.

IBM needed an operating system to run its new PCs. The company approached Microsoft co-founder Bill Gates, then a 19-year-old college dropout. Crucially, however, they left Mr Gates the licence rights. It was only as the operating system grew in volume and power that IBM recognized that it had made a key mistake. In 1985 IBM was the most profitable company in the world, making profits of almost $6.6 billion (Broadbent, 2005). By 1993, IBM reported quarterly losses in excess of $8 billion, caused by increased competition and a changing market. IBM was failing to compete with the new breed of innovative software companies and hardware producers who could make computers much more cheaply. Blackberry was the darling of the smartphone. Established in the early 1990s the business had a stratospheric rise, mainly by making business e-mail central to its strategy and its button keyboard. Then it was caught on the wrong foot by the overwhelmingly positive response to Apple's new iPhone in 2007 with its touchscreen. Apple had rushed the iPhone and in its demo even needed to use a critical path to avoid the glitches in the product so its success was by no means a foregone conclusion. Blackberry had a lot of goodwill and responded quickly but crucially not well enough. Its first touchscreen model Storm in 2008 was critically panned, and the company never managed to create an application (software add-ons) marketplace to compete. The company has lurched ever since. Overall, the devices are no longer phones, they are small tablets that happen to make calls. The new battle appears to be who will make unfolding screens work; Samsung is looking ahead on this with its AMOLED screen.

You can see these innovation-led adaptions happening elsewhere. Microsoft, which used to be just a software licensing company, began making hardware with the Xbox (sure, keyboards were first, but not relevant) and is now building its own Surface tablets, and now owns Nokia's handset business. It is a software-operating writing, tablet-making, phone-building business – just like Apple. Adapting is critical and it requires a culture of innovation.

It is easy to use tech as examples because the speed of change is fast but the same applies to service companies. Look at how the big accountants have now become global consulting firms, including technology with accounting almost as a sideline.

The innovation rulebook

The rulebook for an innovation culture might include the following:

- Absolute clarity on a reinvestment ratio for research and development (80:20 of future profits?).

- Bring in internal and external experts to incubate radical ideas via intense sessions and immersion, away from the grind. Sony is an example of an incubating company and Canon employ similar methods.

- Set the rule that no ideas are daft. The idea that man might fly was once daft, and the fact I can communicate to the other side of the world in seconds undreamed of. Listen to the wacky, there are no rules.

- Kimberly-Clark promotes one-day 'expert acceleration sessions', which bring hand-picked external thought leaders face to face to generate and stimulate scenarios.

- Embrace youth. The new kids on the block will be tomorrow's leaders and they think differently; separating them from leadership based on hierarchy is a mistake and creates 'ivory tower' syndrome. Appoint mentors to help the next generation understand business further but cross-fertilize technology and trend ideas back into the executive team. Who will learn the most, I wonder?

- Behave like a small start-up and accelerate the speed of innovation.

- Establish an open blog with customers. Complaints are feedback. Encourage ideas from suppliers and support service companies. Work in collaboration with other businesses and/or universities and design companies. Unilever is a great example of a corporate that operates an open innovation platform.

- Look at the gaps – the dark matter of what is not being done. This is where the boundless strategic ideas are. Educate the team in this respect.

- Get outside-in perspective, similar to the type of reality-checking investors bring.

- Most importantly, be willing to upset, polarize and disrupt. People can be inherently conservative, and new ideas are often weak at the start; after all, they have not enjoyed years of incremental improvement. I am sure that the walkers who overtook the first motor vehicles must have laughed. The first computers were pretty poor – I can remember waiting 20 minutes for a tape to load a game; try telling your kids that.

- Fight the fear of change and link innovation to your vision. Build a culture of reward for ideas. Consistently ask the team and customers: is there a better way? Then ask again.

- Accept that today's status quo is not tomorrow's and you may design products that make today's way obsolete. If you don't, someone else will.

The business need for innovation combines with both competitive advantage and the underlying human need for sustainability and improvement, perhaps the journey we have undertaken since we discovered art and fire. Businesses, products and markets will only endure where they deliver superior sustainability outcomes and this requires both innovation and investment. The great news is that with the sum of human knowledge at our fingertips, if we can get better at prioritizing the right from the wrong, we should be able to innovate to a future that is, literally, magic. Fire was magic once, then came matches and lighters, what next? Heat without flame, an air source heat pump can efficiently take heat out of freezing air to warm a house or a swimming pool in the depths of winter. How does that work?

Investment in advantage

Being ahead of the competition, innovating and pioneering new products, services, systems or business models all take time, effort and cost money. The uncertainty combined with the investment cost seems to be the main reason many executives turn their back on seeking advantage through being different and adding more value. Big-name innovation success stories can leave leaders frozen in the headlights staring in the abyss of ideas. Which ones and why? Nonetheless, apply scenarios and a process against research with the right questions and advantage becomes easier. With technique and an end in mind, the return from investing in seeking advantage is actually far greater than the cost and remember, if you don't then the market will lead you, if you are lucky, into a gentle decline and if you are unlucky, a sudden death. The online onslaught killed Woolworths in the United Kingdom. It failed to innovate and found itself in the squeezed middle, yet the £1 style stores have captured much of their old market at the lower end using the thrill of bargain hunting to draw customers in. This showed that there was a market but at a lower end than the one Woolworths focused on. Being neither low cost nor premium, in the end no one quite knew what Woolworths quite stood for and what value they brought. The new £1 players have a much better focus on understanding what they need to be to the consumer. It helps them differentiate. If Woolworths' UK high street closure holds one lesson, it is that there is no room for complacency when trends move as quickly as they do today.

Despite the risk inherent in trying new things to seek advantage it is the less risky route, and the less costly, particularly with focus in mind. Being clear on where markets are heading, with more understanding as to why, enables you to build better scenarios and generate better ideas. Combine this with clarity of category, saying no more often and focused research and development against that category and we have a strong prospect of either staying ahead or leading the competition.

Chapter summary and leader questions

You can't stand for something if you chase everything. Use market research, the line of probability and analytics to define your target market and ask what do they really need and where you should focus. Build your management team to look after today's status quo effectively and profitably to create cash flow. Use this cash flow and profit to balance invest and develop products, services and brands that create new customer value in different ways, and advantage and breakthrough will come from your focus.

The world is complex, and we often lose sight of the quiet simple things. Game-changing advantage comes when you find a design, product, service or business model that gives better value to the customers at lower cost to you, in an arena that is either the next big thing or at least growing. Value does not, of course, mean cheap but the benefit that customers secure from the purchase. We can discuss management style, research, analytics, strategy, and how best to implement change but the central and simple question is always, why are you 'better' to your customers and how do you keep costs down while still achieving 'better'.

Many martial arts use the concept of focus. Have you ever seen the small guy charged by the big guy, only to last second stand aside and nimbly nudge; a light touch in the focused way and the big guy's own momentum takes him over? Or the people that smash through pieces of wood as if it was paper by concentrating their whole body force specifically on one point just behind the wood with the strength in the hit coming through the whole body? These martial arts develop and manifest energy from the body in focus (knowing where the market is heading) and then redirect incoming energy (seeing the competition's weak spots and the unwanted customers). In this analogy, game changing is secured by nimble balance and focus, not strength and dominating investment. It is in crafted study and anticipation of the market and the movements that we can see where to focus. In that sense, creating advantage is not always a battle of products, more often it is a battle of focus for the consumer's mind. What are your hidden secrets? What is really different and better, and do you communicate this effectively?

Leader questions

1 What do you need to lose in order to gain?

2 What are your competition really saying and how does this compare to your actual position?

3 Why are you different and better?

4 How do you communicate your difference?

5 What are you quietly passionate about that's working well and how could you concentrate and do more on this?

6 What do you need to disrupt?

7 Where is the market going and how can you get ahead of it?

8 What are your hidden secrets and value drivers?

References

Broadbent, V (2005) How IBM misjudged the PC revolution. Available from: http://news.bbc.co.uk/1/hi/business/4336253.stm [Last accessed 27.08.15]

Clough, R (2015) 3M Beats Earnings Estimate on International Sales Growth. Bloomberg Business, 27/01. Available from: www.bloomberg.com/news/articles/2015-01-27/3m-beats-profit-estimates-as-sales-rise-in-u-s-and-asia-pacific [Last accessed: 27 August 2015]

Encyclopedia.com (2015) Rainforest Café Inc. Available from: www.encyclopedia.com/topic/Rainforest_Cafe_Inc.aspx [Last accessed: 27 August 2015]

Gallivan, R (2015) Shares in Rightmove Leap 10% on Profit Rise. *The Wall StreetJournal*, 27/02. Available from: www.wsj.com/articles/shares-in-rightmove-leap-10-on-profit-rise-1425040053 [Last accessed: 27 August 2015]

Gruley, B (2013) At Chobani, the Turkish King of Greek Yoghurt. Bloomberg Business, 31/01. Available from: www.bloomberg.com/bw/articles/2013-01-31/at-chobani-the-turkish-king-of-greek-yogurt [Last accessed 27 August 2015]

Wikipedia (2015) Pareto Principle. Available from: https://en.wikipedia.org/wiki/Pareto_principle [Last accessed: 27 August 2015]

References

Adaptive organizations

09

Introduction

Achieving planned advantage requires both strategy and looking ahead in the market more effectively to find the gaps and niches. It then requires commitment and focus to quickly exploit the opportunities identified. However, the single biggest challenge often facing the executive team is organizational inertia, which we examine in this chapter. The executive team, and even the whole business, may be able to see what to do earlier than others, but not succeed in shaping the organization to the outcome. The bigger the business, the more this may be a challenge as there will be more people to question the direction and more people to move in a certain direction. We can compare this to the famous story of David against Goliath, where the small shepherd boy David fells the giant warrior, Goliath, with agility and a slingshot. The story seeks to share that improbable victories are possible. On examination, victory was actually probable for the shepherd boy: how could David lose with a far-range weapon if Goliath couldn't get close? On analysis, it is actually the less nimble Goliath who is the underdog when it comes to winning advantage.

Adaptive

Much has been written about business agility. This is because the agile enterprise is one of the best counters to fast-moving times. Essentially the idea is that you specifically design the business systems and culture to move, maintain and adapt goods and services according to customer demand. If we think of the business as a living organism, quite simply we design the business to react quickly to environmental changes. By reacting better and faster the organism secures advantage in that environment. This is the same concept as Charles Darwin's evolution theories from his famous work on the 'origin of species'. It is encapsulated in the famous quote invariably attributed to Darwin: 'It's not the strongest or most intelligent of the species that survive; it is those most adaptive to change.' Interestingly, by a strange quirk of evolution in itself, it is believed the quote was actually first used by Leon Megginson in a management talk in 1963 but has reattributed itself to Darwin because it was stronger than the original words.

> An agile adaptive approach is simply a secure foundation upon which we build our strategic plans.

The key to evolution in organizations is in education; however, most agile initiatives are led from the top of an organization downwards, whereas advantage is likely best secured and certainly more sustainable by building team-driven agility.

Competitive advantage leaders will therefore invest in a business design and a culture that enhance agility and adaption, but they will not rely on them. The thinking presented to us by some agility business gurus (that rapid change means agility is enough) is flawed. Instead, an agile adaptive approach is simply a secure foundation upon which we build our strategic plans to create advantage. This is because while agility is effective, it remains reactive to the environment. Agility requires the environment to change, or at least gives us real signs of change, whereas strategy is more forward-looking and anticipatory.

Agility is actually a reactive, near-sighted state based on observation, usually in the direct vicinity of the environment. Strategy drawing on analysed data and the research into likely market outcomes in the line of probability

FIGURE 9.1   Agility versus strategy

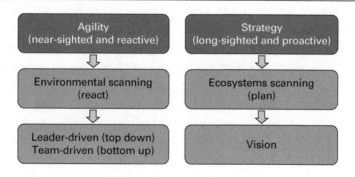

is proactive and over the longer term. Strategy requires leaders to go beyond the environment and assess the whole ecosystems of technology and the competitive transformations that are occurring to then nudge evolution.

Agile at foundations

A culture and business design that encourage, and reward, adaption and agility are the essential foundation of advantage. This is because businesses built around this foundation are easier to drive change through, from the leaders top down but also, from the team bottom up feeding, suggesting and driving change back to the executive team. So, how do we design organizations that are effective at rapidly adjusting to the business environment, naturally and resourcefully?

We tend to think of foundations as very solid; after all they have to support heavy buildings. But interestingly the heavier the building the less we may rely on solidity in foundation construction and techniques such as rafts and friction pilings are used instead. In a raft, instead of a thick immovable heavy foundation directly under the wall, the weight of the building is spread across a whole concrete cast slab, which in itself may move. This means the building can move with soil movements. In friction piling, as demonstrated by the Venetians to create their magical city on water over 700 years ago, wood was used to construct buildings above swamps with no solid ground at all. The wooden log (these days reinforced concrete) is drilled vertically into the ground. The friction of the ground against the length of the log gives solidity and by using a lot of them you can build a house on mud (think what happens when your shoe is pulled off in deep mud or sand). As the buildings get bigger and taller, especially to counter earthquakes, other techniques are employed such as base isolation. Over the last 30 years, engineers have constructed skyscrapers that float on systems of ball bearings, springs and padded cylinders. Acting like shock absorbers in a car, these systems allow the building to be decoupled from the shaking of the ground.

In times of rapid market change, flexibility is key and we can design our own shock absorbers, rafts and pilings, which are deliberately adaptive structures from the ground up in our businesses. These structures include the granting of permissions and the establishment of rewards to 'give change a go' directly at team level. That is, creating reward systems for innovation, along with careful management of the organization's structure from outsourcing to building capacity flexibility whether in headcount, productivity or premises.

The business information and technology platforms also need agility. Today this is becoming easier with the cloud as more and more systems rely on a base with app-based extensions to allow modular expansion.

Outsourcing and capacity planning, along with IT transformation and agile systems, are all large specialist topics so instead in this chapter, I have chosen to concentrate on how we can build agility into our people, teams and culture at foundation with the view that this will then run up through the business. If adaption and agility are embedded in our culture, this is the foundation for team-driven evolution in the environment, enabling the leaders to then concentrate on strategy in the ecosystem. We design a business where, instead of simply being employed to ruthlessly maintain the status quo, the managers are also employed and rewarded for improvement and, perhaps sometimes, failure. The people who do the job are often, after all, the people who can see best what needs to change and why.

The system

There is a challenge in creating truly adaptive cultures, however. We tend to think of an effective business as being ordered, and planned. This is much like a formal garden that is lovingly controlled, maintained and structured. To become a head or senior gardener from education to the corporate ladder we are trained in this formality and it is typically only people that know how to tend such a garden that get to seniority to run the garden, yet the danger is we start to believe that the formality is nature itself enhanced. Without management it would take about 20 years for almost all structure to have dissipated from such a garden. In the United Kingdom, the famous, now reclaimed and much acclaimed 'Lost Gardens of Heligan' took 400 years to cultivate to beauty but after the Great War of 1914–18 took away its gardeners, just 10 years to be swamped by ivy and brambles. Management and leaders have been so trained in the structures to get to be senior in the garden that they become constrained by the very formality they tend. Unless they recognize that, beneath the structure nature and civilization, wild, beautiful chaos is waiting to be unleashed; they can't expect to create adaptive organizations.

This is similar to the Peter Principle; management guru Laurence Peter observed that often anything that works well will be used in progressively more challenging applications until it fails. If applied to people it means that we promote ourselves to our highest level and often slightly beyond before we get stopped. In this idea we essentially get promoted to incompetence. It is only when we recognize this and learn more that we then move on again. What I am suggesting is that in order to be truly adaptive, leaders will recognize this and in their own mindset break through the very formality and structures they used to secure the head position. Exceptional leaders go beyond the system. It is interesting how many truly exceptional entrepreneurs there are who went to good schools but actually failed at them. In the United Kingdom, Sir Richard Branson is one of them. He learned the manners, leadership and ability to communicate but couldn't cope with the exams, instead preferring his own rules and thus the Virgin empire was born. Warren Buffett, who has held the title of richest man in the world, had already made £50,000 in today's money by the time he had finished college, from delivering newspapers, renting pinball machines and investing this money in land, yet he was rejected by Harvard Business School.

Wild side

Beauty and innovation are actually built in the wild garden and in the experimentation of wholly new playful ideas, leading to nature or market-led change. Adaptive organizations need to take their people closer to the wild side. An adaptive culture will set the rule that there are fewer rules than we imagine and it ideally needs to be led from the top. This does not mean the odd creative away day to challenge rules; it means that the need to embrace our wild side a bit more should be embedded in the very core of the business. Google is probably the best business example of an organization that understands chaos and unlimited opportunity. Its headquarters have goats not lawnmowers, it allows people to work anywhere they want to and gives its people 'innovation only' days. Employees can bring dogs into the office and skateboard around the building. Google is a voracious acquirer, having bought over 170 companies including YouTube, Android, Deepmind (AI) and Motorola to secure and maintain advantage. Android is now the most-used smartphone operating system in the world yet the acquisition only cost $50 million in 2006 and in 2014 620 million users hit Google daily, that's half of the world's internet users. There is no dress code, body paint is acceptable and there is a T. rex dinosaur on campus for company. As a result, they employ the best graduates and their list of innovations – including smart watches, translation into 80 languages and robot cars – leaves the competition breathless.

Dynamic markets mean fast change, which requires more openness and acceptance of change. A recent example of this is Snapchat, a photo messaging application developed by Stanford University graduates in 2011. The service has grown so quickly that in November 2013, Google reportedly offered $4 billion for the company, which the company founders declined. Even Google cannot win them all!

Cross-specialist agile teams

People are an advantage: the right people in the right roles at the right time. To create advantage you have to have good people working with you, and they need to understand the agility concept and be capable of driving the business and engaging directly in change. A significant proportion of the businesses I see have essentially stalled, yet they share a common problem. A leader who is too hands on and a second tier that is operating in silos without the full picture, underinvested in training, and worse has a vested interest in the status quo. This creates a gap forcing the leader to have to drive and coerce the business to change rather than the team engaging proactively in delivering change, and both sides then get frustrated.

Many businesses are engaging in shareholder value strategies and the companies that achieve higher values are usually agile team-driven organizations, rather than leader-driven. This is usually achieved via engaging the team earlier in higher-level training and strategy work. The number one drive is to take people beyond their silos. Imagine if your finance director understood the marketing department's capability and challenges 100 per cent and the marketing director the other way around. This not only creates more understanding and sustainability, it increases teamwork as well as enabling the second tier to see the broader components of the organization better and thus adopt more agile methods. If you like, the 'manager specialists' ideas are now generated with a broader and deeper understanding across the business and will therefore be better and more likely to be adopted.

This approach might include sharing the business analytics and dashboard across more players (Chapter 5). Many private organizations prefer to keep the dashboard data, particularly the finances, closed in case they open themselves to salary negotiations against the profits, or fear of performance criticism, but if you have good people they will understand a business must perform and will always negotiate the best salary regardless. With more *open* dashboards, if the organization and team on a broader base know the underlying performance across all areas, more energy and ideas are created. Embedding analytics and the dashboards in decision-making and teamwork ties the data to overall business outcomes. This increases the quality of shared information but also the accuracy of team-driven decisions as they are based on reality not conjecture.

Building cross-division and strategic awareness in the management team and even beneath it takes a lot more time to start with but, if slack is built in to allow this time, the organization becomes far more rewarding. Agile teams require permission to both work 'hands on' in the business and 'hands off'. The hands-off elements are taking more time beyond each division to look across the business and ask collectively what could we do differently, not just what could my team do better.

In this sense the idea presented here is very similar to that achieved in military training in the United Kingdom by the Special Air Service (SAS) or the Parachute Regiment (the Paras). Such teams often need to engage behind enemy lines and away from lines of communication so they are trained to operate autonomously and will all be trained, for example, in the use of explosives, not just the explosives' expert. As well as being taught skills, they are trained how to train others, thus these skills again enhance capability. Managers seek competitive advantage by maintaining or further developing knowledge in the business in a culture that enables and embraces creativity, across specialisms.

A good example of this is Tesco, one of the world's largest retailers. Since 1995, using what is a standard approach today, it has found advantage by innovatively leveraging its customer loyalty card programme to extract purchasing insights. The team applied this insight to a supply chain redesign. As a result and via scenario planning, Tesco can deliver exactly the right type and amount of inventory to the right store at the right time and reduce its risk of stockouts. The business can accurately predict weather-driven buying behaviour at unique stores and can precisely stock them based on a weekend weather forecast. By using this approach and in just one year, Tesco captured more than £100 million GBP in operational cost savings, delivered by a team of just 50 employees who were not only skilled in statistics but also, more crucially, trained in retail processes, enabling the team to apply the analytics insights directly in an agile operational manner (Clark, 2013).

Yet again Google deserve a mention here. The business follows a '70-20-10 rule'. Employees spend 70 per cent of their time on their standard role, one day per week on projects that will develop their technical skills and benefit the company, and half a day per week exploring product and business innovations and ideas. The on-the-job training and improvement requirement ensure agility but also the best employees are attracted, sustained and retained. Figure 9.2 summarizes the foundations for a team-driven adaptive approach.

FIGURE 9.2   Agile team approach

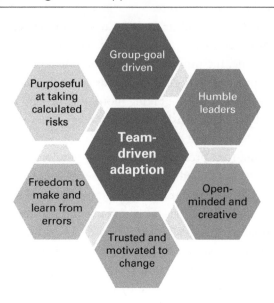

Evolution

Evolution has taken simplicity to complexity biologically, but also in civilization, technology and our business systems. Over a long period of time, the process of selecting what works and deselecting what doesn't has led us from single-cell organisms to complex sentient beings. In business, bartering led to money which led to banks, which, combined with data, led to complex financial global trading instruments, which are hard to understand even for the specialist.

On review, nature's selection process is not random in any way. The variations that give greater health and reproductive success in nature are retained and less successful variations are weeded out. For example, each successive generation of giraffe had longer and longer necks to give them the advantage of reaching the best leaves at the top of a tree. Those with greater success at getting the food, that is those with the longer necks, are able to reach the better leaves, being healthier, breed more. Those with shorter necks were deselected. We can adopt the evolution concept in business in a broad sense by observing how the market favours and selects those who adapt better and faster to the market. Those that don't are deselected, such as IBM and Blackberry, as highlighted in the previous chapter. Using this idea as our base, we can therefore educate everyone in an organization to help in the selection process. This therefore encourages the training, sharing and encouragement of selection and adaption in its workplace products and services. It sounds obvious but by actively and continuously identifying and selecting the aspects that work well, and stopping the elements that don't, continuous improvement should be reached.

The selection idea is similar to the Japanese management principle of Kaizen (defined as both continuous improvement and change for the better), the core idea in Kaizen being that you humanize the workplace to eliminate over-hard work and train people to perform experiments and innovate in an observed way to improve processes and increase efficiency. Kaizen uses selection on a continuous basis, usually at a more departmental level. Much success has been achieved with Kaizen in creating lean manufacturing process but it is just as applicable to all industries and services. By setting the aim that the team have a responsibility to work smart and select the positive traits, you set a culture that encompasses continuous change, thus enabling the business to drive adaption bottom-up as well as top-down, little by little, resulting in transformation. Kaizen and natural selection are both incremental approaches and it is important to make sure we don't get so busy making the small changes that we ignore the bigger and perhaps braver decisions that come from strategy.

It is important to recognize that this selection does not encompass the overall strategy, otherwise you will have empowered chaos, ie everyone adapting but to what aim and in what direction? In this we must avoid being so 'hands off' or free that followers feel they are being left to adapt in a 'fend for yourself' way. The adaptations need to point towards the overarching end vision and goals. We can see that where we spend and focus our time, as shown in Chapter 3, is critical.

Overall the aim is to educate everyone in the organization on the importance of evolution to thrive. This will move people from a *reactive* position-based and reliability outlook to how and why we should use initiative to do it better: a *proactive* outlook to break the status quo and lead selection and transformation. The business might also need to look at its reward and remuneration packages. In most companies, nearly 100 per cent of pay is focused at how well and reliably the 'day job' is maintained. How much reward and pay is focused at adopting and selecting change? One note of caution on this, according to Forbes and a survey from *Human Resource Management*, individual innovation pay and reward are not the answer (Rivera, 2012). This is because creating adaption and selection is a complex creative task that requires outward collaboration whereas individual rewards can create a singular inward focus. Consider a milestone-based team performance bonus, rewarding change delivery that makes an impact.

Team-driven adaption and selection enhance organizational evolution and free up time for leadership to work better on the overarching initiative and strategic changes that are required to secure advantage. Figure 9.3 shows this approach.

FIGURE 9.3   Advantage natural selection

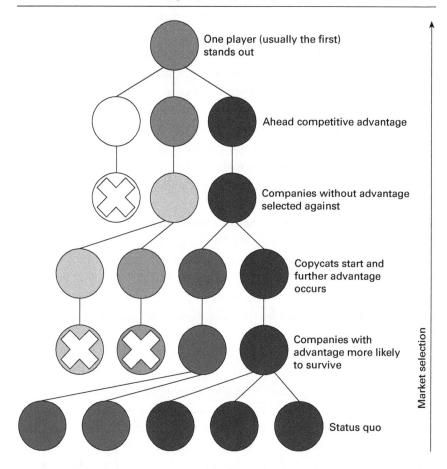

Workplace advantage

In a constantly changing global environment, facing sustained challenges including high costs and low margins, where you work and the design and culture of where you work impact on advantage. In these conditions of fierce competition, the competitive advantage of an organization often rests with its people and how the workforce capability is aligned to the business strategy. The capability and agility of an organization's workforce influence the ability to achieve the goals in each of the business functions highlighted in Figure 9.4. Planning to build that capability is key. The team needs to continually develop to support the achievement of the business direction.

We have increased age diversity, more remote workers, working fragmentation, global resource, changing hours and social expectations. What will the virtual and physical workplace of the future need to encompass? Agile companies are increasingly employing:

- flexible dress codes, open-plan modern hub-and-hive offices, hot-desking;
- innovation awards and rewards;
- social activities to encourage inter-office friends (the highest retention driver);
- ongoing training and development, innovation and career mentors;
- self-managed teams (a trust approach);
- non-hierarchical management;
- age, sex and race diversity particularly at board level;
- trust expenses systems – that is ones that allow common sense not guidelines and work on 'cheap' spot checking not expensive 'auditing';
- job-sharing, part-time, flexible working;
- telecommuting; and tech investment, open internet access;
- innovation days;
- career breaks for up to 12 months and 'purchased leave';
- home working and condensed hours; and
- flexible benefits choice.

A workplace design may also mean letting go a little. Many owners are fearful of flexible working or non-supervised teams but if you trust people and with the right checks, far better results are achieved. A large accountancy practice we recently worked with insisted that staff logged all personal calls on their mobile billing. This was pedantic, annoyed staff and the time actually taken to do the checking far outweighed the savings from the checking. The traditional method was dropped. The billing increased by just 5 per cent but the hours and frustration saved, and motivation gained from stopping the logging by far offset this.

Do you have workplace advantage? If not, how can you design it? The workplace advantage sum is to design environments and a culture that secure excellent retention rates and encourage team-driven strategic initiative and ideas, yet retain accountability and demand optimum results, summarized in Figure 9.4 below.

Changing minds

The line of probability and scenarios should drive the leader's view of how an organization might need to look, behave and what it should do. Sometimes this can result in dramatic or sweeping changes. The downfall of many CEOs is a failure to create the subsequent required change in the business. Designing an adaptive organization from the ground up will help, as will involving people in building the scenario to help all key people *own* the decision. Nonetheless, however adaptive your culture, at some point you will hit conservatism and inertia.

> Far too much effort is put into *selling* the change in order to implement it rather than first creating awareness about the need to experiment, evolve, adopt and adapt.

Senior leaders get training in agility every day by proxy of the inherent fluidity in our businesses. Managers don't, however. They don't see all the numbers and rarely have the full picture. Most of their training and day-to-day activity is actually focused on reliability as opposed to change. Furthermore, people can inherently understand the need to be open to change but lack the motivation to change. It's easy to revert to task or previous habit and subconsciously encourage the inertia wall. This is not necessarily conscious resistance but passive inertia that makes delivering new ways and new advantage initiatives harder to establish.

Far too much effort is put into *selling* the change in order to implement it rather than first creating awareness about the need to experiment, evolve, adopt and adapt; effectively, teaching how to learn, before teaching specifics as to how or why change or evolution is necessary. We can recruit as well as train to a change outlook, which ensures that the foundations of dynamic adaption are inherent in the culture.

FIGURE 9.4 Adaptive workplace environment

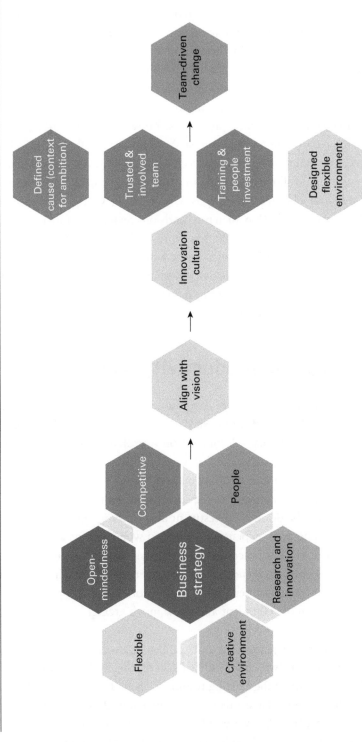

Leaders can create flexible outlooks by example. That is, never lament the past but simply learn from it, reduce ego and over-dogmatic strategic ownership in favour of embracing flow, to look ahead and talk ahead rather than dwell on the good old days. Train yourself to embrace new technologies, ideas and continuously dedicate time to their research. The world is what you think it is, and by immersing yourself in a forward-thinking outlook you will create an innovation outlook and experience in both your life and the organization. The key question is: How can 'I' help 'us' get where we need to go? Humility and a good sense of humour will take you a long way.

By understanding what needs to change and why, you increase acceptance. This is then followed by exploration, workshops, group brainstorms, research and investigative analysis with the team. Options are then explored with team and leadership, then pros and cons reviewed before jointly choosing a path. Overall, advantage leaders work with the organization to share the environment and position, then work with the team to identify the changes needed, thus building a collective vision around the strategy on what can be achieved. They secure alignment by influence, and inspire through transparency, frankness, challenge, praise, reward and belief.

Training and productivity bias

We live today in a knowledge economy; ideas are more valuable and useful than capital. This can lead us back to the biblical David and Goliath story. David won the victory – I contend on a probable basis as he had remote warfare technology whereas the warrior Goliath was weighted down by armour and traditional weaponry. David had the idea and the long-range ability. Adaptive organizations require leaders to share and develop the ideas. This can only be done via investment and training and yet many managers regard training as an expense, squeezed in when surplus allows, rather than allowed for and embraced as an ongoing cost. The right training will increase selection awareness, decrease supervision costs, improve customer service and enhance retention. Well-informed employees make fewer mistakes, are more confident and show much greater proactive adaptability and initiative.

How many organizations have a heavy investment in new staff and recruitment costs, which far outstrips increasing and investing in awareness and productivity in the existing resource? Using Pareto's 80:20 rule, it might look like this: if we have a team of 100 in a consultancy business with a sale per head of £100,000, we would have £10 million revenue. If via training and awareness we could enhance productivity by just 15 per cent per head we would increase to £11.5 million revenue, yet if we recruited five new heads we would only grow by £500,000. This is of course very simplistic but training and productivity gains are usually easier to reach, yet the main focus of many leaders is growth by expansion. Furthermore, the 15 per cent increase through investment in training might well be year on year whereas the recruitment is one-off. Training is very often skills-based and technical, whereas much of the gain can actually be achieved in training business acumen and personal development skills. Employees with enhanced awareness in these areas are more likely to be far more flexible beyond their specialism, or 'on the job' capability.

A win–win scenario emerges, as the organization supports self-skills via a focus on lifelong learning and development. This sustains a shift towards more high value-added activities, such as proactive adaption on the job. In a similar way, schools in most Western education systems are today starting to adapt to this approach. As the digital age places knowledge at our fingertips, individual effectiveness becomes far more about how pupils access, find, sift and apply knowledge as opposed to remembering knowledge by writing it down as previously happened in academic studies. I need basic maths to use a calculator but its computing capabilities far outstrip mine. Education in coding and how to use the calculator is perhaps more important than the direct skill of maths. In these ideas we can see that while we might have a training budget, how much is allocated to learning and how to learn and use the environment, as opposed to just skills-based?

The first step to agility is in getting employees to take the effort seriously by raising awareness to the need to be agile and to learn. Executives can reduce the risks of such investment by insisting on reimbursement for a specified period of time following completion of the training.

Chapter summary and leader questions

In order to secure competitive advantage, looking further ahead and more accurately in the market is great, but it does not guarantee advantage. It is those who successfully adopt the ideas and make them a reality that win. This can be best achieved using team-driven 'selection' and 'agile' adoption to extract from complexity. In plain English, train the team to use common sense, be proactive to create change when things don't work and trust them.

This simplicity can be built from the ground up by making an agile and evolutionary approach an inherent part of the organization's culture, policies and rewards, and embedding the workplace best practices that achieve them. This may be achieved by a mix of breaking formality and hierarchy, training, affording permission to fail or better data and knowledge share. Overall we combine the culture with reward, awareness, sharing and encouraging evolution and selection at a team level. We track and show a keen interest in the selection but encourage a proactive approach and conversation to adaption at all times with the overarching goal and vision clearly in mind at all levels. We can also remember that in the necessary organizational quest for reliability we feed the vested interests of the status, and therefore we must go perhaps further out of our way to feed agility as the counter.

Advantage leaders can help set the rules and environment to address the problems of changing requirements, uncertain outcomes and complexity, through the design of an adaptive business culture and system. This enables goals and approaches to be modified 'in game' or 'on the job' to optimize performance. Knowledge and ideas can be captured by the players during the performance to identify and create new processes or approaches, without continuous intervention and management. That is, the people on the ground apply judgement, 'select', engage and adapt, and the leaders, while they track progress, trust the team to use common sense. The approach takes design in the first instance but becomes self-fulfilling and maintainable as the culture inherently drives the evolution.

Advantage is secured at the foundations by building a flexible operating model at a lower cost, yet allowing permission to try things differently to encourage productivity and innovation. We eliminate or deselect waste and inefficiency and amplify or select the growth areas.

Leader questions

1 How much do you allow a culture of selection?

2 Does your team understand the importance of selection and engage in a regular process to achieve it?

3 How open-minded are you and your team really?

4 How pioneering is your culture, and how much does it accept and learn from failure?

5 What training investment has been made in agility awareness?

6 How much do you rely on team-driven changes?

7 Why are you different and better?

References

Clark, L (2013) Tesco uses supply chain analytics to save £100m a year. Computer Weekly, 30/04. Available from: www.computerweekly.com/news/2240182951/Tesco-uses-supply-chain-analytics-to-save-100m-a-year [Last accessed 27 August 2015]

Rivera, R (2012) 5 Myths of Human Resources Management. Forbes Business, 21/11. Available from: www.forbes.com/sites/sap/2012/11/21/5-myths-of-human-capital-management/ [Last accessed 27 August 2015]

Business by design

10

Introduction

In our work so far, we have examined the line of probability, and we have researched both the data and the competitive arena. We have scenarios and are confident of the market direction. As a consequence we should have new products, services, processes and approaches. This may, however, require an overhaul of the whole business. Will the brand, systems and team cope with the changes we seek? Does the business have the right finances, resources and distribution channels? In this chapter we examine the business model. How can we seek to be both market disruptive and create advantage in the model?

By design

The business model describes a business's infrastructure and organizational strategy to link its products, segments and customers or its operations, distribution, brand and personnel. As with the creation of products, the model requires strategy, design and forward thinking. Where is the market going and how can we design the business around a more effective and efficient model as a consequence? How will the business convert 'investment' inputs such as capital, raw materials, operations, services and labour into outputs, that is goods and services, which are effectively distributed with sufficient profit margin, aligning and using all the resources available?

Advantage can be found in better understanding what is happening and likely to happen in your market and then creating new or improved products and services. However, this is by no means the only way to stand out. Many businesses have achieved competitive advantage by applying better business models against the line of probability research and data. Where are things going, and how do we shape the business from the ground up, enhancing and altering the infrastructure to take advantage? With more market certainty on the line of probability, leaders can essentially carry out an interdisciplinary review backed by the whole context of the business's current direction, scenarios and ideas, and consequently reshape the business accordingly. As we examined in Chapter 3, when we are in leadership not management, we may need to strip away the layer cake of history to future-proof the business model.

Your current model will not be the same in 10 years' time. This will happen over time by evolution, new processes and technology; so how can we control this process, accelerate change and better design the model to efficiency? What brand, look, infrastructure and operation will be most effective in the future?

Alignment

Building and accelerating growth in a business require effort, and lots of it. However, by exerting precisely the 'right effort at the right pressure points, with the right model' it is possible to contribute tirelessly and more effortlessly, aligned or 'in flow'. However, many leaders are too busy to take the time to find those pressure points, leading to overexertion and inefficiency in the model. That is, the infrastructure might fail to match the brand or shareholder aspirations and vision, or product value may fail the customer expectations. A key part of securing advantage is therefore in the design of each of these components and how they then interrelate. In an efficient car, the engine is connected in just the right way to the gears transmitting power to the axles and out to the wheel in the most efficient manner. The chassis and body are balanced to fit the power correctly. We can use this in comparison to business: operations are the engine, sales and marketing the gears and the body and chassis the brand. They are all designed to work in cohesion to create the one efficient unit that flows.

'Flow' is actually a recognized and studied psychological state where an individual becomes fully immersed in an activity, feeling energized and focused. It is a state of enjoyment and complete engagement. Flow was first written about by Mihály Csíkszentmihályi, a psychologist studying and interviewing successful artists on their ability to immerse themselves wholly and positively in their work in order to create exceptional results (Csíkszentmihályi, 1975). In the interviews several people described their experiences as 'flow' after using the metaphor of a water current carrying them along. In a business context, alignment that creates flow can be achieved on individual activities but also by objectively engaging in implementing

FIGURE 10.1   Business by design alignment

Product	Brand and position	Value
What are our key products? Who are our key suppliers? What and who are the true competition? How much do we charge and what 'value' do customers extract consequentially?	What is our culture? What do we stand for? How are we perceived? What is our reputation? What do customers 'actually' say? How clear and unified is our message?	What value do we deliver to clients? Which client problems do we solve and what are they willing to pay for this? What products do we offer? Which customer need do we satisfy and what do they currently pay for this?
Resources	**Revenue Streams**	**Distribution Channels**
What key resources does our strategy require? How strong are our customer relations? How good or strong is our team, and how efficient is it? What brand patents, copyrights, data do we have? What is our financial cashflow and capital structure?	What value are our customers really willing to pay for? What do our customers really pay for? What recurring revenue do we have? How much does each stream actually contribute against what cost?	Which channels do our customers want to be reached by? Which channels are working well and not working well? What is our digital platform and channel? How are our channels integrated? How are we integrating our channels with customer routines?
Costs	**Company structure**	**Premises infrastructure**
What are the most important costs inherent in our business design? Which 'resources' are most expensive? What are our fixed costs versus variable?	What type of relationship do we have with each customer segment? How are they integrated with the rest of our business design? What is our shareholder and legal structure and how aligned is it to the vision?	What is our physical estate and how does it match customer need? How cost-effective is the estate to enable us to deliver value to customers? What are our virtual estate and capital?

Left margin: **What is the line of probability for our market?**

Right margin: **Why is our business design better?**

What design do we need as opposed to have to create alignment?

and designing the right business model. When your model argues with reality you nearly always suffer... when you accept reality and concentrate positively on what you can change to align the model, you achieve flow. Ultimately this requires absolute objectivity in recognizing your own organizational strengths, weaknesses and habits and being prepared to adjust, free from the constraints of history.

> When your business model argues with reality you nearly always suffer.

Business design and innovation in combination

An effective business model creates advantage in efficiency and alignment, whereas new products and research can create innovation advantage. Many companies seem to engage in the pursuit of either product or model innovation. However, employing and seeking the combination are where the world-beating businesses are usually formed. We tend to only think of the product innovators as 'first' but equally organizations which are ahead in the design of their business model, customer service, brand or process create more trust in the minds of their customers and their employees. The design is a systematic review and analysis of the organization's structures to improve and adopt change in business process, target customers, infrastructure, buying, organization, operations and policies to best enable the commercial opportunity.

When the business design is aligned and clear, the organization flows ahead of competition as matters become more effortless. A lack of cohesion results in decline and inefficiency. If production is efficient but the brand is incapable of communicating the value of the products we might still have a lack of success or advantage.

CASE STUDY

Nike is a good example of a world-beating business that has embraced change in its business model and innovation in its products to create advantage from the start. The business was founded in 1964 by the track athlete Philip Knight and his coach Bill Bowerman, as the distributor for a Japanese shoemaker, Onitsuka Tiger (now ASICS). Originally called BRS, they sold shoes from the back of their cars and in 1966, BRS opened its first retail store in Santa Monica, California. Due to rapidly increasing sales, BRS expanded its retail and distribution operations but by 1971, the relationship between BRS and Onitsuka Tiger was coming to an end. BRS prepared to launch its own line of footwear, which would bear the Swoosh logo, newly designed by Carolyn Davidson. The model had moved from distributor to retailer to manufacturer.

In 1976, the company hired John Brown and Partners, based in Seattle, as its first advertising agency. The following year, the agency created the first brand ad campaign for Nike, called 'There is no finish line'. By 1980, Nike had attained a 50 per cent market share in the US athletic shoe market, and the company went public in December of that year. Today Nike sells an assortment of products, including shoes and apparel for sports activities such as football, basketball, running and tennis, but it has also become popular in youth culture supplying urban fashion clothing.

In the 1980s Nike became an 'unbundled' manufacturer. It stopped manufacture and outsourced this throughout the world, concentrating instead on design, positioning and marketing. In 2003, the company bought Converse, the makers of the Chuck Taylor All Stars line of sneakers, for US$309 million (Wikipedia, 2015). The business acquired Umbro, the England football team's kit manufacturer in 2008 for £285 million (Wikipedia, 2015). In 2012 they divested Umbro for half this sum to refocus operations. In this we can see a willingness to embrace what works and stop what doesn't or hasn't worked. Mark Parker, the Nike CEO at the time of the sale, said: 'Umbro has a great heritage but, ultimately, as our category has evolved, we believe Nike Football can serve the needs of footballers on and off the pitch.' In other words, upon review the Nike brand was much stronger in the football industry and Umbro had become a low-growth brand.

Nike has always led innovation in shoes. It recently introduced cricket shoes called Air Zoom Yorker, designed to be 30 per cent lighter than their competitors, and teamed up with Apple Inc to produce the Nike+ a product that monitors a runner's performance via a radio device in the shoe that links to their iPod or iPhone.

Nike continues to interrogate and substantially adjust its business model. The following is lifted directly from Nike's website:

The Future: Closed-Loop Business Model

The financial, social and environmental imperatives for moving to a sustainable economy will dictate how business models evolve over the next decade. We believe that we are entering an era of post-globalization, one in which new business models will emerge based on the overwhelming pressures fuelled by regulation, scarcity, consumer behaviour and innovation. We think the future will demand closed-loop business models that move closer to achieving zero waste by completely reusing, recycling or composting all materials.

Our vision of a closed-loop business model includes up-front design of products that can be manufactured using materials reclaimed throughout the manufacturing process and at the end of a product's life. To fully realize this new model, industry must find new answers to business challenges. Innovators must create new ways to recycle and reuse waste and turn that into new products. Designers must look at new sustainable raw materials. Leaders must examine the impact on supply chains and labour forces. (Nike, 2015)

Beyond agility

The Nike outlook shows that competitive advantage through the business model is as important as product innovation. This is strategically led beyond agility. The above demonstrates their awareness that, in the information age, consumers are knowledgeable and will only choose *good* companies, however well designed their products. Over the next few decades, sustainability will come increasingly higher on the agenda. Ethical sourcing, recycling and value- or ethics-driven businesses that care about their values as much as they do about profits will be the winning businesses. A global economy is a complex ecosystem. If we fight the environment or try and control it rather than live with it there will always be a battle against the odds. Business design will take account of values, sustainability and consumer trends. The model will be led by both the product and the customer feedback, as well as the needs of the organization. Sustainability of the organization's infrastructure becomes symbiotic with the likely market direction.

The reflection for leaders is simple. Where is the market going? What are tomorrow's customers going to want? How does our business model fit this need, and if it doesn't what needs to change in order to create an advantage model? This could be location, distribution, supply chain or route to market. We must be unbiased by history and instead look ahead and design the model carefully and objectively.

Stand-out models

What can we do to the model that's different? Very often this is simply a new way of providing an old product. Britain's YO! Sushi restaurants are a great example. In 1997 they brought the concept of a Japanese 'kaiten' sushi bar that delivered food to customers via a conveyor belt and made it more modern. An old product but a brand new way of presenting it created exponential growth. The business model can be as disruptive as the products to gain advantage. McDonald's achieved advantage in the 1960s by taking a restaurant concept into a process with the sole aim of delivering food more quickly. The same product (though they reduced the menu), but with speed, not flavour, as the key differentiator. Facebook is repeating the model, reducing trade from licensing software, by offering free content and software in exchange for data profiles to advertise against: the software product is the same, but the distribution and revenue stream are different. Leaders can select a combination of strategies, product innovation or business model and brand differentiation. Behind this we have the idea that if cost or quality is the only difference we end up with diminishing yield and potentially slow growth.

Customers expect value and quality but strong growth is only secured when you are operating in a way that's aligned and stands out. Why are you different, efficient with a first-in-class business model as well as product, or how could you be? How aligned is the model?

FIGURE 10.2   First-in-class disruptive models

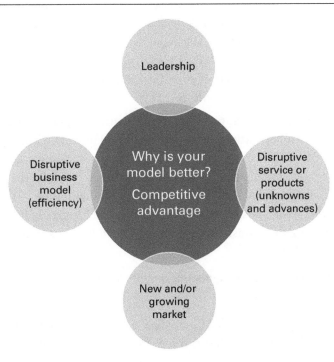

Business model types

There are many strategic options and business model types. In analysis most companies will choose and focus on a predominant approach simply because it's almost impossible to be 'first' in all. There is a myriad of different business models but there are four main recognized strategies:

- Cost – a cost-leadership strategy is to offer products or services at the lowest cost in the industry. Efficient buying and lowest-cost production are essential for this design. The challenge of this strategy is to earn a suitable profit for the company. Primark, Walmart and Skoda succeed with this strategy by featuring low prices on key items. The model is not simply about offering consumer cost savings; it entails configuring every single aspect of their business model in order to drive down cost.

- Difference – a differentiation strategy presents existing products to consumers in new ways that competitors are not yet offering or are unable to offer. An example is Dell, which launched mass customizations on computers to fit consumers' needs, or YO! Sushi food on conveyor belts.

- Product innovation – a product strategy seeks completely new or notably better products or services ahead of the competition. The new products drive sales by being better than the old, thus creating new demand and sidelining the original. Companies such as Tesla with its battery cars or Canon with its extensive research and development budget of over £600 million a year employ this as a primary strategy (YCHARTS, 2015).

- Operations – an operations strategy is focused on performing business and operations better internally and more efficiently than competitors. The design aim is to make the organization easier to 'shop' with and higher margin due to efficiency. Barclays, the world's sixth largest global bank (Source: **www.acuity.com**, June 2015) might consider itself a customer services business but ultimately it is an operations and infrastructure business. (Reed Business Information Limited, 2015).

There are of course many sub-strategies. By no means exhaustive, these might include:

- The middle-man model: Airbnb takes a 3 per cent commission on hotel or bed and breakfast earnings from its hosts and in return charges a booking fee of 6–12 per cent to guests for every booking they make, thus operating a middle-man or broker approach. The model requires an infrastructure that encourages an introduction and then bundles services, usually expertise, around this. Estate and real estate agents operate on the same basis.

- Auctions: The price of the goods is left variable and individuals compete via bids to determine the final value and purchase price. From Christie's, established in London's Pall Mall in 1766, who sold a Picasso painting for US$179 million in 2010 (*Telegraph*, 2011) to eBay, established in just 1996, where you can buy bike lights shipped from China for just £3 each, the model has a diverse range.

- Franchise: The franchisor creates a product and brand and can scale up more rapidly by then selling this on a licence to individuals. The individual benefits from corporate support and the brand name and in return the franchisor receives a royalty. Kall Kwik print and Subway use this model. The first Subway franchise opened in Connecticut in 1974 and the first UK store in Brighton in 1996, yet just seven years later in 2003 there were over 200 UK stores.

- Direct: From Everest Glazing to Encyclopaedia Britannica and Dell, direct sales mean that producers can enhance their margin on retailers and resellers, albeit that it may result in reduced distribution. As a primary distribution channel, the internet has encouraged a re-emergence of direct selling, although with the increasing cost of Google in the search landscape, some argue that it is no longer a direct route. Google don't actually count other search engines as their biggest competitor; they believe it is Amazon.

- The Hook model: The most famous example of this is the razor blade industry selling low-cost razors with expensive blade refills. Gillette led this approach, with a high amount of sales captured in the components. The digital printer industry often works on this basis with low-retail-priced machines and once the customer is locked in, high-price ink cartridges.

- Recurring or subscription revenue: The print copy market operates almost exclusively on this basis with Danwood being the UK's leading provider. By building an infrastructure that customers need for support the organization can then offer 'lock in' contracts to use the service and support. Magazine publishers such as *National Geographic* are also a good example of this model with the publisher increasing regularity and the subscriber usually receiving a discount in exchange. In fact this has worked so well for so long that the brand has also established a retail presence and TV channel.

- The advertising model: Many publishers, TV stations and internet platforms create revenue this way. The latest example and perhaps most exciting recent example of this strategy is Facebook. The social media site now has over 936 million daily active users, or 65 per cent of its total monthly active users. The primary income is advertising and many doubted the social platform could become commercial; however, Facebook has reported a profit of US$512 million (£341 million) for the first three months of 2015. Its revenue was up 46 per cent to US$3.32 billion on the same quarter in 2014 (Market Watch, 2015). ITV, the UK's main commercial TV station, was built successfully on advertising revenue for years; however, the internet was slowly eroding its viewing base. ITV executives responded to the threat by acquiring the social networking website Friends Reunited, based on its 15 million users for £120 million in 2005. The site had a good subscription revenue. The idea was good but the platform's flaw was that it was not generic or free. Facebook could do what Friends Reunited did for free and the membership shrivelled. In 2009 ITV sold the site for £25 million (BBC, 2009).

- Upsell model: easyJet is a good example of this. The aim is to drive significant volumes of customers by charging a very low price. This is achieved by a low-cost focus, for example easyJet's head office is at Luton airport, a peripheral airport on the outskirts of London and thus low cost. Once the volume is secured they combine ancillary sales such as priority seating, baggage charges, Starbucks coffee sales and insurance products to enhance margin. The lead product is priced competitively but there are numerous extras that drive up the final price.

> The best business model changes are those that challenge the value proposition. Not only does the model show its difference to customers, it offers them, and ideally the business, better value.

Advantage through value

In business by design the idea is that competitive advantage may be found by looking at each component of how business is carried out, whether it is distribution, manufacture and service and changing the basis of the infra-structure or process. The change may then create a stand-out position or proposition to customers. The business is different because we access the product in a different way. The furniture giant IKEA achieved this in the 1950s and secured rapid growth by combining the new idea of self-assembly, with a catalogue and showroom combination, thus increasing reach while still insisting on well-designed furniture.

The best business model changes are those that challenge the value proposition. Not only does the model show its difference to customers, it offers them, and ideally the business, better value. A mobile hairdresser could use this approach. The hairdresser would save on the costs of premises or salon enabling them to undercut their high street competitors. The customer saves time, travel and money so has better value.

This example is of course limited as there is only one hairdresser so the model fails to secure scale-up, perhaps the strongest advantage. This is where value drives scale and that enables buying power that reinforces the value by increasing margin and/or the ability to offer lower cost to the client.

'Value' is not the same as 'cheap'. Even a high-end premium brand can offer value. Mercedes lease cars are usually very competitively priced because the perceived quality and higher longevity of their product result in lower depreciation than other manufacturers on most of their standard small and mid-range models.

FIGURE 10.3   Value model combination

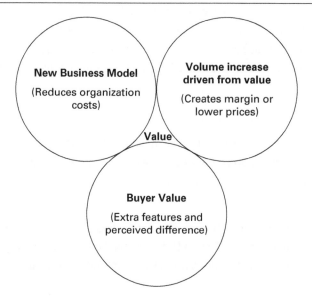

A value model requires careful examination of the supply chain and business infrastructure but it does not necessarily require new products. There is a common view that in order to disrupt you must invent game-changing new products that change the marketplace and as a consequence product innovation can become an overly singular focus. Reinventing the business model has equal and sometimes far greater opportunity. In 1996, Amazon and eBay both fundamentally changed retail with the highly successful combination of mail order and the internet. Before that, in the 1970s in the United Kingdom, Green Shield were an incentive business offering customer loyalty reward stamps via Tesco and petrol filling stations. The collected stamps could be exchanged for goods via its catalogues and stores. However, retail margins came under fire so reward stamps started to decline. Green Shield shifted its model to cash instead of stamps and the highly successful retailer Argos was born using a new combination of catalogues to display goods and depot stores to collect them from.

Game-changing models

CASE STUDY

At the time of writing Uber is one of the world's fastest growing companies with a game-changing business model. As a result of entirely reinventing the way we book taxis, the company is growing even faster than eBay (Blodget, 2014). The business started in 2009 as a luxury car service in San Francisco. It now operates in 58 countries, is valued at US$3.76 billion and operates in more than 300 cities worldwide.

> A value model requires careful examination of the supply chain and business infrastructure; it does not necessarily require new products.

The idea of Uber was born out of frustration by two tech-savvy tourists in Paris, who struggled to hail a cab. Before Uber we relied on the monopoly of city meter licensed cabs or we had to look up a local taxi firm, and make a call. The meter cab required hailing and the further out from the city centre you were, the fewer cabs there were. The local cab company was pot luck and the wait time was often a work of fiction. In both cases this often led to a poor experience. No one thought too hard about this, it was just the way it was, but everyone grumbled. This reminds us that irritations can be a good pointer to business models or products that need looking at.

Uber tackled the grumbles head on, essentially by 'wrapping' the experience and the simplicity of the idea is breathtaking in hindsight. Their smartphone app is integrated with Google maps (yes, Google now have a US\$258 million stake) so that you can see how far away their nearest cars are (Wilhelm and Tsotsis, 2013). You can then get a quote and/or just commit based on this information and even better you can then track the car's progress. The Uber driver calls or texts to confirm the booking. You can choose a low-cost or premium car. Uber has grown organically with very little marketing simply because the product is excellent.

Uber reimagines each step of the taxi process to make it seamless and enjoyable from mobile hailing, cashless payments, no tips and using driver ratings to ensure better driving and usually cleaner cars. The product is the same, the service still offers taxis; however, the 'wrapping' is so wholly different that each change dramatically alters and largely improves customer experience. In my experience, London's metered black cabs are exemplary and possibly the best in the world; probably the cleanest and politest, but... they can require pavement hailing skills and beyond trips in Central London (and London is now very spread out) the meter clocks up, sometimes as you watch with no end in sight. Uber cuts this out by giving an estimate of the cost of the journey when you make the booking. You can get a quote and make a booking five minutes before you leave a meeting or a restaurant, wait for your car, then step in. In cities like Dubai, which has very limited public transport, Uber alters the landscape completely; in the past people booked their taxi but in a large sprawling city the wait was often long. Uber's volume of drivers increases cover, thus reducing wait time and by providing the ability to track the cab on your phone also reduces anxiety. Additionally, the credit card basis of the service cuts out the need to carry cash.

Uber is a traditional product reinvented around a new business with the clever use of technology to enhance the customer experience. Ultimately it is a value innovation. By being more efficient for both the customer and the driver it offers more value at less cost.

Mapping your model

As a corporate you will no doubt have given considerable thought to both the model and the processes employed to drive reliability in the model; however, how future-proof is the model? What processes, steps, supply and channel arrangements create opportunity to surprise or stand out as different, yet might also help customers gain extra value at the same time? An important advantage tool therefore may well be in mapping out each step of your process from raw idea to finished and completed goods or service.

The process review sets out each step then looks at the opportunity to both seek efficiency, highlight elements to delight customers and drive value. The UK retailer Argos, owned by the Home Retail Group, which also owns the DIY chain Homebase, has just brought Homebase into the depot network. You can now collect Argos goods at Homebase. This not only enhances online sales with the benefit of increased depot and collection access beating postal delivery for certainty of receipt but it also pulls customers directly into Homebase.

By mapping out the process in visual steps you can then create different scenarios around the process by taking out and adding in elements. This may result in changes to pricing if the model ends up different but it helps you make business model ideas simpler, more concrete and actionable. Figure 10.4 sets out the components of mapping.

When mapping the process it can be useful to think of the work of Michael Porter, who developed the value chain concept in his seminal 1980 book, also of the name *Competitive Advantage*. The idea of a value chain is that it maps the whole series of activities that create and build value at every step. Porter's value chain concept identifies that we highlight and secure useful activities that create advantage and remove or diminish the wasteful activities.

In activities we look at logistics, processing, sales and marketing, brand and service as well as post-sales work. We also look at or audit the organization's infrastructure, human resources, procurement management systems and technology. To express this more simply, carry out an audit of every component and decide where it contributes. That is, customers value the component or product to pay sufficiently and the internal element is of merit in contributing to the value component. With this common-sense outlook we might then secure in combination the ability to charge higher prices, lower production costs, speed of delivery, quality, margin and a better brand and reputation.

FIGURE 10.4   Mapping the model and reviewing value

Process and resource	Channels	Revenue type
Map out existing steps Human resource and Infrastructure	Review resource, supply, procurement and customer touch points	Review pricing model and positioning versus price

Create a mind map of all the points then change to play out different model and outcome scenarios against the line of probability. Where is the market going?

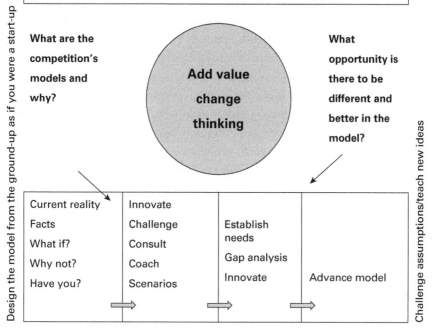

Brand alignment

Reviewing the model against the likely future of the market is not about simply seeking efficiency. There is a risk that in process review all we do is look internally and seek or tune the existing engine or platform for efficiency. Efficiency is critical but changes in the model itself may help clients gain better value. Often these efficiency or model changes occur but are then not communicated, losing a critical benefit to clients and opportunity for the organization to engage. Using the 'engine' comparison we need to market the performance and technology changes that the client is benefiting from better.

Advantage can be gained by innovation in the business model but we must communicate these differentiators to our customers. It is also critical that our communications and branding create the perception of being ahead of others. This is where branding comes into an advantage strategy, not just logos or advertising but a deep understanding of how the organization can present itself to the right people more often, in the right way and ahead of what others are doing. That is, creating a unique name and presentation for a product in our customers' minds with a consistent theme to establish a significant and differentiated presence in the market that attracts and retains customers.

Of course, branding is a specialist subject in itself and it takes a lot of work with the right experts to get right, but one of the most important areas where leaders can make a big difference is by focusing on alignment or as I call it 'one voice'. One voice is about coordination and building trust. Once we have decided who we want to talk to, it is communicating why our products and models are game changers more often and more consistently. Positive familiarity dramatically increases buying, that is consistency builds trust in the mind. If each time and every way your chosen prospects see you with the right advantage or benefit messages you will increase market share. Figure 10.5 summarizes the one voice concept.

FIGURE 10.5 Advantage brands – one voice

Clear vocal brands break out of their category and gain advantage. What are your voice, message and tone? How clear are they, and how do they show your benefits?		
Who are your real target audience and why?	Profile your customer per segment. Give them names and imagine what they do.	**Which customers**
What do your customers currently think and do?		**Identify need**
What do you want your customers to think and do?		**Match needs**

FIGURE 10.5 *continued*

What is it your company really does?	What problem do you solve? How would you describe this quickly, in less than a minute, to gain attention?	**Solve problems**
What benefits do you have?	Features that describe the item. Benefits of the solution you offer. Describe the feature then add 'which means' = benefit	**Which means benefits**
What tone of voice do your targets need?	Imagine the persona of your business? What character does it play, or have?	**Tone and positioning**
Where are your brand and marketing 'heard'?	How consistent and aligned is that voice? Does your website match the customer service? Are your salespeople using the old script? Do your 'past' case studies reflect the customers you want 'tomorrow'?	**Auditory message**
Where are your brand and marketing 'seen'?	A picture speaks a thousand words. How simple, different and clear are your images? Do they show benefits in the right, clear way? Schematics can be very helpful.	**Visual message**
How much time has been spent aligning the brand to the vision to create one voice?		

Once you have designed an effective brand position, everything you do – from your marketing and communications to the way your organization and premises look and feel, how the phone is answered or the sales representatives talks–recalls the brand promise. Why are you ahead, better and different and how do you communicate this?

Marketing mix

In a 'by design' review we may need to look in more depth at marketing throughout the business and examine how this impacts both brand and strategy. The traditional 'marketing mix' thinking is useful as a base for this thinking. This mix is the four Ps of marketing. That is, price, product, promotion and place (and increasingly positioning and people). These elements are the actions that a company uses to market and sell products and to build a brand.

- *Price.* This depends overall on the position and the production costs as well as the supply chain. Typical strategies might include premium, middle or budget, multibuy strategies and loyalty discount strategies. Overall these strategies are determined by the business plan, volume and margin. Your competitors' positioning will also have a heavy influence here. How are you different and why is your pricing better (remember that better does not mean cheaper)?

- *Product.* We have already discussed innovation in the product. How does this give value to the customer and how well designed is it? Good products will not guarantee success but they really help. Why is the product solving a problem and in a better way than others?

- *Place.* This is about location or premises. In retail it refers to the point of sale. Does our location reflect the strategy and how do we stand out, what is the quality of our presentation? In particular in retail or hospitality infrastructure businesses quality of design is essential.

- *Promotion.* Today there are hundreds of promotion methods from the internet to exhibitions, advertising, public relations, direct mail, telesales, commissions and awards to the trade. What are the activities being undertaken to make the services or products familiar and known to the customer?

Overall combining, layering and changing the elements of the mix help us create a cohesive understanding of why you are better and how this is communicated to your customers, ideally so your organization is first in their minds. Creating a mix (see Figure 10.6) that is aligned and presented with one voice will help secure a leading position with customers; that is, they will think of us first. When we are perceived as first or ahead, our customers will buy more from us and recommend us, and it is usually easier to get them to listen to our marketing. The brand creates goodwill by design. Figure 10.6 summarizes the marketing mix.

FIGURE 10.6   The marketing mix

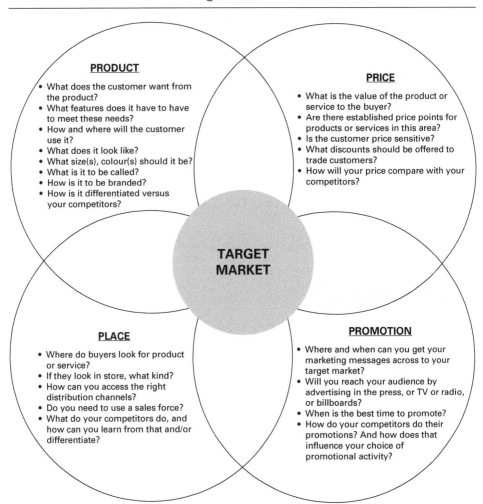

PRODUCT
- What does the customer want from the product?
- What features does it have to have to meet these needs?
- How and where will the customer use it?
- What does it look like?
- What size(s), colour(s) should it be?
- What is it to be called?
- How is it to be branded?
- How is it differentiated versus your competitors?

PRICE
- What is the value of the product or service to the buyer?
- Are there established price points for products or services in this area?
- Is the customer price sensitive?
- What discounts should be offered to trade customers?
- How will your price compare with your competitors?

TARGET MARKET

PLACE
- Where do buyers look for product or service?
- If they look in store, what kind?
- How can you access the right distribution channels?
- Do you need to use a sales force?
- What do your competitors do, and how can you learn from that and/or differentiate?

PROMOTION
- Where and when can you get your marketing messages across to your target market?
- Will you reach your audience by advertising in the press, or TV or radio, or billboards?
- When is the best time to promote?
- How do your competitors do their promotions? And how does that influence your choice of promotional activity?

Chapter summary and questions

Ultimately, dynamic markets require leaders to create flexible structures and enable the structure to be more fluid. Instead of relying on history to create the infrastructure we can look ahead at the likelihoods and build the infrastructure and organization's model to enhance efficiency and also stand out. Advantage does not require disruptive and ground-breaking innovations, it requires strategy combined with discipline, motivation and intelligence. Stand-out businesses can be secured by looking at and innovating in the model as opposed to just the products, and arguably this is equally as successful as creating game-changing businesses.

Much can also be achieved when the model is more efficient, and often this is about understanding how better to join the model together more effectively. I previously used the comparison of building better business models being similar to designing better cars. The idea being that with each component better designed and then better joined the sum creates the advantage position. In this respect the leaders can be like the oil that flows between the parts. They ensure a dynamic moving structure with as much fluidity and as little friction as possible.

Advantage is secured at the foundations by reviewing and designing sustainable efficient operating models, and combining this, where possible, with better products. The design and value drive growth when the brand then successfully aligns around communicating why the model, products and value are better.

Leader questions

1 What are your competition's models and why are you different?

2 How receptive to change is your model, and how flexible is it?

3 How aligned are the components of your model?

4 Where is your model (process, resource, and infrastructure) different and better?

5 How aligned is your brand to the value you deliver?

References

BBC (2009) ITV in £25m Friends Reunited Sale. Available from: http://news.bbc.co.uk/1/hi/8186840.stm [Last accessed 27 August 2015]

Blodget, H (2014) Now I know why investors are going hog wild about Uber. Business Insider, 13/11. Available from: http://uk.businessinsider.com/ubers-revenue-2014-11?r=US&IR=T [Last accessed 7 September 2015]

Csíkszentmihályi, M (2000) *Beyond Boredom and Anxiety: Experiencing Flow in Work and Play*, Jossey-Bass

Market Watch (2015) Facebook Inc. Available from: www.marketwatch.com/investing/stock/fb/financials [Last accessed: 27 August 2015]

Nike (2015) The Future: Closed-Loop Business Model. Available from: www.nikebiz.com/crreport/content/strategy/2-1-3-the-future-closed-loop-business-model.php?cat=cr-strategy [Last accessed 07 September 2015]

Reed Business Information Limited (2015) Bank Rankings – Top Banks in the World. Available from: www.accuity.com/useful-links/bank-rankings/ [Last accessed 7 September 2015]

Telegraph (2011) A brief history of Christie's. Telegraph Finance, 28/01. Available from: www.telegraph.co.uk/finance/newsbysector/retailandconsumer/8287387/A-brief-history-of-Christies.html [Last accessed: 27 August 2015]

Wikipedia (2015) Converse (shoe company). Available from: https://en.wikipedia.org/wiki/Converse_%28shoe_company%29 [Last accessed: 27 August 2015]

Wikipedia (2015) Umbro. Available from: https://en.wikipedia.org/wiki/Umbro [Last accessed: 27 August 2015]

YCHARTS (2015) Canon Research and Development Expense (Quarterly). 30/06. Available from: https://ycharts.com/companies/CAJ/r_and_d_expense [Last accessed 07 September 2015]

Wilhelm and Tsotsis (2013) Google Ventures Puts $258m Into Uber, Its Largest Deal Ever. TechCrunch, 22/08. Available from: http://techcrunch.com/2013/08/22/google-ventures-puts-258m-into-uber-its-largest-deal-ever/ [Last accessed: 27 August 2015]

Decisive action

11

Introduction

With accelerated change business models and products changing faster than ever, companies cannot rely on past success or existing processes and approaches. New logic and changes are required. The line of probability and data will give us strategic insight and we now need to implement tactics and actions to achieve the strategy. This requires decisive and often immediate action. Organizations that spend too long debating the strategy can miss opportunity. Strategy needs to translate to decisive action. In this chapter we examine how this is best achieved.

Decisive action

Decisive action requires effective, clear and concise communication. Advantage leaders create followers. They secure the buy-in or command the authority, ideally both, to get people to take action to change and follow, even if the objectives are challenging. This requires communication that motivates, inspires and creates the clarity needed to accomplish objectives. Communications that determinedly share today's realities (where you are now), then envision the objectives (where the organization could be). Finally we share the decisive actions that will achieve the objectives step by step.

Today Kimberly-Clark is a highly competitive consumer brand owning products such as Huggies and Kleenex; however, this was not always the case. The business started as a paper company and in the early 1970s was struggling. At this time Darwin E Smith was named chief executive. His name is not famous because he was shy and mild-mannered; however, he transformed the business.

> There was no 'personality' CEO, just a brave decision on the future of the
> market, which challenged the status quo and was backed by clear
> communication and decisive action.

Smith and his executives concluded that the company's traditional core business – coated paper – would struggle. The market was too narrow with weak margins and they needed to develop a consumer paper products business. While this area had more competition, the margins were significant. Smith decisively announced that Kimberly-Clark would sell its paper mills, which met with much criticism. All proceeds would be thrown into the consumer business and an action plan developed to transform the business over a 20-year period. Today the business is a global organization. A new direction was identified which was quietly yet determinedly articulated and backed by decisive action. There was no 'personality' CEO, just a brave decision on the future of the market, which challenged the status quo and was backed by clear communication and decisive action. Jim Collins, in his business classic *Good to Great*, covers a lot of the thinking around what it takes to make a great CEO. He also wrote about Darwin Smith (Collins, 2001).

Setting the direction

Fast-moving turbulent times create noise and complexity. The most important counter is designed simplicity. That is, that the plan and direction message is carefully designed by the leadership. It is then well articulated to motivate the business going forward.

Advantage leaders are great communicators. They set the direction and share the vision in ways that inspire. This does not mean you have to be a natural world-class speaker. It means being very clear on the direction and why, then consistently repeating the simple message to ensure commitment. To achieve simplicity we need designed communications that quietly share the data, research and probabilities to demonstrate the 'why change' picture. From this context we then move rapidly to the 'what to change' picture to drive action. Context is the basis. It matters because it creates the setting for the content – the decisive action required.

Dynamic markets create very broad options. Context, as well as explaining why, also enables us to narrow those options, which then enables simplicity in the 'what' to do. In simplicity for example, an oil company might say:

'Carbon-based technology is the energy of the past. Renewable energy using the earth's natural resources such as hydro, solar and wind are the future. Every action we take will focus on contributing to this future to create a clean planet for humankind.' Today, British Petroleum (BP), one of the world's largest oil companies says this (BP, 2015):

> **What we do** – We find, develop and produce essential sources of energy. We turn these sources into products that people need everywhere. The world needs energy and this need is growing. This energy will be in many forms. It is, and will always be, vital for people and progress everywhere. We expect to be held to high standards in what we do. We strive to be a safety leader in our industry, a world-class operator, a good corporate citizen and a great employer. We are BP.

> **What we stand for** – Above everything, that starts with safety and excellence in our operations. This is fundamental to our success. Our approach is built on respect, being consistent and having the courage to do the right thing. We believe success comes from the energy of our people. We have a determination to learn and to do things better. We depend upon developing and deploying the best technology, and building long-lasting relationships. We are committed to making a real difference in providing the energy the world needs today, and in the changing world of tomorrow. We work as one team. We are BP.

I shall be contentious: the statement with 'high standards and safety' at its core is highly mindful of the Deepwater Horizon disaster. In 2010, the offshore oil rig Deepwater Horizon exploded and sank, killing 11 people. The loss of the rig left an oil gusher in the sea floor, which leaked at 1,600 m below the surface for 87 days before a way could be found to cap it. The spill caused huge environmental damage with an estimated discharge of 4.9 million barrels and is accepted as the largest oil disaster in history. The disaster has left a scar on BP and the planet. BP is a large enough company to easily absorb the clean-up costs, and the rig was a tiny part of its operations but the statement does not show how they intend to move forward. It is reflective not visionary.

To be visionary BP needs to drop 'Petroleum' from the company name. It's time to rebrand. Yes we need oil and they can profitably continue to benefit from that but overall the mission must be to diminish this. The spill reinforces this direction as much as global warming statistics. Renewable *clean* energy is the future and BP is not owning the decision above. They can see it's coming with the statement 'energy in many forms', but does the above show clear drive to the organization over the next 50 years? In 2015, BP have spent US$20 billion on projects worldwide but only a fraction went into activities other than fossil fuel extraction, despite the fact that in 2003 they changed their slogan to 'Beyond Petroleum' (Macalister, 2015).

BP's research and investment into renewables are almost negligible. Whereas, for example, Tesla's plans for low-cost home-energy batteries make the future of solar look far more promising, BP appears to have made a choice to profit from our overdependence on oil, rather than to seize the day and help humanity go clean. Yet the company has the world-beating profits, infrastructure and engineering brains to do this. There is no simplicity in the BP message because they are opting for short-term profits in the wrong direction, and have not made the decision to 'disrupt' themselves. They remain highly mindful and contrite about Deepwater. This ignores the context that it is the right thing for humanity to care more for the environment, if at the least for its own benefit and therefore the content of the BP plans is flawed and one of the world's largest companies will ultimately fall to new visionaries.

Tough conversations

The BP example above is a great example of avoiding tough conversations. Renewable energy is less profitable today and requires huge infrastructure and shifts in mindset, and so it might mean stock values and profits drop while the long-term view is taken. One suspects that the BP board knows this but they are not having the tough conversations needed.

Tough conversations require a focus on *context* as opposed to *content* and can only exist in truthful and open environments. The debate is embraced rather than resisted. Most organizations avoid debate as it is seen as contentious and disorganized, but debate is where the changes are found. In Chapter 9, I suggested that the greatest advantage comes from outside the formal garden (the process organization) and from inside the wild garden (positive chaos) and debate forms part of that chaos. Encourage debate and tough conversations but then be very clear that whether you agree or disagree, the outcome will always be a clear, decided-upon course of action which will be carried out in reasonable time.

The more open you have been in securing the direction, the better. Respecting others' ideas and encouraging them even if they are passionately different shows strength, but also by this openness, the organization is better able to understand what reality is all about.

Different perspectives and constructive confrontation lead to a better direction and message. It is not the role of the leaders to avoid debate, or reduce the row. It is their role to manage the dialogue and ensure that perspective is kept during and afterwards with the clear mindset that challenge or confrontation must 'positively' deteriorate into agreed action in a reasonable timescale.

Long-term competitive advantage requires truth. If changes are challenging, trust can only be built with sincerity. For every great idea there are invariably areas of the organization that may be adversely affected. This also requires frankness. The position is the organization's future and its sustainable contribution is greater than anyone's vested short-term interest, including the leaders. BP might look to recruit a CEO from a renewable energy company to start to redress the balance, or to be even more radical, from Greenpeace.

Tough conversations include the concept of tough love. That is doing the right thing even if it hurts people. For example, there may be a tendency to step in when a less experienced colleague is having trouble. Sometimes it seems it is just easier to do the work yourself or go around the problem and allow subordinates to pick up the slack. There may also be an unwillingness to restructure an organization out of loyalty to long-serving colleagues. Tough love means we do what is right because we love the organization more than any one individual or department.

Tough love may also mean moving beyond the self-esteem culture, where we praise too much to make people feel good. Of course people need praise but leaving them basking in satisfaction will not create advantage. Advantage actually requires a state of agitation, in an environment of high expectations. Tough conversations may mean we tell people more clearly where they are failing yet in a supportive way.

> Tough love may also mean moving beyond the self-esteem culture, where we praise too much to make people feel good. Of course people need praise but leaving them basking in satisfaction will not create advantage.

Strategy boards

Ultimately, setting the direction and taking decisive action are agreed upon in the strategy engine of the business, that is the board. We have come a long way from the first board meetings. The word originated in the English language c1200 AD, from the planks or boards used as early tables. Today, as well as better tables, the chairs are also more comfortable and I mean this perhaps both physically and metaphorically. Securing advantage should ultimately mean that things start to work. This should mean that you become successful, which in turn can lead to being over-comfortable and perhaps arrogant about the success. The status quo and company become your friend, when in business this is actually often the most dangerous state. A board will seek to be both entrepreneurial and drive the business towards advantage while keeping appropriate control and risk management.

The board will set strategy and implement the plans by directing the company's affairs to gain advantage, while also meeting the appropriate interests of its shareholders and relevant stakeholders, employees and society. The role requires awareness, responsibility and balance with many interests at work so the potential for contradicting interests is high. Each member will also personally contribute to leading to advantage by standing back 'hands off' as described in Chapter 3 and taking the long-term strategic view against all the various pressures, including competition and market movements.

Strategy meetings may of course be workshops with the team but board meetings are where the decisions are sanctioned, and they should have a clear agenda with a strong focus on the difference between management and leadership. It is therefore important that they are professionally chaired. The chairperson's role will determine the final content of the agenda, in conjunction with the managing director, and manage the timings of the meeting and agenda against the importance of the content. The meetings could include:

- an agenda focused on agreeing a strategy and assessing performance against strategy;
- creating open discussions by introducing each item in a balanced, positive way;
- creating a balance and blend of conversation to ensure all views are heard, not just those of the senior or most charismatic people;
- summarizing what has been decided to check there are no misunderstandings;
- objectively identifying any deficiencies in the strategy and the board's approach;
- allocating responsibilities and ensuring that they are carried out;
- checking at the next meeting that all decisions have been implemented; and
- agreeing communications and update plans.

In some companies the chairperson and the managing director are the same person. While this may be entirely practical, a separate chairperson can increase objectivity and stop the managing director from dominating all decisions to create a more balanced view of strategy with a clearer agenda. Non-executive directors can also play an important part in assisting the chairperson by regularly and rigorously assessing the effectiveness of the board's processes and activities, as well as being more objective, thus increasing accountability and perspective.

The board's role

As well as strategy, the focus will include:

- Ensuring that company operations are in line with strategy.
  Are the business model and resource in line with the objectives?
- Making sure procedure, ethics, sustainability and compliance are appropriate.
- Clearing communications strategy and the willingness to take tough choices objectively.
- Risk assessment. How are risks best managed against resource?
- Monitoring performance.
- Ensuring accountability to shareholders and stakeholders.

The regularity of board meetings may depend on both your resources and ambitions. The observation is perhaps that there is a squeezed middle. Many start-ups spend a lot of time on strategy and research, as they figure out how to survive. Corporates are compliance led and therefore formal meetings are legally essential, but without this discipline or requirement many mid-tier businesses fall out of the practice. They are the squeezed middle, too busy managing the business to worry about strategy. The result of effective strategic boards is to establish collectively and decisively a clear strategy and vision, aligned to the values and resources of the organization in order to drive towards competitive advantage.

Communicating the strategy

Once the leaders and board have agreed the overall direction, decisive action is where change occurs. Fast deployment of action is critical in competitive and dynamic environments. Speed depends on effective communication; not what you say but what is heard. Beyond failure to get buy-in, failure to clearly articulate the strategy comes a close second as a barrier to advantage. How many great ideas get lost at buy-in stage because the message is not carefully designed and is over-convoluted in the presentation? Advantage is

FIGURE 11.1   the role of the board

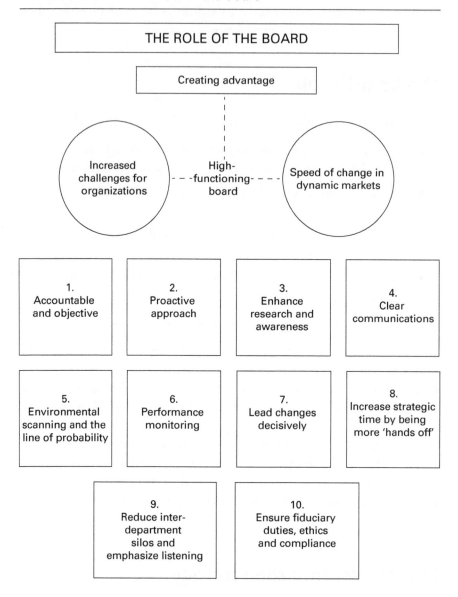

THE ROLE OF THE BOARD

Creating advantage

Increased challenges for organizations

High-functioning board

Speed of change in dynamic markets

1.
Accountable and objective

2.
Proactive approach

3.
Enhance research and awareness

4.
Clear communications

5.
Environmental scanning and the line of probability

6.
Performance monitoring

7.
Lead changes decisively

8.
Increase strategic time by being more 'hands off'

9.
Reduce inter-department silos and emphasize listening

10.
Ensure fiduciary duties, ethics and compliance

gained when leaders reduce complexity to simplicity by articulating simply the key messages and actions required to secure competitive advantage.

It does no good to create a vision without a plan to engage people with it. Repetition is also essential. People are usually absorbed in their own problems and this means that it can take time for them to relate to your challenges. This means taking the time to polish your message so it is compelling and persuasive, then repeating it. Not everyone has this skill and so employing help may be critical. The message is not just verbal; it may also need to be followed through in visual and written communication. The objective: simple, positive, powerful messages that create absolute clarity.

Possibly the most famous speech of the 20th century is Martin Luther King's 1963 'I have a dream' speech in which he called (ultimately) to end legal race segregation and combat racism in America. Fifty years on, the speech is still widely known and quoted. It has appeared in the West Bank conflict zone of Israel/Palestine and posters of King with 'I have a dream' words were used by protesters in China's tumultuous 1989 Tiananmen Square protest for democracy. Martin Luther King's speech starts six successive paragraphs with 'I have a dream' and seven with the words 'let freedom ring'. In fast-moving and noisy times simple messages are louder and have greater impact. The effort to design strong messages and repeat them can have profoundly positive consequences in delivering decisive action.

Simple messages: strategic framework

Your company needs to work as a team to deliver actions to achieve the desired change and ultimately this requires action plans. In my years as a professional adviser it is amazing how many lengthy business plans I have seen that show growth forecasts and identify direction yet ultimately fail to communicate or detail the action steps required to achieve the growth, yet these plans are often used to communicate the organization's objectives. Advantage requires action plans that identify clear next-step waymarks and actions, as opposed to persuasively crafted, but out-of-date, textbooks with beautifully modelled, but flawed, financial hypotheses.

Many businesses engage in business planning but when they realize that the effort for such detailed plans is high, and find that the plan is invariably overtaken by events, they can lose faith in the process and stop doing them altogether; yet nothing can be achieved in a vacuum. In conclusion, in dynamic markets, plans should be short and highly action-orientated and leaders should be clear and concise in their articulations, setting both the actions and the directions. A message, actions and plans that are designed, concise, practised, focused and drilled.

Setting the direction requires the reduction of complexity to simplicity. This may be best reinforced by visuals. Putting the message clearly and succinctly in writing takes time but it is critical as it forces you to really work out what needs to be said and why it is different. A strategic framework page, as shown in Figure 11.2, can be extremely useful in both encapsulating and communicating the vision, mission and the top-line snapshot of the resulting plan or key drivers.

FIGURE 11.2   Strategic framework

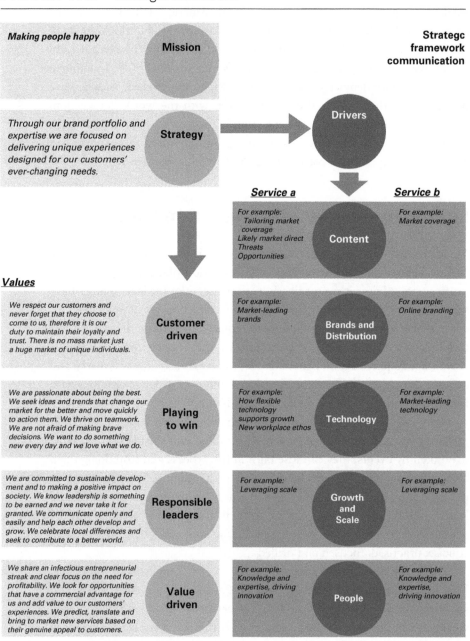

A vision is not a statement. A vision is a set of ideas that describe a future state that helps stretch minds and capabilities; it is the overall direction of travel and should actually be a moving goal. If it is achieved, what is next? A mission is more immediate and therefore much more important to decisive action to gain advantage. This should be simple.

The Walt Disney Company used to have a very clear mission statement: 'Make People Happy.' Today their mission is 'to be one of the world's leading producers and providers of entertainment and information. Using our portfolio of brands to differentiate our content, services and consumer products, we seek to develop the most creative, innovative and profitable entertainment experiences and related products in the world' (The Walt Disney Company, 2015). Despite Disney's huge overall success, how is this memorable? Does it motivate?

> A vision is a set of ideas that describe a future state that helps stretch minds and capabilities; it is the overall direction of travel and should actually be a moving goal. If it is achieved, what is next? A mission is more immediate.

The action chart

Creating advantage requires higher than normal amounts of change projects, particularly for existing businesses. Such change or decisive action requires clarity and organization. In large, complex organizations, tasks can involve countless numbers of people and resources. In dynamic markets those plans can be overtaken by the market; this increasingly means that projects are fluid with re-scoping and agility. This makes the need to manage the most critical delivery path even more important. Most leaders will be familiar with project management tools such as a Gantt chart, and critical path analysis, as shown in Table 11.1 and Figure 11.3. These develop the schedule, key delivery steps and roles and responsibilities. They don't replace communication as the plans progress. You have to remember that any document that you create for a project is a living document, from the requirements all the way down to the lessons learned notes, until you are finished closing out the project.

TABLE 11.1   Gantt chart

Task name	Dec 14	Jan 15	Feb 15	Mar 15	Apr 15	May 15	Jun 15	Jul 15
Planning		•	•	•				
Research			•	•				
Scenarios				•	•	•		
Decisions						•		
Engage							•	•

FIGURE 11.3   Critical path analysis example

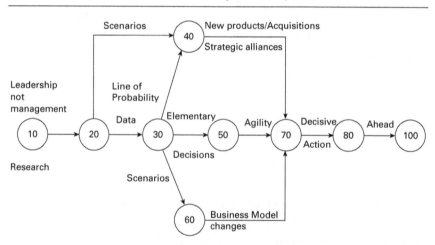

Group your actions and plans together, probably led by division, then agree the priority of each project. Define each project. This should include:

- finalizing project details;
- developing the project plan, including success measurements;
- assembling an effective project team with the relevant skill sets;
- defining critical project steps and paths with evaluation at the end of each phase;
- agreeing processes, sign-off and process documentation;

- identifying and managing potential project risks and appropriate contingency plans;
- re-scoping where required as you progress, ensuring updated tracking;
- deliverables should be tested at every critical point; and
- evaluation.

Change for advantage

After identifying direction, getting people to do things differently and implementing effective change are the number one challenge faced by leaders and managers. Generally people are not dynamic, with perhaps the majority being risk averse, seeking and being motivated by security rather than ambition. They might complain about being bored, or worry about their lack of promotion but are they really prepared to adopt the changes, or take the risks that are required to fulfil their personal or their organization's ambitions and change?

A bad strategy implemented well will almost invariably outperform a good strategy implemented badly. At some point we have all experienced this in one way or another by engaging in strategies of one sort or another that struggle. The usual approach when initiatives struggle is to simply double the effort, and increase the conversation. If the initiative still fails we then conclude that the strategy was wrong and cease it. This may be the right thing to do, but it is perhaps as likely that the implementation was flawed as much as the strategy. There are many contributors to implementation success or failure but the few that stand out are set out below.

1 *Execution*. Great strategy but poor tactics – when we have a good idea and product but fail to create the actions behind it that secure success. Is it really the strategy that's at fault, or does the problem lie with how you executed it? Make the changes you need, and try again. The Pixar story is a good example of this. Pixar pioneered electronic computerized animation to cut out hours of laborious studio time spent sketching; however, Pixar was struggling to sell its computers with losses at one point of over $100 million. The idea was arrived at to extend their demonstration films to commercial films. In 1995 the magical film *Toy Story* was released by Pixar, in association with Disney, and earned $361 million worldwide. Every one of Pixar's releases has been a box office hit with each averaging over US$550 million gross worldwide (Metacritic, 2015).

2 *Resource*. The implementation of a new strategy often involves hiring or promoting someone who is specifically tasked with the implementation of that change. A designer, for example, will lead the new commerce website and integrate it into operations and IT, or perhaps a sales executive with new product sales. The professional may be excellent, but often we simply get the wrong person. Not only do they have to have the expertise to deliver the specialism but they have to have the experience and intuition to understand quickly the dynamics of the business and its culture. When we get the resource wrong, the strategy fails and we may conclude incorrectly that it is better to stop the strategy rather than resolve the resource challenge. One of my clients, a distribution business, was struggling to capture business from the internet when it was first launched. On analysis they had used the wrong agency and were not paying enough to do it right. A more heavyweight solution has led the internet to be by far their best marketing campaign. It is costly but the return on investment has far offset the costs.

3 *Communication*. Good communication is not something that just happens. Implementing tactics requires clarity on who is doing what, why and when. Regular updates and reviews are essential, backed by effective and accessible project management tools with attentive managers and leaders. We can delegate tasks but fail to track their progress or hold people accountable in their delivery. Energy is lost through lack of awareness or efficient progress or failure to address poor results and the strategy fails.

Ultimately, when we look at the collapse of Enron in October 2001, at the time the seventh largest corporation in the United States, poor communication lies at the heart of the failure. The business's operational performance failed to match its surging stock prices based on poor, overinflated performance reporting. To maintain stock value and thus their own wealth, executives became complicit and were forced to continue inflating results. The lack of communication of effective moral values in the senior team and honest conversations effectively led to them lying to shareholders and the markets. Once the duplicity was discovered bankruptcy became inevitable.

4 *Timing*. The strategy is implemented too slowly, or it takes too long. We miss the moment or we simply run out of steam. We stop a good idea because we have not nurtured it well or allowed it the space and time it needs to be successful. Patience can be required, yet at the same time speed of action to implement it is critical. Being fast in implementation and patient in results can be fruitful. In fast markets operating speed has increased. Speed requires an executive team that is aligned in outlook and supported by effective information and systems. It requires openness to challenge and discussion of problems and accountability to keep reality absolutely in view.

5 *Financial*. The subject of finance has to be covered at some point in any strategy book. It is important, but also the topic is extremely well documented so I have chosen not to spend significant time on the subject. Money allows businesses to take advantage of opportunities to grow, reinvest and employ resource. From cash flow, funding types and its management, it is a resource, a hindrance and an opportunity. The strategic use of financial instruments, such as loans and investments, is key to the success of every business. It also has a large bearing on delivery. We can overinvest, underinvest, not deliver fast enough for our reserves or have insufficient reserves for our ambitions. To deliver decisive action, we must analyse the return on investment from that action and the resource we have available to reinvest while remembering that ultimately it is the customers that give us the money.

6 *Learning*. Businesses rarely secure advantage without risk and risk may mean investments or efforts that don't work out. Remember that, and use mistakes as part of the learning process. When your initial idea doesn't flourish take what you have learnt and try several different approaches to find the one that does work. If on re-engagement the initiatives still don't deliver, then it is time to try something entirely different.

Tipping-point leadership

Decisive action needs people to support it. Whether via consensus or hierarchical command, people need to act in support to carry out change. We have seen that resource may impact on this, but it is also inevitable that some people will block the change. How many times have we all seen a management initiative fail simply because people ignored it? This is ultimately a lack of respect or professionalism from the team. If people don't deliver change they probably first lack the training, or are incompetent (or unsupported incompetent). If problems persist after training then we must consequently ask whether they are incapable or insubordinate. Habits take time to change so when replacing the old with the new, insist on constant training and conscious application. Finally, review then embed.

Beyond individuals struggling to make changes, we also have group inertia, or politics. Usually this is because the leadership has tried running before they can walk; perhaps selling the need for change or better results but not objectively backing and influencing the need for change with the right strategy, resource and training. Such leaders hit the inertia wall. Firstly, what is it most important to change and why change? What is the data, the analysis and where is the research? Share the findings then workshop to agree the changes, secure new ideas and innovate and we should secure the tipping point. If all else fails we may have to revert to politics ourselves. You can't persuade large groups but you can influence small groups so by working at the extremes, taking aside and converting the extreme doubters and encouraging the advocates, the middle ground can be best influenced and tipped to change.

FIGURE 11.4   Tipping point

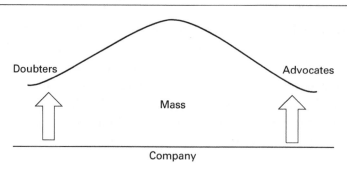

In 2009 and 2010, Toyota had to carry out the largest ever recall of vehicles in the United States (Kelly, 2012). To much outrage, 5.2 million vehicles were recalled due to floor mats catching on the foot brake pedal and a further 2.3 million vehicles were recalled when it was discovered that the accelerator pedal could stick, both causing potentially dangerous and unintended acceleration. The damage to the brand seemed irretrievable but instead of relying on a PR firm, Mr Lentz, the CEO at the time, offered a live conversation on one of the most popular communities on the web: Digg. Digg is well known for its hostility to corporations so this was a brave move. More than a thousand challenging questions were submitted and Mr Lentz answered as many as possible in the given time. It was a completely transparent interview that helped Toyota move from a tarnished brand to a positive brand. By concentrating on tipping the highly vocal minority in such an open and public way the interview did much to refloat the sinking brand.

Contrast this approach with that of BP chief executive, Tony Hayward. Just 48 hours after a hostile interrogation by a US congressional committee on BP's Gulf Coast oil spill, he insensitively attended a yacht race on the Isle of Wight (UK). This tipped his and the company's reputation deeply backwards; Mr Hayward no longer works for BP.

The skills of advantage leaders

To find opportunity, leaders will operate against a secure knowledge base and on a broad set of facts to see what impacts there are in the environment. They will then gain strategic clarity on the priorities in the business. What conclusions and opportunities can be seen that others can't see and how do we arrive at these more quickly?

In this context the outlook of the advantage leader is influential, in that they will always believe that you have to keep working at success, and keep moving, never shying away from the challenging questions; quietly, keenly and ably looking for the opportunities. Advantage leaders apply practice and discipline to their approach, combining this with a strong level of self-awareness and the right values. In today's open, ethics-driven and legislative world, these values are primarily altruistic not egotistic. The word 'altruistic' is derived from the old Italian word *altrui*, 'of or to others', extended from the Latin *alter*, also meaning 'other'. Ego is Latin for 'I'. In this principle or practice of unselfish concern for or devotion to the welfare of others and the organization, advantage leaders can do what it takes to challenge the status quo with the greater good at the centre.

Beyond an altruistic approach, advantage leaders are more observational, they listen more yet fundamentally they remain more decisive but without losing empathy. They are prepared to drive change and accept that this causes challenges but keep the greater good in mind.

Advantage leaders spot opportunities more quickly. 'How can we help?' and 'How can we do it better?' should always be the underlying approach.

TABLE 11.2   Advantage Leadership approach checklist

	Advantage Leadership	
	Notes	✓
Courage and objectivity	The ability to see reality, the bravery to speak the truth and the openness to challenge people to drive change	
Integrity	The openness to engage in all dialogues, and the honesty to create trust	
Delivery	Do what you say you are going to do	
Visibility	Making sure you take the time to engage with everybody and listening when you do. Being seen to care and act	
Humour and empathy	Fun contributes to motivation. Humour is not about being good at jokes but smiling more and seeing the funny aspects better. Empathy to relate to the challenges others see	
Communicate	Communicate consistently, repeat the messages in memorable ways. Listen more to understand today's reality better	
Anticipate	Carry out environmental scanning and review the data to see the connections then scenario plan to create the strategy	
Flow	Have the discipline to pace yourself, and the organization skills to anticipate ahead to free up the time to connect with people calmly in the moment. A 'stressed' boss does not inspire	
Decisive action	Being clear who needs to do what by when, tracking progress and holding people accountable to delivering in budget and on time. Action and direction	
Talent	Recognize who the right people are for the right role	
Risk	It is not avoiding risk but managing it that creates advantage. Assess risk from low to high and implement strategy accordingly	
Goals	Set and monitor key priorities and objectives, and monitor the progress throughout the year	
High expectations	Good is not good enough. Focus on performance, innovation and why your proposition is better	
Add value	Seek solutions that help people. Listen to how you can help your customers, ensuring an external strategic focus. Why is your organization better?	
Altruistic	Focus on the collective success and collaboration. We, not I	
Context	Respect people enough to share the real reasons, tell people the truth and the reasons why	

Chapter summary and leader questions

Today change is unmistakably faster than at any other point in the 200,000-year history of modern man, primarily due to the innovation of printing and now the digital revolution, batching and leveraging ideas in real time. Leaders need to spend time with their teams discussing and examining the 'real-time change' challenge at source, or the context. By sharing *what* is happening we can then see better *why* it is happening. This context in turn leads to a stronger understanding of *how* to take advantage. The *how* is the decisive actions required to deliver an advantage transformation.

With an understanding of *why*, people are less questioning and more involved. They are then better motivated to drive the *how*. This is essentially designing the team and organization's mental outlook via constant simple messages, an outlook that is determined, action-orientated and focused on high standards and speed. The world has changed – and will continue to change at pace – and therefore our strategies, systems, processes and structures need to adapt too. Today, from complexity we focus to extract why, what and how to drive decisive action and gain advantage.

Leader questions

1 How clear is your mission and direction statement?

2 What tough conversations are being avoided?

3 What are your simple messages on why change, what needs to change and how?

4 What is the board's contribution to the strategy process?

5 How clear are the board on where they spend their time?

6 How good is your project management?

7 What 'advantage' leadership training have you and the executive team had?

8 What barriers to change exist in your organization and how can you reduce these?

References

BP (2015) Our values. Available from: www.bp.com/en/global/corporate/about-bp/company-information/our-values.html [Last accessed 1 September 2015]

Collins, J (2001) The misguided mix-up for celebrity and leadership. Available from: www.jimcollins.com/article_topics/articles/the-misguided-mixup.html [Last accessed 1 September 2015]

Kelly, A M (2012) Has Toyota's image recovered from the brand's recall crisis? Forbes Leadership, 05/03. Available from: www.forbes.com/sites/annemariekelly/2012/03/05/has-toyotas-image-recovered-from-the-brands-recall-crisis/ [Last accessed 1 September 2015]

Macalister, T (2015) BP dropped green energy profits worth billions to focus on fossil fuels. The Guardian 16/04. Available from: www.theguardian.com/environment/2015/apr/16/bp-dropped-green-energy-projects-worth-billions-to-focus-on-fossil-fuels [Last accessed 1 September 2015]

The Walt Disney Company (2015) Investor relations. Available from: https://thewaltdisneycompany.com/investors [Last accessed 1 September 2015]

Metacritic (2015) Available from: www.metacritic.com/ [Last accessed 1 September 2015]

The advantage sum

12

Boundless flux: boundless opportunity

When we think of great business leaders, we think of charismatic, passionate, audacious people. We think of powerful individuals who encourage and inspire through strength of personality. We also think of people who build 'advantage companies'; innovators and visionaries that got the 'new' right. However, these thoughts and visualizations can be unhelpful and rely too much on talent. In the complexity of rapid change, today's successful leaders are more observational, better listeners and understand strategy better. It is not force that creates competitive advantage but intelligence. The intelligence to strategically understand how your organization is or can be better and articulating this well, continuously combined with securing effective change. Advantage also requires patience. 'New and improved' may also be based on years of trial, error and failure to learn how to succeed.

Increasingly advantage lies in ideas as opposed to capital or products. It is the ability to harness these ideas and knowledge that becomes the most creative force in our businesses and the environments they operate in, not the personalities behind or in charge of the business. Our organizations face an unparalleled and unprecedented pace of change, driven by our ability to communicate and share know-how instantaneously and globally. We can choose to respond with energy, enthusiasm and agility to keep pace, but this is tiring. Instead we can pause, take stock, research, analyse and ask how we can be better and get ahead of the market rather than chase the market. In essence: be strategic.

With accelerated change we have boundless opportunity but many of us feel our economic lives are out of control, dominated by constant change overload and organizational flux, combined with an underlying dissatisfaction at a predominantly capitalistic output. To regain control and satisfaction and drive competitive advantage we must strategically adopt new practices, processes and thinking. Flux is defined as being in a state of continuous movement or change. Fast change is the new normal, so the counter is to create businesses that are more fluid and to look further ahead to where the movement is likely to take us. In the line of probability and the data lie the answers and context to where advantage is. In operating as leaders we must design organizations that allow us the time to go and seek these answers and then through traditional strategy and clear communication, engage and share the ideas and knowledge secured on our quest.

By sharing this context our organizations can see more clearly the reality as to what is happening, and why it's happening in our environments, and they are then better placed, on an agile basis, to figure out how to be better as a consequence.

The new

There are many business thought leaders still talking about the *new* knowledge economy or the *new* digital age and arguing for *new* approaches. However, with fast change and flux as normal, *new* is inevitable and therefore it is old. The knowledge or digital economy is no longer *new*, nor is the accelerated pace of change, yet in so many areas of business we insist on sitting on old models. Whether this be the hierarchical senior male 'elder statesmen'-dominated boards, or our reluctance to embrace flexible working and lack of investment in pioneering areas out of fear of failure. Many owners only accept onwards and upwards as a method of growing a business and rarely in these days of immediate return take long-term decisions. However, the organizations that fast-track tend to be established correctly from the start, or shake the legacy of their history and reinvent themselves, but this may mean going backwards or working downwards first to create better foundations – and then onwards and upwards. Cuts, changes, or 'sell off' consolidations may actually be the first step in onwards and upwards to create advantage as you change the business model.

We are compromised when we are driven by tradition or history, which leads us to piecemeal incremental change and growth. As much as we advance to advantage, environmental change disadvantages us and we make little headway. In the advantage sum, we create organizations that put aside history, take out the old assumptions, reduce the silos and by joining the interconnections secure and maximize new ideas and knowledge. We then strategically harvest these efficiently to accelerate growth and gain advantage via agility, investment, clear communication, investment and focus. Quality of product or service still matter and still create good businesses. However, today they are only a source of competitive advantage when they are combined with the right business model, positioning, distribution and brands. It is the strategy, ideas and intelligence that give them value to create exceptional advantageous businesses.

Strategic leadership

Michael Porter published his ground-breaking book *Competitive Advantage* in 1985. The book asks us to look at our organizations as a series of activities which link to create 'a value chain', with the focus that each link in the chain should add value – it contributes something that a customer is prepared to pay for. The chain will include non-product areas such as distribution and training. Each link in the chain could create competitive advantage in its own right. The theory is sound; however, unless we continuously look at what our customers want now and are likely to want in the future it can result in incremental efficiency thinking. Understanding each component of your value chain is important to gain sustainable advantage but fast-moving markets require us to look beyond what adds value today and try and identify what will add value tomorrow. This is where our work on the line of probability, scanning, researching and asking what is likely to come based on the current macro picture are so important.

If we combine this with the micro picture, the analytics and trends analysis, we secure a far more focused picture on why things are changing, what the implications are, and then through scenario planning how we can gain advantage. The combination of macro insight from the line of probability and micro insight from data means our educated guesses are more likely to be accurate. With this assessment of where things are going we can then use concepts such as Porter's 'each link in the chain' and ask whether each element of our business adds value with tomorrow in mind.

Advantage steps

Essentially leaders and executives research which innovation, new products, strategic alliances and customers are likely to bear the most fruit going forward, while designing the business to work in an agile way with team- and management-driven change, as opposed to leader-driven change to then take advantage. The scenario work and planning help us identify how to be better with greater clarity.

In 'elementary thinking' the leaders connect the thinking, identify the better strategy and communicate in what areas and why the organization can be better, while the managers identify, via scenario work, the specifics of how to capitalize the business model and operations around these areas and directions. An agile team approach with latent flexibility then combines with fresh thinking, not wedded to the legacy of history and the status quo, to capitalize more efficiently on the knowledge and ideas gained in the process and, crucially, before the competitors do. With a first move and speed to market approach to implementing these ideas, we gain market share which gives us economies of scale, which in turn help build further advantage through buying and branding power and build sustainability (so long as success doesn't lead to complacency).

The traditional view of strategy can be inwards and looking for incremental improvements in the chain, but by looking outwards at future customer demand and trends we can create businesses that gain advantage on a market- and team-driven basis. Overall, conceptually, we place the business in the way of advantage as we can see it more as it comes through the market, rather than reaching or grasping for it from behind. In my previous book, *Navigating the Rivers of Cash*, I used the analogy of the river being the market and flowing. All the time we are in the 'current' managing, we can't see where the flow is going and thus set a better course: leadership. If we get out of the fast-moving current and look upriver more, we can see the easiest course and plan where to gain the best current ahead, in order to secure advantage. Competitive advantage is best secured if we think more moves ahead than our competitors, as shown in Figure 12.1.

FIGURE 12.1   Competitive advantage strategy

Competitive advantage strategy	
Research and scenarios	**Execution**
Reconstruct market boundaries Focus on the big picture Go beyond the numbers Reach beyond existing demand Get the strategic sequence right **New products/strategic alliances/ new territories/acquisitions/ business model changes**	Overcome key organizational hurdles Review business model Seek first moves Build execution into strategy Communicate why, what, how

Purposeful value

When we think or look several moves ahead, we might also need to consider the purpose of business, particularly as knowledge consumers become more driven by ethics and transparency. Capitalism mostly has a free market economy. This means people buy and sell goods and services under their own freedom of choice according to what they most value. In the market, we barter and exchange work for money, which enables us to purchase the things we both need and also want. Consumerism is the assumption that the more goods or services exchanged the better off that society is. However, increasingly overconsumption and greed are being negatively attributed to both capitalism and consumerism.

The context of this negative view is that perhaps too many of us in the world are materialistic and acquire too much for vanity as opposed to need or even comfort. Many people suggest that people with more material goods are the least happy, the most notable of these being the Dalai Lama, the spiritual leader of the Tibetan people, in his book *The Art of Happiness* (2003). His observation is that the more goods you own, the more they own you and it takes too much time and energy to earn the money to buy the goods and run, maintain and repair them, which results in unhappiness. If this is true in an age where human knowledge is so free it is surprising that materialism has become so prevalent, but I am not surprised. There is almost no commercial interest in the Dalai Lama's view that we might need less, and huge commercial interest, which means lots of money spent on telling us that we need more. That is, much of the knowledge shared is actually marketing to encourage us to buy more discretionary goods and services.

Overt materialism may actually be a symptom of uneven wealth distribution as our connected world has led to an overall surge in living standards but, as it is new, it is unfairly distributed and we are still working on that distribution. One solution presented is socialism, an economy underpinned by state not private ownership, with the aim of the state increasing distribution. To me, however, this is flawed as it ignores the fact that wealth is created when individuals are allowed to compete fully and freely. This competition invariably leads to big winners, particularly as once you have capital it is easier to make more capital, that is, it is easier for the rich to get richer. In my opinion, the solution to create both wealth and advantage is for capitalism to select moral self-responsibility; that is a free market where people and companies compete to create wealth, combined with leaders who are more values driven, leading to a less materialistic and more altruistic form of capitalism. One where we value the ideas and contribution as much as we value the material goods. Two of the world's richest men are leading this charge, with their giving pledge: the website **www.givingpledge.org** contains letters from some of the world's richest people and these are extraordinary. Bill Gates and Warren Buffett have both given away at least US$25 billion apiece in their lifetimes (Lane, 2013).

To add value or be of value

In Porter's business classic *Competitive Advantage*, the thesis is that each element or chain of the business should add value in order to secure advantage. In purposeful value, as capitalism matures and consumers have more knowledge and more choice, we may be required or, even better, choose each element that *adds value* also be *values*-driven. That is, we seek strategies that gain advantage while also focusing on ethics, purposefulness and being useful. In seeking advantage, organizations design each element or link in the chain to both secure advantage and to contribute to society's betterment wherever it can. As an example, a client I have worked with offers standard telephone networks and calls. They have chosen to specialize in sports clubs. This gives them expertise in the requirements of sports clubs, with many towns having two or three of one type or another. At the same time they have pledged to give half of their profits from calls back to the club, which enables the club to claw back some of its costs. The volume they get from the pledge means that they win far more clubs as customers and make a difference to local sport by enabling clubs to have a more commercial set-up than otherwise possible. The business, club and local sport do well which benefits all.

> As capitalism matures and consumers have more knowledge and more choice, we may be required or, even better, choose each element that adds value and be values driven.

The word 'capital' meaning 'something of value' is originally from the Latin word 'caput', meaning 'head'. It was used when calculating how many 'head' of cattle a rich person owned, from the days when cattle were traded in place of money. Capitalism was first used as a word in the 19th century. The system has existed for millennia; however, increasingly we must ask what it really means. The free market has required heavy government intervention to maintain, sustain and create economic growth; that is the continued expansion of our system to supply goods and services. During the Great Depression in the US in the 1930s a form of quantative easing (QE) was used by the Federal Reserve to stimulate the economy. This was used again in 2009 by both the Federal Reserve and the Bank of England in the UK to stimulate an economy on the verge of collapse after the credit crunch. The credit crunch occurred when liquidity between banks almost collapsed as people rightly feared that many banks' balance sheets were overinflated with too much bad debt sitting on their books. QE is where the state's central bank buys financial assets, mainly debt from commercial banks, thus 'creating money' and directly injecting it into an economy. If we need to create or effectively print money to maintain a free market, many argue it is no longer a free market. Are these interventions, compounded by the environmental impact of overt materialism, actually signs that overt and free capitalism is creaking?

Our recent history would seem to suggest that state intervention in our economies is inevitable from time to time. Global warming and finite natural resources also signpost that materialism is in contradiction to sustainability with a global population of 7 billion today, forecast to increase to 9.6 billion by 2050 (**www.worldwatch.org/node/6038**). In combination do we accept that capitalism actually has to be 'managed' more, as opposed to left 'free'? It is not acceptable for companies to simply make money, they must contribute as illustrated by this quote from Tesla Motors: 'As we work to lessen global dependence on petroleum-based transportation and drive down the cost of electric vehicles, we are committed to instituting a closed loop battery recycling system. A closed loop of material use involves manufacturing of battery cells, assembly into battery packs, then vehicles, and finally, recycling into raw materials for future use' (Tesla Motors, 2011).

This statement shows a full organizational awareness that the choice of customers is now moving beyond the strength of the product or just its value cost to the overall 'idea' of the product itself and its total impact. We buy the product based on its use and the brand but also, increasingly, the brand values. How the goods are made, sourced and recycled informs our buying choice as does how the organizations use the consequent profit and also how they pay tax. The view is that the value chain is becoming transparent in the knowledge age and that has the potential to fundamentally enhance capitalism beyond the pursuit of corporate profits to a force for responsibility and good.

Some countries, such as Singapore, already have what some might call 'managed' capitalism whereby the government carefully regulates the economy.

This approach minimizes the kind of excesses that many Western countries, such as the United States, see but may limit entrepreneurship.

Many organizations are inherently aware of the need to act responsibly and many have established corporate social responsibility (CSR) policies and departments to assist in setting and maintaining its values. This is a step in the right direction but in my version of competitive advantage this approach also has an inherent challenge. This is because a department is a silo and the CSR department becomes the police. In a truly values-driven business we should not need police as each element of the business is defined by its choice of ethical values as much as its profit. Regardless of this and in the long term, informed customers will demand that companies have the right values in their buying criteria and therefore advantage can only be achieved if we also seek purposefulness.

For years, individuals such as Warren Buffett and Bill Gates have chosen their ethical values and contribution to society as a consequence of these. Business leaders now face the same opportunity in their businesses. I would suggest that strategic advantage can no longer be easily secured without also asking and answering the questions about how we will contribute to a better society and life. Many will say that from a position of luxury it is acceptable to make this statement but if we look at the way overall society has improved over the decades, from the reduction of child poverty or the realization of Martin Luther King's dream of no racist segregation, we do over time seek and usually realize improvements, but they can take a long time. Over time, companies are also likely to be expected to contribute beyond financial success to secure advantage.

Complexity to simplicity

As systems mature they become more complex but often actually appear simpler. I am writing this on a solid state hard drive (SSD) laptop that is lighter than the average hardback book. SSDs have no moving (mechanical) components. This distinguishes them from traditional electromechanical magnetic disks such as hard disk drives (HDDs), which contain spinning disks. Compared with electromechanical disks, SSDs are typically more resistant to physical shock, run silently and have lower access time. Without moving components they appear and operate much more simply, yet the technology took over 40 years to develop. If we compare this progress to capitalism perhaps we will settle into a more sophisticated model where we value material goods less and value ideas, experience and the knowledge that contributes to them more. The rise of the 'experience' product, whether this is an adventure sport or tourism, would suggest that this is the trend, and the virtual online world is giving the physical world a run for its money.

If we redefine success in business beyond profit and a shareholder value to social contribution, companies have a stark choice. I am confident that capitalism and society will mature and are maturing beyond their current infantile overt materialism to a more sophisticated value system, and it is the values themselves that we will trade as much as the goods and services. When we ask why and how we can be better or gain advantage we must also ask how we can contribute more. Can we create advantage organizations that choose to do the right things, not because customers demand it, but because the businesses want to?

Summary

In this analysis, creating advantage is not about talent or luck or thus finding the brilliant new 'saviour' product. Instead, we strategically work to seek better understanding of where the market is heading and thus what actions need to be taken to make our organizations better. We research more, using better environmental scanning techniques and data analysis, and we consequently spot the clues to secure clarity and understanding of the probabilities.

The understanding and clarity create the insights, which create the plan, energizing the changes required to deliver advantage. Effective and respected leaders have a clear starting point – they know the performance and behaviours essential to achieve their vision, but today they need the better strategy. This takes:

- vision and determination to create something better beyond the immediate;
- dissatisfaction with the status quo;
- being prepared to act in opposition to convention;
- open minds, careful observation and intense listening;
- clear roles and responsibilities with the permission to strategize;
- acceptance that failure is part of learning;
- research, creativity, analysis and intuition;
- leaders who 'manage' yet embrace risk to achieve;
- willingness to disrupt or change, even when things are working;

- a completely open mind about values and the future;
- the space to write the script as opposed to follow, or just orchestrate, the show; and
- teamwork, focus, responsibility and belief.

FIGURE 12.2   Leadership approach

Approach		Focus
Open leadership		Differentiation
Teamwork and vision		Disruptive products and business models
Research, analysis and intuition		Future focus

FIGURE 12.3   The process of creating competitive advantage

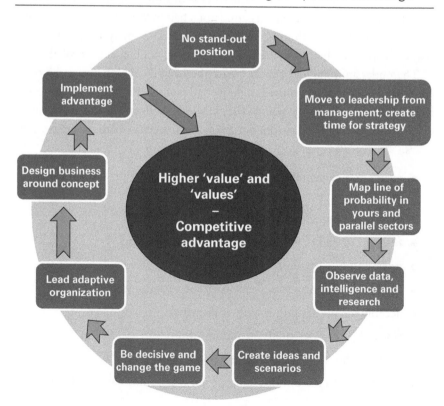

Markets move rapidly and this means that today's plan will be out of date tomorrow. An agile approach can be mistaken for an effective counter; however, it is insufficient. By engaging and investing in research and data analysis we can increase our perspective of tomorrow and therefore re-engage in effective strategic thinking. Figure 12.2 shows the leader mindset required.

I wonder if we put aside hierarchy, our egos, and the vested interest of the status quo and instead, through research, scanning and data looked ahead further at the line of probability, what we could become? If I had 'a dream' it would be that through re-engaging in effective strategy, and understanding its simplicity rather than complexity, we might create more flexible, capable and extraordinary positive and purposeful organizations that contribute ahead. Where is your market going and consequently why and how can you be better?

References

Randall Lane (2013) The 50 philanthropists who have given away the most money. Forbes Business, 18/11. Available from: www.forbes.com/sites/randalllane/2013/11/18/the-50-philanthropists-who-have-given-away-the-most-money/ [Last accessed 1 September 2015]

Tesla Motors (2011) Tesla's closed loop battery recycling program. Tesla Blog, 26/01. Available from: www.teslamotors.com/blog/teslas-closed-loop-battery-recycling-program [Last accessed 1 September 2015]

INDEX

Italics indicate figures or tables